The Psychology of Rumor Or How The Flying Saucer Phenomenon Spread Throughout The Nation

Gordon W. Allport & Leo Postman

SAUCERIAN PUBLISHER
Original Sources in Ufology

ISBN: **978-1-955087-32-2**

2022, Saucerian Publisher

Al rights reserved. No part of this publication maybe reproduced, translate, store in a retrieval system, or transmitted in any form or by any means, electronic, mechanical, photocopying, recording or otherwise, without prior written permision from the publisher.

PROLOGUE

Today, many Americans spend most of their time at UFO conventions, UFO pilgrimages, and New Age gatherings. Cities and local people have learned to capitalize on their UFO phenomena. Rumors of the 1947 crash of a flying saucer draw tourists to Roswell, New Mexico, which holds an annual UFO festival and sports its own UFO museum. However, there is no study of the role played by rumor in the development of the Flying Saucer phenomenon.

In July 1947, the renowned psychologist Dr. Gordon W. Allport from Harvard University was once interviewed by a reporter from The New York Times about his book: *The Psychology of Rumor.* During the interview, He pointed out that: "The book concerns itself "with how current rumors are born and grow and how flying saucer epidemics spread throughout the nation." The author finished his book at the end of WW II and the dawn of the UFO age. The main concern during this time was national security, and Alpost's main emphasis given to his work was the menace of rumors during wartime. Also, he feels the social atmosphere that permeated those years with the Roswell incident (1947) and Kenneth Arnold's (1947) first widely reported modern unidentified flying object sighting.

However, his book was not intended to deal directly and is not about Flying Saucer rumors; the author realized that the social forces that produce rumors during wartime are also at work during peacetime and could be applied to the flying saucers phenomena. He knew the catastrophic consequences of the rumors spread throughout America in Orson Wells' radio drama "The War of the Worlds" of 1938 about an alien invasion from Mars. Therefore, he knew the dangers that could cause rumors of an alien invasion or an extraterrestrial visit.

Also, rumors are building blocks of belief systems. The reader could take a closer look at Cicero's Cat comic sequence on page 150, in which the cat's rumors exaggerate the character of a dog. The same social interaction observed in Cicero's Cat works for the creation of rumors among flying saucer devotees. This dynamic could explain the changes reported in alien bodies and flying saucer shapes throughout time.

We have republished, as a facsimile edition, Allport's original work of 1947 under a new title: *The Psychology of Rumor Or How The Flying Saucer Phenomenon Spread Throughout The Nation* following the author's comments to The New York Time reporter.

This book has been formatted from its original version for publication. **IMPORTANT, although we have attempted to maintain the integrity of this title accurately, the present reproduction could have minor errors due to the age of the original scanned copy.**

Editor
Saucerian Publisher

Book-Authors
The New York Times (New York, N.Y)
21 July 1947.Page. 15.

Books—Authors

The third volume in Hervey Allen's projected six-volume historical novel about Colonial Pennsylvania and the Indian Wars will be published by Rinehart next March. Its title will be "The City in the Dawn," and with its predecessors, "The Forest and the Fort" and "Bedford Village," it will complete the first unit, to be called "Sylvania." All six books will eventually be titled "The Disinherited."

"Motion Picture Acting," by Lillian Albertson, a textbook on the technique of movie acting, is scheduled for November publication by Funk & Wagnalls. Miss Albertson is a former Broadway actress. In Hollywood she has taught many stars, among them Clark Gable.

Holt will publish on Aug. 4 "The Psychology of Rumor," by Gordon W. Allport. The book concerns itself with "how current rumors are born and grow, and how flying saucer epidemics spread throughout the nation."

The Ziff-Davis $500 contest for Western and mystery stories has been won by John Jameson Jr. of Big Horn, Wyo., and Winnetka, Ill. The prize was awarded at the annual Midwestern Writers Conference for his Western story, "Peace-Loving Man."

THE PSYCHOLOGY

OF RUMOR
OR HOW THE FLYING SAUCER PHENOMENON SPREAD THROUGHOUT THE NATION

GORDON W. ALLPORT
Professor of Psychology, Harvard University

LEO POSTMAN
Instructor in Psychology, Harvard University

From *Vergilius,* Opera (ed. by Sebastian Brant).
Strasbourg: Grüninger, 1502.

"Swift through the Libyan cities Rumor sped.
Rumor! What evil can surpass her speed?
In movement she grows mighty, and achieves
Strength and dominion as she swifter flies.
Small first, because afraid, she soon exalts
Her stature skyward, stalking through the lands
And mantling in the clouds her baleful brow . . .
Feet swift to run and pinions like the wind
The dreadful monster wears; her carcase huge
Is feathered, and at the root of every plume
A peering eye abides; and, strange to tell,
An equal number of vociferous tongues,
Foul, whispering lips, and ears, that catch at all . . .
. . . She can cling
To vile invention and malignant wrong,
Or mingle with her word some tidings true."

(*Aeneid,* Book IV. From the translation by
Theodore C. Williams, by permission of
the publishers, Houghton Mifflin Company.)

PREFACE

A LARGE part of ordinary social conversation consists of rumor mongering. In our daily chitchat with friends we both take in and give out whole lungfuls of gossip—sometimes idle, sometimes not. Idle rumors are an unverified, casual type of discourse serving no purpose other than passing the time of day with a friend. When we pass on a bit of hearsay, we may mean nothing more than we signify by our innocent greeting, "Good morning. Fine day, isn't it?"

But social discourse that expresses nothing in particular except vague feelings of friendliness toward our interlocutor, at the same time avoiding the embarrassment of dead silence, is only one of the forms that rumor takes. Most rumors, and most gossip too, are far from idle. They are profoundly purposive, serving important emotional ends. Just what these ends may be both teller and listener are usually unable to say. They know only that the tale seems important to them. In some mysterious way it seems to alleviate their intellectual uncertainty and personal anxiety.

Although rumor spreading is at all times a social and psychological problem of major proportions, it is especially so in time of crisis. Whenever there is social strain, false report grows virulent. In wartime, rumors sap morale and menace national safety by spreading needless alarm and by raising extravagant hopes. They menace the security of military information and, most damaging of all, spread the virus of hostility and hate against loyal subgroups within the nation. In the years of postwar strain rumors are only slightly less destructive in their effect.

It was the problem of wartime rumors that led us originally to undertake the experimental investigations reported in this book. But when we began to interpret our experiments in relation to both wartime and peacetime tale spreading, we were struck by the lack of systematic treatment of the subject in the literature of social psychology. Up to now no one seems to have attempted a unified and coherent account of the primary phenomena of rumor. Hence, we have felt obliged to gather together in the form of a basic textbook all the relevant information that concerns this important topic.

Under no circumstances should rumor be thought of as a mere oddity, as a quaint but trivial divagation in man's otherwise sensible social conduct. Quite the contrary, the rumor principle turns out to be of widespread applicability. Its characteristic course of distortion in recall, forgetting, imagination, and rationalization is precisely the same course of distortion that we find in most forms of human communication. Take, for example, legends. Legends are enduring tales of exploits or events that serve as a focus for the cultural pride and tradition of a family, tribe, or nation. The motives that sustain legends, the course of change they take through the years, are basically the same as those encountered in transient rumor spreading. In courtroom testimony, in recounting past experiences to friends, in witticisms and in autobiography, in proverbs and aphorisms and biography, and even in the writing of history and in the creations of the artist we find the same essential principle at work as in ordinary rumor distortion. The tendencies to *level*, to *sharpen*, to *assimilate* to personal and cultural contexts are found operative in all

PREFACE

forms of human communication that are not rigidly constrained by objective and impersonal standards of truth.

Although in the following chapters we try to point out the wider applications of the rumor principle, for the most part we center attention upon those unverified propositions for belief that are ordinarily designated as rumors. By fixing the reader's mind upon this narrower range of examples, we hope he will become so thoroughly conversant with the rules involved that he can readily apply them to all related forms of human communication.

A *rumor,* as we shall use the term, is a *specific (or topical) proposition for belief, passed along from person to person, usually by word of mouth, without secure standards of evidence being present.*

The implication in any rumor is always that some truth is being communicated. This implication holds even though the teller prefaces his tidbit with the warning, "It is only a rumor, but I heard . . ."

The medium of transmission is generally word of mouth. True, rumors are occasionally printed in newspapers or magazines, or find their way over the radio waves. Responsible publishers and broadcasters, however, are learning to guard against hearsay reports and, for the most part, to avoid the communication of rumor. On the other hand, slanderous pamphlets and the irresponsible portions of the press are common carriers of harmful tales.

Our definition calls attention to the fact that rumor is ordinarily specific and topical, and for that reason generally of only temporary interest. Rumors come and go; sometimes the same ones recur. But almost always they deal with events or with personalities. The protagonist of a rumor is ordinarily well identified: Mrs. X, a movie actor, the Russians, the stranger who moved in next door, a Federal agency—these are typical targets of rumor. There are few stories that do not have personal and clearly identified victims. And there are few that fail to specify clearly the character of the action or deed that provides the tenor of the tale. Hearsay reports of happenings, gossip, slander, and hopeful or dire predictions of coming events are among the concrete forms that rumor takes.

The central feature of our definition is its insistence that rumor thrives only in the absence of "secure standards of evidence." This criterion marks off rumor from news, distinguishes "old wives' tales" from science, and separates gullibility from knowledge. True, we cannot always decide easily when it is that secure standards of evidence are present. For this reason we cannot always tell whether we are listening to fact or to fantasy. A date-lined news item available to all readers in a reputable newspaper may ordinarily be taken as a secure standard of evidence. But when, in telling a friend about the item, I depart from the news item as printed, rumor is started. If my oral account parallels closely the printed item there is no rumor—unless, of course, the original news item itself departed from secure standards of evidence and is itself rumor!

Thus, in order to decide whether we are listening to information or to rumor we must judge the closeness or remoteness of the evidence upon which the report rests. In rumor the source of evidence has grown dim. Often it has receded to nothing more substantial than "They say . . ." Especially when the standard of evidence is represented by a dangling pronoun (without clear antecedent), watch out for rumor. So, too, in other cases where the criterion of evidence is elusive, as in the familiar formula, "I have it on good authority . . ."

Since the standards of evidence sometimes exist within the

PREFACE

informant himself, we are often forced to judge whether our informant really knows whereof he speaks. We can be fairly sure that a scientist telling us about his specialty is not passing along rumor. Our physician is less prone than our lay friends to believe or to tell rumors of magical cures or of improbable epidemics. A veteran of Okinawa is less likely than others to believe or pass on imaginary versions of that island battle, although even veterans tend to depend on their imagination in telling about a battle. All individuals have within themselves secure, or relatively secure, standards of evidence concerning matters in which they are expert. But it is often difficult for an outsider to judge the degree of their expertness and impartiality.

On most matters we are all inexpert, and to that extent are rumor prone. We have neither time nor patience to check what we hear against outside standards of evidence, even when such standards exist and are available. Since this is so, our only dependable defense against rumor is a generalized skepticism of all hearsay reports. A wholesome degree of such skepticism, we hope, will accrue to readers of this book.

In gathering our material we have benefited by the experience of R. H. Knapp, who in the early days of the war worked on the problem of rumor for the Massachusetts Committee of Public Safety. For helpful criticisms of the manuscript we are indebted to Ada and Robert Allport and to Dorothy L. Postman. The latter, as well as Sylvia B. Korchin and Lorraine Lerman, helped in the preparation of the manuscript. Aid in obtaining illustrations was generously given by Dr. Arnold Weinberger, Mr. Ross E. Taggart, Mrs. A. Raphael Salem, of the Houghton Library, and Dr. Jakob Rosenberg, of the Fogg Art Museum at Harvard. We wish to thank Mrs. Eleanor D. Sprague for her assistance in the preparation of the manuscript, and Mr. Charles Wadsworth for drawing the stimulus pictures used in the rumor experiments.

We wish also to thank the following publishers for permission to reprint illustrations or textual passages from copyright works: The Bell Syndicate, The Bobbs-Merrill Company, Cambridge University Press, E. P. Dutton & Company, Inc., Houghton Mifflin Company, Alfred A. Knopf, Inc., and Princeton University Press. We also thank the editors and publishers of the following organizations and periodicals: Associated Press, Boston *Globe*, Boston *Herald*, *New York Herald Tribune*, *New Yorker*, *PM*, *Public Opinion Quarterly*, *Science*, *Syracuse Post-Standard*.

G. W. A.
L. P.

December 1, 1946
Harvard University

TABLE OF CONTENTS

1. **RUMOR IN WARTIME**   1
   Pearl Harbor Rumors—Rumors and National Morale—Rumor Defense—Rumor Offensives—Rumor in the Armed Services
2. **WHY RUMORS CIRCULATE**   33
   The Basic Law of Rumor—Motives in Rumor Mongering—Projection—A Generalization of the Rumor Formula—Secondary Reasons for the Circulation of Rumor—Home-stretch Rumors
3. **TESTIMONY AND RECALL**   49
   Testimony—Perceiving, Remembering, Reporting—Individual *vs.* Social Memory
4. **AN EXPERIMENTAL APPROACH**   61
   The Problem—The Laboratory Approach—Standard Procedure
5. **RESULTS OF THE EXPERIMENTS: LEVELING AND SHARPENING**   75
   Leveling—Limits of Leveling—Sharpening
6. **RESULTS OF THE EXPERIMENTS: ASSIMILATION**   99
   Definition of Assimilation—Relatively Unemotional Assimilation—More Highly Motivated Assimilation

7. RESULTS OF THE EXPERIMENTS: CONCLUDED — 116
Shift of Theme—Inventions and Elaborations—Effort After Meaning—Verbal Misunderstandings—Time and Place Errors—Children's Reports

8. THE BASIC PATTERN OF DISTORTION — 134
Universality of the Three-part Pattern of Distortion—Creative Embedding—Is a Rumor Never True?—Exaggeration—Elaboration—Condensation—Conventionalization

9. RUMOR AND SOCIETY — 159
Rumor and History—Rumor and Legend—Metaphorical Significance of Rumor and Legend—The Classification of Rumors—Fusion of Passions and Antipathies—Rumor Publics—Whispering Campaigns—The Press and Rumor—Labeled Rumor—Rumor and Humor—Rumors and Riots—Summary

10. THE ANALYSIS OF RUMOR — 200
Seven Case Studies—Guide for the Analysis of Rumor—Originals for Solution

BIBLIOGRAPHY — 227

APPENDIX — 233
Standards for Agencies Working on the Prevention and Control of Wartime Rumor

INDEX — 241

1 RUMOR IN WARTIME

RUMOR became a problem of grave national concern in the tense years 1942 and 1943. At that time a high official in the Office of War Information gave a reason for rumor and a recipe for its control that were partly —but only partly—correct. "Rumor," he said, "flies in the absence of news. Therefore, we must give the people the most accurate possible news, promptly and completely."

It is true that rumor thrives on lack of news. The almost total absence of fear-inspired rumors in Britain during the darkest days of the blitz was due to the people's conviction that the government was giving full and accurate news of the destruction and that they, therefore, knew the worst. When people are sure they know the worst, they are unlikely to darken the picture further by inventing unnecessary bogies to explain their anxieties to themselves.

At the same time, it would not be hard to prove that rumor also flies thickest when news is most plentiful. There were few rumors about our desperate losses at Pearl Harbor until the papers themselves had published an official report on the disaster. Although there were scattered rumors of Hitler's death before the papers told of the assassination attempt in the summer of 1944, there were many more immediately afterward. The deluge of peace rumors in late April and early May, 1945, coincided with the open discussion of the approaching collapse of Germany in the press. Similarly, a flood of rumors swamped the country during the final hours before V-J Day. Premature stories of the war's end spread faster than they could be officially denied.

One of the odd episodes in the history of rumor was the spreading of tales of the death of many notable persons, including General Marshall, Bing Crosby, and Mayor La Guardia, within a few hours of the release of the news of President Roosevelt's sudden death on April 12, 1945. If public events are not newsworthy, they are unlikely to breed rumors, and in certain circumstances the more prominence the press gives the news—especially momentous news—the more numerous and serious are the rumored distortions this news will undergo.

The OWI official made his error in assuming that rumor is a purely intellectual commodity, something one substitutes, *faute de mieux*, for reliable information. He overlooked the fact that when events of great importance occur the individual never stops at a mere acceptance of the event. His life is deeply affected. In his mind the emotional overtones of the event breed all sorts of fantasies. He seeks explanations and imagines remote consequences.

And yet the official did state, inexactly and too simply, a part of the formula for rumor spreading and rumor control. Rumor travels when events have importance in the lives of individuals and when the news received about them is either lacking or subjectively ambiguous. The ambiguity may arise from the fact that the news is not clearly reported, or from the fact that conflicting versions of the news have reached the individual, or from his incapacity to comprehend the news he receives. In the summer of 1945 the atomic bomb was the subject of many rumors, especially among the uneducated. It was rumored that lethal radiations hover for a long time over an area hit by an atomic blast, making all life impossible. A public opinion poll records the belief of one-fourth of the population that the discovery might cause the earth to explode in one huge atomic blast. Scientists went to a great deal of trouble to discredit these stories. There were also many Utopian rumors about vast improvements in the standard of living that would immediately result from the harnessing of atomic energy. People were simply unprepared to evaluate the news they had received from Nagasaki and Hiroshima.

Most important of all, especially in wartime, rumor will race when individuals distrust the news that reaches them.

PEARL HARBOR RUMORS

In January and February, 1942, rumors of fear deluged America. Their burden was always the same: our losses during the Pearl Harbor raid were much greater than the authorities admitted. Some versions claimed that the entire Pacific Fleet had been sunk at Pearl Harbor on December 7; others that 1000 planes had been destroyed on the ground that same day. It is now known that the full extent of the losses sustained at Pearl Harbor was not divulged in the first official reports, probably for reasons of military security. The stories grew out of the suspicion that such was the case. Distrusting the news, the public had no secure standards of evidence by which to check and control its frightened imagination. So widespread and upsetting were the tales that President Roosevelt felt it necessary to devote part of his fireside chat delivered on February 23, 1942, to a repudiation of these bogy rumors. Even then the President could not tell the whole story, but he did his best to allay the fears of the people by divulging as much of the truth as he could without endangering national security. What effect his assurances had we shall indicate shortly.

First, let us apply our rumor formula to the Pearl Harbor

stories. We find—as in all rumors—that although the incident had great importance in the lives of the people, the news pertaining to it was subjectively ambiguous. In this particular case the ambiguity arose out of three conditions operating at the time: (1) Many people were profoundly distrustful of the administration in Washington, of its erstwhile reforms, of its interventionism, of its alphabetical agencies, and of its "long-haired" experts.[1] (2) In general, people were uncertain of the news policies of the government in wartime. Even those who were not opposed to the administration did not have full confidence in the official handling of news. In the early days of the war, distrust may have had some justification.[2] (3) Most of all, people's lives had been profoundly upset by the coming of the war: families were disrupted, plans altered, a dark and uncertain future loomed ahead. More specifically, a great deal of fear was felt by citizens who were not sure of our capacity to ward off bombing attacks or even an invasion. *To explain this fear* it was necessary to find a plausible cause. The one most readily at hand, most concrete, and most reasonable was the assumption that our defensive forces were in fact almost totally destroyed. We were virtually defenseless. Since no engagement other than Pearl Harbor had occurred, it must have been at Pearl Harbor that we were rendered helpless. It was easier to believe in con-

[1] That rumors reflecting misconduct of the war were in fact believed more readily by citizens who opposed the Roosevelt administration than by those who were friendly toward it is a fact established by a research conducted by F. H. Allport and M. Lepkin (1945).

[2] That a considerable distrust of official news dispatches existed throughout the war is shown by a series of public opinion polls asking the question, "Do you think the government is giving the public as much information as it should about the war?" Three days after Pearl Harbor only 68 percent of the people were ready to answer "yes" to this question. The number answering "yes" fluctuated throughout the war, never exceeding 70 percent, and going down as low as 51 percent in March, 1944. (Data supplied by the Office of Public Opinion Research, Princeton University.)

crete, recent, dramatic causes rather than in the more distant, less identifiable cause, i.e., our own failure to prepare for national defense. Thus a strong emotion accompanied by an "effort after meaning" negated such news as was received.[8]

The need to rationalize post-Pearl Harbor fears was strong enough in many people to withstand the formal reassurances of the Commander-in-Chief. Quite unexpectedly an experimental opportunity was created by his fireside chat of February 23, 1942. It so happened that on February 20 a group of 200 undergraduate students had been asked the question, "Do you believe that our losses at Pearl Harbor were greater, much greater, the same, less, or much less than have been officially stated?" The results in summary were:

> Greater or much greater .... 69 percent
> Same or less .... 31 percent

Then came the President's talk to which the majority of Americans listened. On February 25, an equivalent group of 200 students (the same group not being available) were asked precisely the same question, and at the same time were asked whether they had heard or read the President's speech. Among those who were unfamiliar with his statement *no change* in the percentages occurred. Among those who had read or heard the assurances, the results were:

> Greater or much greater .... 46 percent
> Same or less .... 54 percent

Here was an unusual opportunity to measure the effectiveness of a solemn voice of authority speaking through the

[8] One of the most important psychological sources of rumor spreading is people's desire to understand and simplify the many complicated events and developments which follow each other, often with bewildering speed. Rumors serve to make things simpler than they actually are. This striving for simplicity and understanding we shall call "effort after meaning."

powerful medium of the radio in a time of crisis. If the experiment is representative for the country as a whole (and there is no reason to suppose that college students are atypical in this matter), we may say that the President with a few reassuring words succeeded in changing the belief of 23 percent of the citizens. From one point of view, this is a dramatic achievement. To allay suspicion, to reduce fear, to obliterate a defeatist belief among perhaps 20,000,000 citizens in so short a time is a tribute to the prestige of the President and to the effectiveness of radio as a medium.

At the same time, the majority of those believing the deleterious rumors kept on believing them, in spite of the President's best efforts. In these individuals, we must assume, the subjective anxiety was so great, or their personal distrust of Mr. Roosevelt so intense, that even news conveyed with the highest voice of authority did not break the hold that the rumor had over them.

RUMORS AND NATIONAL MORALE

PEARL HARBOR rumors, along with all other rumors of excessive casualties, may be classified as fear (or "bogy") rumors. To this group belongs a story circulated in New England in 1942. The kernel of fact was that a collier had been sunk as a result of an accident near the Cape Cod Canal. But so great was the anxiety of the New England public that this accident became a fantastic tale of an American ship being torpedoed with the loss of thousands of nurses who were aboard her. The story had other versions equally gruesome.[4]

To the fear rumors belong also the stories of "basket cases." A woman, it was said, had received a War Department notifi-

---
[4] Cf. R. H. Knapp (1944).

cation to meet her returning soldier husband at the town railroad station. She did so and, according to the story, the husband was delivered to her in a basket with both arms and both legs amputated.

This grim tale, made out of the whole cloth of macabre fantasy, circulated widely in 1944. During the entire war, there was but one case in which all four limbs suffered amputation. And the reality in this single case was very different from the imagined helplessness of the victim and alleged heartlessness of the War Department. The true facts are told in an Associated Press story of August 12, 1945.[5]

ARMLESS, LEGLESS WAR VET GIVEN $60,000 IN CASH

M. Sgt. Frederic Hensel, only soldier in this war to lose parts of both arms and legs in combat, and his wife, Jewell, received some $60,000 in cash gifts today as they celebrated their third wedding anniversary at the Army's Percy Jones Hospital.

Hensel captured the public's admiration when he arrived here from Okinawa five weeks ago and announced he was going into the chicken farm business despite what seemed insurmountable handicaps.

In tribute to his courage people from all over the country began sending contributions to help him. More than $26,920 received by the *Detroit Free Press* and $25,000 by the *Chicago Herald and American* were presented to the Hensels. Al Greenberg, Louisville, Ky., businessman, said he had collected nearly $4000 and direct contributions to the Hensels totaled more than $4000.

This account makes no mention of the medical, prosthetic, and financial aid given by the government to rehabilitate this courageous (and far from helpless) veteran.

Bogy rumors, especially in the early days of the war, were somewhat more numerous than rumors of wishful thinking ("pipe dream" rumors). These latter usually took the form of predicting an early end to the war. Lloyds of London, it

---

[5] Reprinted by permission of the Associated Press.

was said, was quoting odds of ten to one that the war would end before Christmas (1942). An absurd little story was told all over the country, to the effect that a certain fortuneteller predicted that Hitler would be dead within six months. The man to whom she made this prediction, the story ran, seemed skeptical. But the seer persisted and added, "Yes, Hitler will be dead in six months' time, and that is just as certain as the fact that you will soon have a corpse in your automobile." Not long afterward, the tale continued, the skeptical patron while out driving picked up an injured man along the road to transport him to a hospital, but on arriving found that the man had died in the car.

It seems odd that this bizarre bit of nonsense should have been found interesting enough to merit widespread repetition. The explanation lies partly in the importance of Hitler's possible death to the rumor spreaders, partly in their wish to believe in his early demise, partly in the subjective ambiguity that surrounds the date of anyone's death, and partly in the need to rationalize—to make plausible—the wish itself. Plausibility is secured through devious logic to the effect that if the fortuneteller was so successful in predicting the corpse in the car, presumably her clairvoyance respecting Hitler's end was something to be trusted.

On the whole, wish rumors, with their characteristically optimistic coloring, were relatively few until the collapse of Germany was imminent. During the month of April, 1945, however, rumors of Hitler's death and of the unconditional surrender of Germany came in a mighty flood, aided near the end by the hair-trigger press and radio which "jumped the gun" two or three days before the actual end.

In the case of these final peace rumors we are dealing with a special phenomenon of rumor which we may call the *goal gradient effect* (see p. 47). Although sustained and speeded by desire and by ambiguity of news, these peace rumors were partly the product of simple expectancy. When we are awaiting a piece of news, it is easy for us to believe it has arrived. How many people "think" they have heard the telephone ring when they are momentarily awaiting a call?

The goal gradient effect due to expectancy is illustrated in the following editorial from the Boston *Globe,* September 6, 1944.[6] The account also calls attention to the fact that rumors may have a "kernel of truth." In this case 9000 Germans did surrender at Mons—but not the entire German army!

FALSE DAWN

A rumor starting from the Brussels radio gave a false thrill to many people yesterday because it announced that the Germans had capitulated. Two hours later a flat denial came from Supreme Headquarters and there was an apology from the station that had first sent it out. The apparent origin was the surrender of 9000 German soldiers at Mons.

There will be other reports that the Germans have given up, but it may be a considerable time before the real unconditional surrender is announced to an expectant world. It is quite possible that some of the ill-founded rumors will have even less to support them than that of yesterday. The Germans are being beaten, but nobody knows how long a substantial force will stick it out, continuing to fight.

Meanwhile the rest of us, civilians as well as those in uniform, will do our parts by carrying on without paying attention to the tales that fly about, pleasing though they may be.

Fear rumors, like wish rumors, had an important effect on home-front morale during the war. The former, alarming in character, tended to inhibit one's confidence in the successful outcome of his own war efforts. Engendering need-

[6] Reprinted by permission of the Boston *Globe.*

less anxiety, they sometimes led to a defeatist point of view.

Wish rumors, on the other hand, with their Pollyanna optimism, sometimes led to a debilitating complacency. The readiness with which people "let down" at the receipt of good news is shown by the falling off of blood donations after the news of important Allied victories. Whenever people believed rumors of impending success or the approaching end of the war, they tended to slacken their efforts and reduce their sacrifices.

Important as are the consequences of fear and wish rumors for national morale, they are relatively slight compared with the effects of the third, and largest, class of wartime rumors, stories reflecting *hate* and *hostility*—"wedge drivers."

Table 1, prepared by R. H. Knapp (1944), gives a percentage distribution of 1000 rumors collected from all over the United States during the summer of 1942.[7]

Knapp's analysis indicates that approximately two-thirds of all rumors current in 1942 were hostile in their intent and divisive in their effects. About 9.3 percent were anti-Semitic, 3.1 percent anti-Negro, 21.4 percent anti-Administration, 19.6 percent anti-Army or Navy. Complaints and accusations were directed in an unceasing stream against groups of fellow-Americans, all of whom were, in truth, making sacrifices to win a common war. The effect of these stories could be only harmful to national unity at a time of crisis. Victims of the stories grew embittered, and suspicion and recrimination became common just at a time when they could least be tolerated.

[7] This table is based on reports from every state in the union received in response to a request printed at the end of a story in *The Reader's Digest*, September, 1942, entitled, "Boston Makes War on Rumor." It is reprinted here by permission of the *Public Opinion Quarterly*.

RUMORS AND NATIONAL MORALE 11

> The Navy (reasons unexplained) has dumped three carloads of coffee into New York Harbor.
> The Army wastes whole sides of beef.
> The Russians get most of our butter and just use it for greasing their guns.
> The President is Jewish.
> The Red Cross charges the boys in Iceland outrageous prices for the sweaters knit at home.
> The Jews are evading the draft.
> The Negroes are forming Eleanor Clubs, in which they assemble guns and ice picks for a charge upon the Capitol.

These are only a few of the monstrosities current early in the war. With variations they were heard throughout the war, and their descendants are heard even today.

Do fear, wish, and hate stories really exhaust the supply of wartime rumor as our discussion and as Table 1 imply? Not quite. There is in addition a small group of rumors that are unclassifiable. These are largely of pseudo-news variety, and most of them might be called *curiosity* rumors. A few samples follow:

> The *Queen Mary* sailed yesterday with 7000 troops.
> They say schools may close so children can assist with the harvesting.
> I heard they're planning to build a big army camp over near Middletown.

It is probable that rumors of this order were much more common than Table 1 indicates. It may be that the rumor reporters did not think them "hot" enough to submit. Nor are they particularly significant for morale unless, of course, they imply a violation of the security of information (see p. 16).

TABLE 1

CLASSIFICATION OF 1000 RUMORS REPORTED FROM ALL PARTS OF THE COUNTRY DURING THE SUMMER OF 1942

(Each entry in the table represents the percentage that a given type of rumor constituted of the total regional sample.)

	U.S.A.	New England	Atlantic Seaboard	South	Middle West	Far West
Wedge-driving Rumors (Total)	65.9	63.2	62.0	61.6	72.5	67.8
Anti-Semitic						
Draft evasion	3.6	7.2	6.6	.9	3.2	1.1
Others	5.7	6.4	7.0	4.2	4.6	6.9
Total	9.3	13.6	13.5	5.2	7.7	8.0
Anti-British	7.3	9.6	9.4	5.2	7.0	5.8
Anti-Administration						
Roosevelt personal	3.1	2.4	2.0	3.3	6.3	....
Salvage and rationing	6.1	4.0	3.5	8.9	6.7	6.9
War bonds and savings unsafe	3.7	1.6	2.7	1.4	6.0	5.8
Selective service: grievances, abuses	2.2	2.4	.8	1.8	4.2	1.6
Graft, waste, inefficiency, accidents	4.4	3.2	2.0	4.7	5.3	6.9
Total	21.4	13.6	10.9	20.2	28.4	22.3
Anti-Negro	3.1	.8	2.3	8.5	2.1	1.1
Anti-Army and Navy						
Government leaders incompetent	3.1	1.6	2.0	2.3	4.2	4.8
Abuses of soldiers and sailors	6.7	8.8	9.8	5.6	5.6	4.2
Drunkenness and immorality	2.6	1.6	2.7	2.8	1.8	4.2
Supplies, equipment: no good, lacking	6.0	4.0	4.1	7.5	7.0	5.3
Supplies, equipment: wasted, misused	2.1	2.4	1.2	2.8	1.8	3.2
Total	19.6	17.6	20.7	21.2	20.3	20.7
Anti-Red Cross	2.2	4.8	2.3	.5	2.8	1.6
Anti-labor	1.6	.8	.4	.5	1.8	4.8
Anti-business	2.3	1.6	2.3	.5	2.5	4.8

TABLE I (*Continued*)

CLASSIFICATION OF 1000 RUMORS REPORTED FROM ALL PARTS OF THE COUNTRY DURING THE SUMMER OF 1942

(Each entry in the table represents the percentage that a given type of rumor constituted of the total regional sample.)

	U.S.A.	New England	Atlantic Seaboard	South	Middle West	Far West
Fear Rumors (Total)	25.4	28.2	26.9	33.8	20.3	19.6
In armed forces						
Suicides	.6	....	1.2	....	1.1	....
Insanity	1.0	....	.8	1.4	1.8	.5
Plagues and epidemics	1.2	....	2.0	2.3	.4	1.1
Excessive casualties	5.1	9.6	9.9	2.8	4.6	.5
Total	8.0	9.6	12.9	6.6	7.7	2.1
Fifth-column activities						
"Bread and submarine" story	2.0	1.6	1.6	6.1	.4	.5
Supplying the enemy	.7	2.4	.4	1.4	....	.5
Spy activity, sabotage	4.2	6.4	2.0	8.5	3.5	2.1
Total	6.9	10.4	3.9	16.0	3.9	3.2
Atrocities						
"Tongue and stamp" story	3.7	....	1.6	3.8	6.0	5.8
Others	1.0	1.6	.8	.9	1.1	1.6
Total	4.8	1.6	2.3	4.7	7.0	7.4
Unrevealed enemy action						
Secret weapon or plans	1.2	.8	.8	1.4	1.4	1.6
Shipping losses	1.0	.8	1.2	2.8	....	1.1
Unrevealed enemy activities	3.3	5.6	5.9	2.3	.4	4.2
Total	5.7	7.2	7.8	6.6	1.8	6.9
Pipe-dream Rumors (Total)	2.0	2.4	3.9	1.4	.7	1.6
Peace rumors	.6	.8	2.0	....	....	....
"Corpse in car"	.4	....	.8	....	.7	....
Enemy sub washed up, destroyed	.6	.8	.4	.9	....	1.1
Victory rumors	.5	.8	.8	.5	....	.5
Miscellaneous Rumors (Total)	6.7	5.6	7.8	3.8	6.0	11.6

RUMOR DEFENSE   It is small wonder that government officials and patriotic citizens became alarmed at the potential damage of rumor to home-front morale. Though they believed that rumor mongering was somehow a natural and inevitable symptom of wartime jitters, they did not know how far it might go in breeding defeatism, apathy, or internal disruption within the nation.

One wartime study in the spread and acceptance of rumor was conducted by Ruch and Young (1942). Certain statements from the Axis broadcasts were circulated, such as "More than 300 draftees recently deserted from Fort Dix in New Jersey." A "circulation index" was computed for each Axis rumor. In New York this index (i.e., the percentage of people interviewed who had heard the rumor) was 8 percent, in Boston 5½ percent. Nearly 23 percent of the total sample had heard at least one of the rumors. Did they believe them? An "acceptance index" was computed by asking whether the subject thought a rumor true (whether or not he had ever heard it previously). The average acceptance in New York City was 9.4 percent, in Boston 3.8 percent. It turned out that both circulation and acceptance were greater among poorer people than among the more prosperous, among those over forty-five than among younger persons, and among Jews than among non-Jews. The rumor proneness of the Jews in this investigation is probably to be explained by the fact that the rumors were chiefly of the "bogy" variety, easily assimilated to the insecurity and apprehensions of many Jews in the early days of the war.

Government agencies with their widespread intake of

public opinion from all over the country were aware of the spread of damaging rumors, but what action to take was a perplexing problem to them. On one occasion, we have seen, the President himself took to the radio to deny a specific rumor. Again, later in the war, he referred explicitly to rumors reflecting racial and religious animosity and attempted to discourage their circulation. *Divide and Conquer* and other publications of the short-lived Office of Facts and Figures were antidotes to rumor, and for a short time the Office of War Information assigned one of its units to rumor control, with Mr. Leo Rosten in charge.

The philosophy of this agency was somewhat different from that underlying the privately organized "rumor clinics," whose story we shall shortly tell. The clinics concentrated their effort upon the refutation of false stories. The OWI, on the other hand, pinned its faith on the formula, "Rumor flies in the absence of news," and centered its energy upon improving the quality of news releases and increasing the confidence of the public in them. Although the OWI expressed doubt about the wisdom of repeating rumors for the purpose of refuting them, it refrained from interfering with the operation of the popular newspaper rumor clinics. The OWI's philosophy held that to smother a rumor with facts is better than to single it out for disproof, lest in the process it become unduly advertised. The rumor clinic philosophy leaned in the opposite direction. People won't see the relevance of facts unless it is pointed out to them. Name the rumor and pound it hard was the policy. Both agencies perhaps erred in placing too much faith in facts and logic. Information and argument are seldom sufficient to obliterate rumors that feed upon fears and hates. When an anti-Semite charges that the Jews are evading the draft, and is then confronted with irrefutable facts proving that Jews are represented in the armed services fully in proportion to their numbers in the general population, what does he do? He shifts his rumor (not his hostility), and now says, "Yeah, but they hold all the cushion jobs in the Army." Since it is impossible to determine who had the "easy" jobs and who had the "tough" ones in the Army, refutation is no longer possible, even if it were profitable. It takes more than correct information and logic to silence the tongue of a motivated rumor spreader. But in a democracy (unlike a totalitarian state) all agencies, governmental or private, are duty bound to make a maximum appeal to the rational capacities of all citizens.

By and large the information agencies of the government used an indirect attack upon the problem of rumor. Relevant facts were issued. The cause of national unity was pleaded in poster and pamphlet. Undercover investigations by the Federal Bureau of Investigation and by the intelligence branches of the Army and Navy pursued the trails of particularly venomous rumors.

Most of the effort that the OWI devoted to rumor was concerned with a very special aspect of the problem, namely, "security of information." Many arresting posters of the type shown in Figure 1 were produced and distributed. Newspaper and radio cooperation was secured. Eloquent slogans were invented, perhaps the most striking being "Zip Your Lip and Save a Ship." Loose talk diminished. Many observers expressed surprise at the way in which an essentially unregimented people learned to guard war secrets. Our ability to do so became a matter for national pride, as the following news story from the Boston *Globe* of August 9, 1945, indicates.[8]

[8] Reprinted by permission of the Boston *Globe* and the Associated Press.

Fig. 1. Typical security-of-information posters (OWI).

HOW BEST-KEPT SECRET OF THE WAR WAS KEPT

Byron Price, Director of Censorship, says the long work on the atomic bomb was the best-kept single secret of the war.

For keeping the secret he gives special praise to the newspapers, radio broadcasters, magazines, book publishers. Says Price:

"The secrecy results obtained by the newspapers and broadcasters should be sufficient answer to anyone who thinks voluntary censorship cannot work."

These groups accepted at war's start, voluntarily, a censorship code. They agreed not to publish or broadcast anything to hurt the war effort.

All censorship during the war, under Price's direction, has been on that voluntary basis. It continues that way.

About 20,000 news outlets—11,000 weekly newspapers, 2000 dailies, and thousands of radio stations, magazines, religious organs, trade publications, college journals, and book publishers—were asked:

Not to publish or broadcast about "new or secret military weapons . . . experiments."

This request was followed. It resulted in silence on a number of experiments, such as radar, and particularly about the atomic experiments, although at that time not too many people knew about that.

Then it was decided to build large plants—two in Tennessee and one in the state of Washington—to carry out the work the scientists were devising.

This meant hiring 125,000 plant workers, numberless contractors and subcontractors around the country, and obtaining the help of some universities.

So in June, 1943, Price's office sent out a confidential note to its whole list of 20,000 news outlets. This note said:

"You are asked not to publish or broadcast any information whatever regarding war experiments involving:

"Production or utilization of atom smashing, atomic energy, atomic fission, atomic splitting, or any of their equivalents.

"The use for military purposes of radium or radioactive materials, heavy water, high voltage discharges, equipment, cyclotrons.

"The following elements or any of their compounds: polonium, uranium, ytterbium, hafnium, protactinium, radium, rhenium, thorium, deuterium."

By surrounding uranium—the heart of the atomic experiments—with those of other elements, all legitimate although funny-sounding, direct attention on uranium was avoided.

About 250 newspapers and radio stations—in the area around the experimental plants in Tennessee and Washington and around a testing ground in New Mexico—

received special requests from Price's office to avoid speculation on the work being done there. So all over the country—although thousands of people wondered what was happening and some others may have guessed—the secret was kept.

Although the campaign for security of information was undoubtedly a success, it was found not to be easy to design methods for combating the less definable and more insidious types of rumor that are subtly divisive and enervating in character.

The best-known attempt was the rumor clinic. Credit for initiating this journalistic weapon of defense belongs to Mr. W. G. Gavin of the Boston *Herald-Traveler*, who between March, 1942, and December, 1943, edited a weekly feature with the aid of local psychologists and other public-spirited citizens. The idea caught on and was imitated in more than 40 newspapers and a number of magazines in the United States and Canada. Often the rumors nailed were simple in type and the replies brief. Occasionally, however, as the following samples show, a psychologist wrote the column, attempting to popularize some fragments of the professional knowledge necessary to an adequate understanding of the more complex and insidious rumors. The first example is slightly condensed from the Syracuse *Post-Standard*.[9]

THE RUMOR CLINIC

CHIVALRY TOWARD WACS

Today's clinic in charge of the Professor of Political Psychology at the University of Syracuse

Few items of subversive gossip have given your Rumor Clinic more dismay than the false rumors which are now circulating about the WACs. Here are some examples: RUMOR: "Over 500 WACs

[9] Reprinted by permission of the Syracuse *Post-Standard*.

have been discharged from the service because of illegitimate pregnancy." RUMOR: "500 pregnant WACs have been returned from North Africa." RUMOR: "General Eisenhower says the WACs are his greatest source of trouble and are of no value to him." There is, of course, not the slightest shred of evidence to support such tales as these.

The rumor concerning the WACs in North Africa is false, for one thing, because it is a mathematical impossibility. The entire number of WACs stationed in this war theater is considerably less than 500. (The exact number is a military secret.) As for what General Eisenhower really said, we have it on record that he considers the WACs a highly superior organization and wishes that he had more of them in North Africa.

The next time you hear rumors of this kind, ask the one who tells them how many cases of WAC delinquency he knows about by direct and reliable evidence. Then ask him how many WACs he actually knows. You will be convinced by such inquiries that these rumors, which tar an entire service organization, are just another case of imagination, hearsay, or of jumping to conclusions.

Rumor of wholesale WAC immorality are absurd upon their face and are refuted both by the facts and by their own lack of logic. Yet strangely enough, they are widespread and increasingly malicious. Something must be radically wrong with our American standards of chivalry, to say nothing of our intelligence.

Not Stopped by Facts

These WAC rumors, unlike many others, are not stopped by the thoughtful presentation of facts. The trouble lies deeper; it goes down into our own inner emotions, and is based upon things which most of us carry around inside of us without being aware of it. Objective evidence will not cure it; we must have insight into ourselves.

We human beings are complex creatures. A good deal of the time we are disturbed about something, but we do not know just what is bothering us. Tho grown up, we are in some ways still like babies, who are frightened, frustrated, pained, or restless, but don't know what it is all about.

There is a special reason, however, why we grown-ups cannot always be clear about our own inner feelings. "Society" makes demands upon us. We want to stand high in other people's estimation, and also in our own. Many of the perfectly natural feelings which we have we are ashamed to recognize or to admit even to ourselves.

This attitude (which is called "repression") makes us inclined to imagine or to exaggerate the presence of these very tendencies in others. We think that the trouble lies in someone else—not in us. We do not like to admit, for example, that we are afraid; and we sometimes do violent things and make sweeping accusations to cover up this fact. Witness the cruelties perpetrated and "justified" by tyrannical leaders when they are put on the defensive.

We do not like to admit that we are narrow-minded, prejudiced, or selfish. If, therefore, we can outwardly blame some group to which we are hostile for alleged acts of selfishness, we can thus divert attention from our own inner prejudice against this group, and at the same time we can overlook the selfishness which lies within ourselves. We do not like to recognize that we have defects or inferiorities. And so, if we can point out imperfections in others, it helps our own self-esteem. Many of us are ashamed or afraid of our own impulses; and that may lead to accusations of irregularities in others.

Real Cause Found

Instead of admitting these natural human qualities in ourselves, many of us tend to shut them up in forbidden compartments of the mind. We just pretend that they are not there. We keep the "front parlor" of our minds open for our conscious use; but we have our secret "back-hall closet" which we do not like to enter. We receive our respectable callers by the front stairs; but the back stairs are reserved for an entrance to this forbidden closet.

Right here we find the real explanation for many of the false rumors of hate and prejudice, the "anti" rumors, which drive wedges between us and our fellow Americans. It is not the true outer facts which drive us to distrust and smear certain groups of our fellow-citizens, but the feelings which we have cooped up in the back-hall closets of our own minds. Up the backstairs come rumors of the short-comings or immorality of others. They play upon our fears and the insecurities we feel about ourselves. But we keep the whole mess out of the front parlor.

Without realizing it we refuse to believe that we have any such weakness; we believe, instead, what the rumor-monger says about someone else. We "project" upon some relatively innocent victim the things which we don't like in ourselves. And, to make ourselves feel still more secure, we join in the same hue and cry against the victim. We pass the rumor on. Sometimes we even embellish it.

Here is something that is even stranger, but equally true. If we have some kind of desire which we think is bad or dangerous, and so keep it shut in our back closet, we do not kill the desire. We have shut it out of the parlor; but that does not mean that it is not going to be indulged or satisfied. On the contrary, every bit of "juicy" gossip we hear helps to "feed" it.

Our Impulses Responsible

In short, we can enjoy these forbidden pleasures, at least in im-

RUMOR DEFENSE

agination, so long as we keep them out of the front parlor. In fact, shutting the closet door gives us a better opportunity to enjoy them. This is true so long as we are not clearly aware of the impulse which we are thus indulging. If we should suddenly start to become aware of it, we are likely to become frightened. We may then find some scapegoat to "project" it on, and become "righteously" indignant at somebody else.

We can then say that the British, the Russians, the Jews or other groups are secretly getting what they want out of the war—we have no feeling about it except the most noble kind of patriotism. We can say—"Those horrible, immoral WACs!—how different they are from sober respectable people like us, who are not sex-minded." But if we have shut our sex life in the back-hall closet, the chances are 10 to one that we are getting secret enjoyment in contemplating these "terrible practices" of the WACs —in believing them, and in talking about them.

Need to Understand

Slanderous rumors, which divide Americans against one another, are not made merely by incidents, nor by the false and careless words; nor by Axis agents; they are a part of the stuff which is inside those who listen to them. When we learn to know ourselves we no longer enjoy such backstairs gossip, nor are we shocked by it. We do not pass it on to others as something spicy or dramatic. Since we understand what it comes from inside those who tell it, we do not believe it.

Every American, thru self-knowledge, can play this part in the stopping of dangerous, wedge-driving rumors. Each one of us can help to uphold the honor and dignity of our women's army corps —to protect these loyal women of America from the back-hall closets of the human mind. Will you do your part?

The second example is reprinted from the Boston *Sunday Herald*, July 18, 1943.[10]

THE RUMOR CLINIC

Today we consider a composite rumor. Some part of it you've surely heard.

RUMOR: *Some minority group (Negro), (Jew), (Catholic) (or other) is not loyal to America, but is (planning a riot), (plotting to get control of the government), (evading military service).*

Fact: Not one shred of tenable evidence has ever been produced to justify any one of these slanders

[10] Reprinted by permission of the Boston *Sunday Herald*.

against special groups of our fellow-countrymen. Such rumors are bigoted and treacherous lies.

Analysis: Even though they are totally unsupported by evidence, these morale-shattering stories are so common that there must be some mental quirks that account for their spread. We have asked a psychologist to explain why today, just when Americans need most to join hands, many of them instead are busy spreading hate-rumors against their fellow-citizens. The Chairman of Harvard's Department of Psychology answers some important questions. His replies reveal the unsavory situation that makes us prey to racial and religious slanders.

Q.—Are racial rumors really dangerous?

A.—Of all the rumors now loose in America, racial rumors are the MOST DANGEROUS. A spreader of racial rumors can do more damage than a saboteur who blows up a factory. The Detroit slanderers, for example, not only lost countless hours from the war industries, but they roused mobs that behaved like the most bestial of Nazis. Worst of all, they embittered the lives of one-tenth of our population, lessening their faith in American democracy and fair-play. If there are many more such incidents, we may lose the war (and deserve to). Hitler's only hope now is civil disunity in the United States.

Q.—Why do some people have racial hates and indulge in racial slander?

A.—The answer is not simple. Perhaps the basic reason is that the racial-gossip feels insecure in his job or deprived of the good things of life. He develops a deep-seated anger. Oddly enough, he doesn't know exactly what he is so angry about or whom to blame. Hence he picks out some more or less innocent bystander and "lets go." He may pick out his wife or children, or even the family cat. Race-haters are those insecure folk who pick out some strange-looking group of people who, because of different religion or color, are conspicuous. They vent their aggression against these innocent mortals who have the misfortune to have "high visibility." For example, we may safely say that Negroes are seldom, if ever, the cause of Negro-hate; the cause lies in the economic, family or personal tangles of the hater himself.

Q.—Why is it that racial rumors flourish in wartime?

A.—The principal reason is that we suffer more confusion and more irritations. Instead of putting the blame for our jitters where it belongs—on the enemy—we pick out a nearer victim whom we see daily. Things seem strange and uncertain to us, so our tabloid mentality tells us that the "strange and uncertain" group that lives across the tracks must be to blame.

Q.—Does everyone who spreads racial rumors feel, consciously or unconsciously, insecurity or guilt?

A.—Not all. The ring leaders undoubtedly do, and some of them are first-class paranoiacs. But other people may be merely the sheep that follow. They like to conform, and they gain a perverted feeling of security by joining the persecutors. Their egos get inflated when they ally themselves with the "whiter," "more Christian," "better" group, forgetting that in so doing they are prigs for considering themselves better than the other fellow, and cowards for attacking a smaller and more defenseless group.

Q.—How, in your opinion, can scapegoating be controlled in this country?

A.—In various ways. First, both adults and children should be taught the truth regarding racial differences (which are few and negligible), and they should be taught the simple psychology of scapegoating I have attempted to outline. Then, we should let ourselves learn the good traits of our neighbors across the tracks. The casualty list is an answer to the question: Who is a loyal American? For a real cure, however, we shall have to provide plenty of economic and educational opportunity for all Americans so that no one group will be tempted to blame another for its frustrations. Finally, we must demand laws protecting the rights of minorities and laws against racial slander, as well as police vigilance in enforcing these laws. Especially in these difficult days police must be alert, reassuring, and impartial in dealing with our many mixed populations.

Magazines of wide circulation gave considerable additional publicity to the purposes of the rumor clinics and through feature stories helped make the public temporarily "rumor conscious." Rumor clinics required channels of continuous intake. Most of the clinics invited their readers to become "rumor reporters," and interested readers became their principal source of supply. In certain centers a Division of Propaganda Analysis or some similar bureau was established under the local or state Committee of Public Safety. In some localities air-raid officers or other individuals selected as "rumor wardens" were solicited once a month to report the crop of stories they had heard currently in their neighborhoods. Bartenders, taxi drivers, and barbers sometimes turned out to be fertile reporters.

There proved to be, however, certain serious drawbacks in using untrained citizens as rumor wardens, or rumor reporters. For one thing, many people have an aversion to "snooping" in any form. Even though this commendable abhorrence would scarcely seem to apply to reporting where the name of the rumor spreader is not asked for, still the aura of tale bearing somehow persists, and many people find the assignment unpleasant. More serious, it was discovered that few untrained people are able to recognize, write down, and transmit a rumor when they hear one. Particularly if people think what they hear is "true" they are disinclined to call it a rumor. On the other hand, well-documented truth may thoughtlessly be branded as rumor or propaganda when the fact is unpalatable to the listener. Finally, it takes considerable initiative and self-discipline to participate continuously in rumor defense after the first flush of novelty is gone. Yet, in spite of these difficulties, many who participated in rumor-control work not only felt a satisfaction in their contribution to morale building but themselves learned to avoid irresponsible gossip.

In the course of experience with rumor clinics, psychologists learned to recognize the pitfalls. A badly run column could do more harm than good. Thus it became necessary to devise standards for the establishment and conduct of clinics. In the Appendix are reprinted the standards observed and widely distributed by the Boston *Herald-Traveler* Rumor Clinic and its collaborating agency, the Committee on Propaganda Analysis of the Massachusetts Committee on Public Safety. They were devised principally by R. H. Knapp, who at that time was director of the Committee on Propaganda Analysis.

Four questions are commonly asked concerning the work of the clinics: (1) Did they not run the risk of spreading false stories? (2) Did they actually prevent rumor spreading? (3) Why did they rapidly diminish in number after 1943? (4) Were the stories reported ever traced to a source in Axis agents?

1. In nailing a rumor did the clinics inadvertently spread it? So far as printed columns are concerned, it seems unlikely that the vivid context of negation, ridicule, and shame in which each printed rumor was set could be overlooked by the reader. The columns were read by the more rational portion of the population, whose motives were basically patriotic, and whose minds were potentially critical of propaganda provided they were given aid in recognizing it. The columns were educational in intent and form. No rumor was cited except in a context of rebuttal. Each printed story was clearly labeled "a phony," "sucker bait," "food for propageese." There was always an objective analysis of the rumor or a factual refutation to catch the eye. In short, when adequate standards are observed in the handling of rumor, it seems safe to say that unwanted credibility can scarcely result. The precautions needed, as the Appendix indicates, include, besides a vivid context of negation and authoritative rebuttal, attention to typography and style. It is well, for example, not to print the rumor in boldface, and even more important to destroy the rhythm and slogan-like quality of some of the more scurrilous jingles and witticisms.

Concerning rumor clinics on the air, the situation is different. A source of danger lies in the dial-twisting habit of the American public. A listener may tune in after the introduction of the program and off before hearing the refutation. Although there were many potential commercial sponsors for radio rumor clinics, all authorities, psychologists and OWI officials alike, discouraged their development.

One experiment, conducted for the OWI, showed that this negative attitude was sound. Experimental rumor programs were privately presented to typical audiences of men and women. An analysis of their reactions showed certain unsatisfactory trends. For one thing, the listeners were not very successful in recalling the refutations heard on the air. Even for the rumors which they disbelieved at the beginning, they could recall only one out of every three refutations. Of the rumors broadcast in this experiment, 70 percent had never previously been heard by members of the audiences, or else had already been rejected by them as false. Of the remaining 30 percent (already heard and believed), 14 percent were still considered to be true or possibly true even after they had been exposed on the air. (It is noteworthy, however, that half of the rumors previously believed were successfully scotched.)

On the whole, the experimenters reached an unfavorable judgment of radio rumor clinics. Many more rumors, they believed, were planted than were properly debunked. Without further experimentation this conclusion cannot be said to apply to *printed* rumor columns. For we know that difficult and controversial material is better understood when presented to the eye than to the ear.[11] But so far as radio rumor clinics are concerned, the experimenter's conclusions seem to confirm the common-sense view that they are unwise.

This conclusion does not mean that the radio cannot play its part in rumor control. Far from it. Generalized programs on rumor may be both entertaining and instructive. A playlet, "How the Story Spread," was successfully dramatized for radio, and many other variations of the same theme were employed to impress their general moral upon the radio

[11] H. Cantril and G. W. Allport (1935), Chap. 9.

public. It is only the specific, current, damaging rumor that must be excluded from broadcasting.

2. Did rumor-clinic columns cut down rumor spreading? Their sponsors would like to think so, but it is hard to obtain conclusive evidence. The problem of evaluating *any* educational or propaganda campaign is a perplexing one. Does the study of Latin do any good? Does social work do any good? Did Nazi propaganda have any profound effects in this country? Did rumor clinics help to diminish rumor? Such questions are hard to answer with finality.

There are only two lines of evidence at hand, and so far as they go, both are favorable to rumor clinics. In cities where these columns flourished it was clear that the public became rumor conscious. Conversations often contained some good-natured mention of the matter. Upon hearing a rumor, the listener might say, "That's a good one. I must send it to the rumor clinic." Innumerable incidents of this sort indicate that a certain kind of generalized immunity was a by-product of the clinic's effort.

Only one experimental attempt was made to test out the rumor immunity of clinic readers.[12] In the city of Syracuse, a representative section of the population was interviewed regarding its belief in certain current stories dealing with waste and special privilege supposedly characteristic of local OPA officials. In the course of the investigation, it was found that those who were regular readers of the *Post-Standard* clinic believed these rumors less than the nonreaders by 6.5 percent. When regular and occasional readers were combined, they showed a 4.4 percent greater immunity. Though the differences are not large (and may be affected by educational level), they nevertheless take on significance when it

[12] F. H. Allport and M. Lepkin (1945).

is pointed out that only about 27 percent of the population accepted the rumors in the first place. Hence the actual difference *in credulity* among regular readers was 25 percent as compared with nonreaders.

Assuming that the clinics produced a certain degree of generalized immunity, did they perhaps go too far and engender an attitude of suspiciousness toward *all* news? We recall that something of this sort seemed to happen after World War I. The public became so propaganda conscious that it spied a propagandist behind every bush and under every bed. This resistance extended into World War II to such a degree that even the most perfectly authenticated reports on concentration camps and other Nazi atrocities were rejected by many as inventions of propagandists. There is no evidence that rumor clinics had any comparable effect. The essential technique of the clinics was to offset rumor by news, to check irresponsible tales by fact. The public was helped in keeping this distinction in mind. Even if in a few cases a slight hypertrophy of rumor consciousness developed, the resulting skepticism was probably the lesser of two evils compared to the detrimental effects of overcredulity.

3. Why did rumor clinics decline after 1943? There was no syndication of the columns. Each was run independently according to local needs and the pattern of the sponsoring newspaper. In some cases editors found it too complex and too time-consuming a feature to maintain; others lost interest or found that the number of rumor reporters dropped. Most agreed that the crop of rumors declined after 1943. As the danger of defeat gradually vanished, jitters subsided, and as people became busier at war jobs, they grew less rumor prone. It is only in times of crisis and confusion that *importance* and *ambiguity* are high. As the war effort

succeeded and as confusion waned, the tide of rumor correspondingly subsided.

4. Were some of the most damaging rumors planted by Axis agents? It is always difficult, and usually impossible, to track a rumor to its source. Civilian sleuths land themselves in trouble, for in attempting to trace the chain of rumor they deal with resistant personalities at every step. The Federal Bureau of Investigation traced an occasional harmful story to its source, but the source was often found to be innocent enough, for the original tale was frequently mild and even truthful compared with the later distortions and accretions that occurred.

It is unlikely that any Axis "rumor factory" existed in this country. However, the "line" of the Axis short-wave radio and the nature of current rumors corresponded closely. Dark hints of the President's sanity were noised at home at about the time Goebbels was airing the same suspicion on the air. It is not clear whether such tales originated in Berlin and were picked up and spread in this country by Axis sympathizers, or whether Berlin was notified of the prevailing complaints and distrust in this country and proceeded to exploit the same themes. The fact remains, however, that America's wartime rumors often seemed to reflect the current line of Axis propaganda.

RUMOR OFFENSIVES

IN modern warfare rumor defense on the home front has its counterpart in rumor offense directed against the enemy. The psychological warfare waged by the Nazis was marked chiefly by the strategy of *divide and conquer* and the strategy of *terror*. Rumor was a prominent tactic in both. In his *Strategy of Terror*, Edmund Taylor

(1940) tells how in preparation for a blitz, the Germans smothered their victims with defeatist and terrorist tales. By radio one rumor followed another into Poland, France, the Low Countries. The tales reported impending invasion and at the same time impending peace negotiation. Confusion was their aim—confusion and demoralizaton. They cast doubt upon the sincerity of the Allied governments and upon their ability to aid the countries in distress. At the same time they falsely reported stories of great Polish or French successes, which raised hopes unduly and led soon to disappointment and terror. In the cocksure days of early German victory Nazi radio propaganda was highly stratified. That is to say, it varied according to the country to which it was beamed and according to the social group in each country to which it was making its appeal.[13] Though this propaganda was not exclusively designed to plant rumors, most of it had this effect, for rumor in wartime is often nothing but propaganda stories at second, third, or fourth hand. The propositions planted were generally crisp and brief, easy to repeat, and calculated to travel rapidly in the chaotic atmosphere of threatening invasion. Fear, confusion, contradictory purposes, and pell-mell retreat followed.

As compared with the strategy of terror, the strategy of "divide and conquer" requires more guile, more build-up, more repetition. The rumors implanted are calculated to stir up animosities within a country so that its downfall can be accomplished more readily. At one time Hitler boasted that America's ruin could be brought about as an "inside job." But he was to learn that the divisive rumors were not enough.

American psychological warfare rested to a much less ex-

[13] J. S. Bruner (1941).

tent on rumor planting. The tactic developed late, and played but a small part in the total strategy of what came to be called "black propaganda." Our use of this below-the-belt strategy, in turn, was slight as compared with our reliance upon direct and open appeal, fortified above all else by the logic of news and irresistible deeds.[14]

RUMOR IN THE ARMED SERVICES

NEARLY every veteran remembers that floods of rumors engulfed him from the day of his induction to the day of his discharge. While civilians were being sprinkled with pipe dreams, bogies, and wedge drivers, men in service were being immersed in them. The reason is simple. The stream of events in which they were caught was of momentous significance to them, but the course of this stream was hidden from their view. Importance of the ideas and ambiguity of the facts were at a maximum.

Especially in faraway lands, cut off from usual sources of news, rumor was the only source of "information." On a ship, officers on the bridge may have been "in the know," but the common sailor was at the mercy of current scuttlebutt. Troops waiting to move (to where?) supplied their destination out of their hypersensitized imaginations. Anxious aviators waiting to be briefed gave vent to their fears in stories of the dangerous targets that awaited them, in rumors concerning the inadequacy of their equipment or of the menace of new enemy antiaircraft defenses.

Many commanding officers became concerned about the threat to morale. Some sought wisely through lectures, demonstrations (like that described in Chapter 4 of this book),

---

[14] For an interesting account of essential differences between propaganda issued by totalitarian and democratic states see F. C. Bartlett (1940).

and through a policy of plentiful news releases to achieve rumor prophylaxis. Rumor boards were instituted in some camps and on some ships. The morning's crop would be posted. In broad daylight they looked a bit silly. In some units rumor clinics were instituted. When well handled, they added a bit of fun as well as instruction to the day's routine.

In one prisoner-of-war camp in Germany, for example, a rumor clinic was part of the regular entertainment program and proved an invaluable morale booster.[15] Prisoners were kept well informed about events in this camp, and false hopes of impending liberation were not allowed to develop prematurely.

[15] Stalag IXb, at Wegscheid, near Bad Orb, Germany. The camp's entertainment was under the direction of Mr. Bryan Patterson.

2 WHY RUMORS CIRCULATE

In the last chapter we indicated the two basic conditions for rumor: first, the theme of the story must have some *importance* to speaker and listener; second, the true facts must be shrouded in some kind of *ambiguity*. This ambiguity, as we have said, may be induced by the absence or sketchiness of news, by the conflicting nature of the news, by distrust of the news, or by some emotional tensions that make the individual unable or unwilling to accept the facts set forth in the news.

To be sure, in rumor there is often some residual particle of news, a "kernel of truth," but in the course of transmission it has become so overlaid with fanciful elaboration that it is no longer separable or detectable. In the rumored story it is almost always impossible to tell precisely what the underlying facts are, or indeed whether there are any at all.

THE BASIC LAW OF RUMOR   The two essential conditions of importance and ambiguity seem to be related to rumor transmission in a roughly quantitative manner. A formula for the intensity of rumor might be written as follows:

$$R \sim i \times a$$

In words this formula means that the amount of rumor in circulation will vary with the importance of the subject to the individuals concerned *times* the ambiguity of the evidence pertaining to the topic at issue. The relation between importance and ambiguity is not additive but multiplicative, for if either importance or ambiguity is zero, there is *no* rumor. For instance, an American citizen is not likely to spread rumors concerning the market price for camels in Afghanistan because the subject has no importance for him, ambiguous though it certainly is. He is not disposed to spread gossip concerning the doings of the people in Swaziland, because he doesn't care about them. Ambiguity alone does not launch or sustain rumor.

Nor does importance. Although an automobile accident in which I lose my leg is of calamitous significance to me, I am not susceptible to rumors concerning the extent of my injury because I know the facts. If I receive a legacy and know the amount involved, I am resistant to rumors that exaggerate its amount. Officers in the higher echelons of the army were less susceptible to rumor than was G.I. Joe, not because coming events were less important to them, but because, as a rule, the plans and strategies were better known to them. Where there is no ambiguity, there can be no rumor.

In wartime, as we have said, the conditions for rumor are optimal. Military events are of the greatest importance. Yet military secrecy, together with the natural confusion of a nation on the march, and the unpredictable moves of the enemy, help create profound ambiguity in precisely those matters that are of greatest concern to us.

The law we have presented is highly dependable. There are certain conditions, however, under which its operation

THE BASIC LAW OF RUMOR

will be weakened. If a population is under close surveillance, say by the Gestapo, and if heavy penalties are placed on rumor spreading, people may to a greater or less degree restrain themselves.

Again, since rumor moves only among like-minded individuals, in a population that is exceedingly heterogeneous with little communication between component groups, rumor may avoid crossing social barriers and therefore have a restricted circulation (see the discussion of rumor publics, p. 180).

For yet another reason, the law may not operate. It sometimes happens that as soon as a man understands what makes him behave in a certain way, he proceeds to behave differently. It seems almost as though in the process of realizing that he behaves like an automaton, man is freed from the necessity of being one. Thus some students of psychology, having discovered why they have this or that objectionable mannerism, have forthwith given it up. Or, people who set out to observe whether the course of a particular emotion corresponds to a psychologist's prediction find that the emotion neither feels nor acts naturally. And so it is that a person who is "rumor wise," who understands that he is likely under conditions of importance and ambiguity to believe and spread rumors, is for that very reason less likely to do so!

It would not be correct to conclude that self-knowledge, or insight, automatically cures all our evil habits or confers a sudden and unlimited freedom of the will upon us. And yet it is a fact, too little observed by psychologists, that knowledge of the operation of a law frequently alters, and sometimes negates, the law in question.

In this fact—that people who are rumor conscious are less

likely to be victimized—we find a justification for all the educational work done during the war by psychologists, magazine writers, radio speakers, and rumor-clinic editors. Here too lies an argument for including a basic study of rumor in programs of social studies in the schools and colleges. Young people who know the law of rumor may be able to safeguard themselves in many types of situations where evidence is insecure. Pains should be taken, however, that caution and healthy skepticism do not degenerate into uncritical negativism. One who is too suspicious of rumor may develop a distrust of even the best authenticated reports.

MOTIVES IN RUMOR MONGERING

WHEN we say that rumor does not circulate unless the topic has importance for the individual who hears and spreads the story, we are calling attention to the *motivational factor* in rumor. Any human need may provide the motive power to rumor. Sex interest accounts for much of gossip and most of scandal; anxiety is the power behind the macabre and threatening tales we so often hear; hope and desire underlie pipe-dream rumors; hate sustains accusatory tales and slander.

In August, 1945, a rumor spread to the effect that Russia declared war on Japan only because Russia received in exchange the secret of the atomic bomb. Those who believed and spread this tale were people who disliked the Russians and, perhaps to only a slightly less extent, disliked the Administration in Washington. Gnawing hatred motivated the rumor. But instead of saying candidly, "I hate Russia," or "I hate the Democrats," the rumor spreader seized upon a story that would *relieve, justify,* and *explain* his underlying emotional tension.

It is important to note here the complex purpose that rumor serves. By permitting one to slap at the thing one hates it *relieves* a primary emotional urge. But at the same time—in the same breath—it serves to *justify* one in feeling as he does about the situation, and to *explain* to himself and to others why he feels that way. Thus rumor rationalizes while it relieves. "Why shouldn't I dislike Russia? It came to our aid only at the cost of an enormous bribe. . . ." "Why shouldn't I feel panicky? Our fleet was wiped out at Pearl Harbor. . . ." "Why shouldn't I distrust the Jews? They are so clannish. . . ." "Why shouldn't I feel superior to my neighbor? I don't indulge in his irregularities of living. . . ."

But to justify our emotional urges and render them reasonable is not the only kind of rationalization. Quite apart from the pressure of particular emotions, we continually seek to extract *meaning* from our environment. There is, so to speak, intellectual pressure along with the emotional. To find a plausible reason for a confused situation is itself a motive; and this pursuit of a "good closure" (even without the personal factor) helps account for the vitality of many rumors.[1] We want to know the why, how, and wherefore of the world that surrounds us. Our minds protest against chaos. From childhood we are asking why. This "effort after meaning" is broader than our impulsive tendency to rationalize and justify our immediate emotional state. Curiosity rumors result. A stranger whose business is unknown to the small town where he takes up residence will breed many legends designed to explain to curious minds why he has come to town. An odd-looking excavation in a city

[1] We experience a good closure when we find satisfying explanations and when our view of a situation is clear and stable.

inspires fanciful explanations of its purpose. The atomic bomb, but slightly understood by the public, engenders much effort after meaning.

To sum up, rumors often assuage immediate emotional tension by providing a verbal outlet that gives relief; they often protect and justify the existence of these emotions which, if faced directly, might be unacceptable to their possessor; they sometimes provide a broader interpretation of various puzzling features of the environment, and so play a prominent part in the intellectual drive to render the surrounding world intelligible.

This threefold dynamic is seldom, if ever, understood by the rumor spreader. He does not know why a certain rumor seems intensely interesting to him and urgently to merit widespread repetition. And he is unaware of the extent to which he is reflecting himself in the stories he spreads, for he does not understand the mechanism of projection.

PROJECTION

WHEN a person's emotional state is reflected, unknown to himself, in his interpretation of his environment, we speak of *projection*. He is failing to employ exclusively impartial and objective evidence in his explanations of the reality surrounding him.

In dreams everyone projects. Only after we awaken do we recognize that our private wishes, fears, or revengeful desires have been responsible for what came to pass in our dream imaginations. The child asleep dreams of finding mountains of candy; the inferior youth asleep triumphs on the athletic field; the apprehensive mother dreams of the death of her child.

PROJECTION

Daydreams too are projective. Relaxed on a couch, we let our mind picture events that actualize our hopes, desires, fears. We find ourselves in fantasy successful, satisfied, or sometimes defeated and ruined, all according to our temperament or the type of emotion that is for the time being steering the associational train of thought.

Rumor is akin to the daydream at second hand. If the story we hear gives a fancied interpretation of reality that conforms to our secret lives, we tend to believe and transmit it.

In the following example Karl Menninger (1930) shows how an unrecognized element of wish can simultaneously both drive and channel a gossipy yarn: [2]

MRS. ADAMS to MRS. BECK: "Where is Mrs. King today? Is she ill?"

MRS. BECK to MRS. CLARK: "Mrs. Adams wonders if Mrs. King may not be ill."

MRS. CLARK (who does not like Mrs. King) to MRS. DAVIS (who does): "I hear Mrs. King is ill. Not seriously, I hope?"

MRS. DAVIS to MRS. ELLIS: "Mrs. Clark is saying that Mrs. King is seriously sick. I must go right over and see her."

MRS. ELLIS to MRS. FRENCH: "I guess Mrs. King is pretty sick. Mrs. Davis has just been called over."

MRS. FRENCH to MRS. GREGG: "They say Mrs. King isn't expected to live. The relatives have been called to her bedside."

MRS. GREGG to MRS. HUDSON: "What's the latest news about Mrs. King? Is she dead?"

MRS. HUDSON to MRS. INGHAM: "What time did Mrs. King die?"

MRS. INGHAM to MRS. JONES: "Are you going to Mrs. King's funeral? I hear she died yesterday."

[2] Reprinted from page 282 of *The Human Mind* by permission of Alfred A. Knopf, Inc., publisher.

MRS. JONES to MRS. KING: "I just learned of your death and funeral. Now who started that?"

MRS. KING: "There are several who would be glad if it were true!"

As a slightly more complex instance of projection, let us take a rumor from World War II. The majority of all recorded rumors in this war, we saw in Chapter 1, were hostility rumors, containing accusations of malfeasance against some special American group: the Jews, the OPA, the Negroes, the Catholics, the Administration, the Army, the Navy, the Red Cross—or against our allies, principally Britain and Russia. Though the logic is more involved, it seems likely that the dynamics of projection also sped these rumors on their way.

Suppose a housewife said over the back fence (and many of them did):

> I hear that out at Camp X they have so much meat that they throw whole sides of fresh beef into the garbage.

Just what might this woman's motivation be?

In the first place the meat shortage was a matter of *importance* to her and her household. Further, the evidence in this case was *ambiguous;* she was not in a position to know the facts of the matter. What is more, she was genuinely inconvenienced by the meat shortage, being frustrated in the planning and preparation for her meals. When she feels frustrated, she knows there is usually a cause. Hence in her "effort after meaning" she endeavored to find the culpable source. Of course, she might have blamed the Axis or Hitler; but these villains were not only remote but their misdeeds were on so grand and abstract a scale that she could scarcely picture their relation to her immediate, concrete annoyance. Besides, if there were better management, wouldn't there be meat enough for all? Perhaps she has known some irresponsible and greedy army officers, or perhaps she doesn't like the way the Army has treated her Johnny. At any rate, a tangible, near-by, plausible villain emerges, and the Army is accused of causing the meat shortage. She thus explains it herself and fixes the blame. Such a process has been called *complementary* projection.[3] Complementary projection is not ascribing one's own emotions to other people, but rather finding in the supposed conduct of others a "reasonable" *explanation* of one's feelings. (It is in this manner, to cite an extreme case of complementary projection, that the paranoiac, filled with suspicion and hate, accuses others of plotting against him.)

But we may not yet have the entire explanation for the woman's chatter. Suppose she has failed to save the kitchen fats (as the government asked her to), suppose she has cheated a bit by withholding ration coupons while buying meat, or bought a bit on the black market. Being at heart a decent and patriotic citizen she cannot avoid pangs of conscience. Or can she? (Most people keep their consciences as quiet as they can, and in order to do so, fall, at least occasionally, into the trap of *direct* projection.)

Direct (not complementary) projection of our own guilt is one of nature's weird provisions for avoiding the uncomfortable pangs of conscience. Emerson pointed it out when he wrote, "What we call sin in others we call 'experiment' in ourselves." Others sin; not we. (Or if we do, how small a sin it is compared with the wickedness of others.) Now our lady, quite unknown to herself, might well have been

[3] H. A. Murray *et al.* (1938).

quieting her own conscience, in effect saying: "Why should I feel guilty? What do my petty evasions of food regulations amount to? Just look, the Army wastes whole sides of beef. By contrast my guilt is negligible."[4]

There is also some experimental evidence concerning the importance of guilt evasion in rumor belief. Allport and Lepkin (1945) found a tendency among people who believed certain rumors relating to waste and special privilege in the OPA to be people who admitted chiseling on their ration allowances and at the same time *denied feeling any guilt or shame for having done so.* Conversely, among people who admitted cheating and confessed to *feeling shame,* there was less belief in the rumors concerning the malpractice of others. In short, when we believe the worst about others, we are managing to escape a guilty conscience in ourselves. If we take the blame ourselves we are less rumor prone.

Confirmation of the same principle is found in the experiments of Frenkel-Brunswik and Sanford (1945). These investigators discovered that among a group of outspokenly anti-Semitic college women there was a tendency to avoid assuming blame and responsibility for their own shortcomings. Conversely, in a group of students who were notably free from anti-Semitic bias there was a marked tendency for them to be "intropunitive," that is, to take blame upon themselves for their misfortunes and failures. People who refuse to face their faults find scapegoats; those who know their own weaknesses, do not seem to need scapegoats.

---

[4] It is, of course, very difficult to prove that people who tell accusatory rumors, are themselves guilty of the very crime which they ascribe to others. It is, however, a matter of common observation that people seem singularly self-righteous when they are criticizing other people for faults which we know they themselves possess.

A GENERALIZATION OF THE RUMOR FORMULA

We may summarize our discussion thus far in the following way:

Rumor is set in motion and continues to travel in a homogeneous social medium by virtue of the strong interests of the individuals involved in the transmission. The powerful influence of these interests requires the rumor to serve largely as a rationalizing agent: explaining, justifying, and providing meaning for the emotional interest at work. At times the relationship between the interest and the rumor is so intimate that we may describe the rumor simply as a projection of an altogether subjective emotional condition.

Having thus established the close connection between rumor and subjective emotional conditions, let us glance again at our formula:

$$R \sim i \times a$$

This mode of analysis closely resembles McGregor's (1938) approach to the factor of wishful thinking in the making of predictions. In the latter's experiment people were asked (it was in the year 1936) whether they thought Hitler would be in power a year from that date. About 95 percent thought he would be. They were also asked whether their personal attitude toward Hitler was favorable. Most hated him. The point is that the dislike people felt did *not* affect their predictions *because there was little ambiguity in the situation*. Hitler's hold on Germany at that time was firm. On the other hand, the subjects were asked to predict the likelihood of King Edward VIII of England's announcing plans for marriage within the year, and were asked whether they thought he *should* marry. Of those subjects who were opposed to the King's marriage, 32 percent predicted in the affirmative, whereas of those who favored the King's marriage 80 percent predicted "yes." At the time of the experiment the news about the King's marital plans was highly ambiguous and contradictory. *Unguided by objective evidence, most people will make their prediction in accordance with their subjective preference.*

McGregor writes, ". . . the influence of subjective factors upon prediction is limited by the degree of ambiguity of the stimulus situation, but also [by] the *importance* for the predictor of the issues involved. If either importance or ambiguity is zero, the influence of subjective factors upon prediction would presumably be zero. In the former case there would be no wishes to influence prediction, and the predictor would simply record . . . the ambiguity of the existent stimulus situation. If ambiguity were zero, on the other hand, the stimulus situation would be completely coercive. Even an intense wish would be inoperative."

McGregor's work leads us to the conclusion that rumor is following a more generalized law of social psychology which may be stated as follows:

> *Subjective emotional distortion in the perception and interpretation of the environment can occur only in proportion to the combined effects of importance and ambiguity.*

Projection and wishful thinking are not unlimited tendencies. They operate only when the conditions permit. Men will fortify their desire with belief, will rationalize, project,

A GENERALIZATION OF RUMOR FORMULA

and spread false rumors, *only in proportion to the ambiguity of the subject and its private importance.*[5]

Thus rumor, as one of the less rational forms of social activity, turns out to be a limited phenomenon. Like wishful thinking in McGregor's experiment, it flourishes only when ego involvement is felt and when objective evidence or knowledge does not place rational constraints upon judgment and report.

In this connection it is well to recall likewise that a number of rumors seem to betray an intellectual hunger rather than an emotional need (cf. p. 37). Because people are curious and want to know, a condition of *importance* is established. But since they do not know, and since they find the topic in question ambiguous, they are susceptible to rumor. The quaint stories that children tell concerning their interpretations of the workings of nature, the mind, the Deity, partake of this character of "curiosity" rumor. Myths and legends, though by no means always free of emotional tendency, also seem often to be little more than primitive versions of science. In short, the "effort after meaning" can by itself constitute the factor of "importance" that underlies rumor (or myth) spreading. Important needs are not exclusively visceral; they can be intellectual as well.

[5] Readers who are familiar with the so-called projective techniques in psychology will recognize at once a similarity between rumor and projective tests. These tests are based on *ambiguous* stimuli. An ink blot is amorphous; therefore, its meaning is supplied by the individual who interprets it. Similarly the Thematic Apperception Test elicits a thinly disguised personal story only if the stimulus picture is susceptible of *many* interpretations. Unless the stimulus figures are highly ambiguous, the subject will not interpret them according to his own needs. It is a serious question whether some of the currently used "projective" methods (including the Thematic Apperception Test pictures) are sufficiently equivocal.

SECONDARY REASONS FOR THE CIRCULATION OF RUMOR

It would not be safe to assume that every individual rumor spreader is motivated by the dynamic pattern we have described. In certain instances, the motivation may be quite special and bear no thematic relation to the story told. For example, the rumor spreader may merely be seeking attention. "I know something you don't know" is often the child's prelude to rumor spreading. To be "in the know" exalts one's self-importance. While telling a tale a person is, for the time being, dominant over his listeners. Such gratification may be quite irresistible to individuals whose lives are otherwise colorless and uneventful. Further, the rumor spreader may find himself able to bestow a favor on some friend who loves tidbits of scandal, or who has a fondness for macabre stories of death and disaster. Indifferent to the rumor himself, he passes it on for the delectation of his friend.

Again, a person may find it convenient to fill an otherwise awkward gap in the conversation by repeating what he has just recently heard. People who do not share the emotional tendencies implied in the rumor may nonetheless keep it moving. Such meaningless social discourse would not in itself account for the existence or form of the rumor, but it would serve to keep the rumor traveling across a "dead spot" in the chain.

At a time when the United States was still at war with Italy, it was found that 25 percent of the members of a certain poor Italo-American community listened regularly to Radio Roma and passed along the Axis propaganda to their neighbors. At first sight it would seem that the loyalty of the group should be gravely questioned. But the motivation behind the situation was discovered to be simple and uncomplicated. People whose radios were good enough to pick up the Italian station enjoyed superior prestige in the community. To maintain this prestige they took pains to listen and felt pride in passing along what they heard to their envious neighbors.[6]

HOME-STRETCH RUMORS

RUMOR is most frenzied when the public is expecting a momentous event to occur. The frenzy is enhanced by the entry of the press and radio upon the scene. The Armistice of 1918 was preceded by a false press announcement four days in advance. In 1945 at the time of both V-E Day and V-J Day the same thing happened. In all these cases premature celebrations resulted. Aside from the understandable desire of the news services not to be caught napping and to bring the good news at the earliest possible moment to the public (before a competitor does so), there are psychological reasons underlying the tendency of all people to "jump the gun" so far as important anticipated news is concerned.

We encounter here the powerfully dynamic condition of anticipation in the individual's mental life. When, after a long, long wait there is only one more piece to fit into the jigsaw puzzle, we are all "set" for the completion. We are like the animals who, in running a maze to reach their food box, speed up as they near the end of the experimental labyrinth. Like them we have our "goal gradient." Even those who are disciplined in news gathering cannot wait, as the United Press experience prior to V-J Day shows: [7]

[6] J. S. Bruner and J. Sayre (1941).
[7] Reprinted by permission of the Newspaper *PM* Inc.

PHONY FLASH SETS OFF PREMATURE CELEBRATION

At 9:34 P.M. Sunday (EWT) United Press sent the following over its news teletype wires:
FLASH
WASHINGTON—Japan accepts surrender terms of Allies.

Two minutes later, at 9:36, an urgent note was sent through.
FLASH
EDITORS:
Hold up that Flash.

But the bulletin had been broadcast over the air and immediately sirens and whistles began blowing throughout New York.

Managers of many movie houses stopped the shows to announce the "news" and thousands more poured into the streets to join the premature celebrations.

At 9:40 P.M., United Press bulletined:
EDITORS:
Our Washington Bureau advises they did not send the flash just transmitted on our leased wires. We are investigating to ascertain the origin.

By this time the radio stations had put out urgent announcements that the report was false. Apparently all the broadcasts were based on the United Press flash.

Meanwhile, the United Press teletypes were as though paralyzed. For at least 20 minutes not a word came through.

At 10:05 P.M. UP sent this note:
EDITORS:
We are still checking on the Washington flash but as yet have not been able to determine its origin. We will carry an explanatory story as soon as possible.

Goal gradient rumors do not contradict the principles we have described, but merely illustrate them in a special case. The expected finale is of great importance to many people. The fact that official news is momentarily anticipated actually enhances the present ambiguity of the situation (Has it come or hasn't it?). News gatherers and news customers are concentrated wholly on the expected finale, and it takes but a slight stretch of credulity to assert and believe that the end has come.

3 TESTIMONY AND RECALL

B<small>Y</small> definition rumor is a social phenomenon. It takes at least two people to make a rumor. Yet, at any given moment, one individual is the vehicle of the tale. What goes on in his mind is the crux of the whole matter. To be sure, a chain is more than the sum of its links; yet it is the separate links that constitute the stuff and substance of the chain. Hence we cannot expect to understand rumor fully without a careful analysis of the typical operations which take place in the successive individual minds that constitute a rumor chain.

TESTIMONY

A<small>LTHOUGH</small> until the recent war psychologists paid little attention to serial (multi-individual) reproductions in rumor, they have for some time been interested in the basic pattern of perception-retention-report as it occurs in the individual. It was about fifty years ago that they undertook seriously the study of testimony, or *Aussage*, as the first German investigators called it.

Testimony, the study of the "observer as reporter," was a field in which a great many psychological interests met, for, as Whipple said,[1]

---

[1] 1909, p. 169.

the report arises from processes of perception and thereby involves the whole psychology of sensation, attention, and apperception; it hinges upon retention and recall, and thereby involves the whole psychology of memory; *it issues in verbal statements, and thereby involves the psychology of language and expression; it is conditioned by numerous subjective factors, temperamental tendencies, sentiment, susceptibility to suggestion, etc.*

At the time Whipple wrote, psychologists found themselves attracted to the study of testimony, one suspects, because it was about the only applied field involving many higher mental processes where they felt they could put their science to practical uses. It gratified them to be able to illuminate an issue arising in the hustle and bustle of the courtroom and the newspaper office.

Among the early pioneers two names stand out—Binet and Stern. Binet (1900) called attention to the need for a systematic experimental study and was among the first to carry out such investigations. He was a pioneer in the use of the "picture test," through which the fidelity of report on pictorial material is investigated. His materials included also object-description tests and tests of memory for verbal material. The ability to report was included in his scale of measurements and still constitutes a part of the Stanford-Binet Intelligence Tests.

Another systematic investigator was William Stern, whose *Zur Psychologie der Aussage* (1902) is a classic in the field of testimony. It is primarily through Stern's influence that *Aussage* developed along two principal lines—picture tests and reality experiments. In picture tests the subject is shown a scene which he must describe from memory as accurately as he can. To make conditions more lifelike the reality experiment enacts some vivid incident and the subjects are

TESTIMONY

unaware of the fact that the "incident" they are witnessing has been carefully rehearsed. One typical "close-to-life" experiment involved the following incident: During a meeting of a scientific seminar two stooges among the students engaged in a quarrel. Their discussion became increasingly vehement until one participant drew a gun and threatened to shoot his adversary. At that point the professor separated the antagonists and asked the witnesses to describe the incident in detail.

In examining the observer's ability to report, two methods have been used: (1) the narrative, or free account given by the subject without aid, guidance, or interruption from the experimenter. This type of report has the advantage of being uninfluenced by suggestion. It does not, however, probe the subject's remembrance as thoroughly or as exhaustively as the second type of report, viz., (2) the interrogatory or cross-examination (*Ausfrage*) which consists of a series of prepared questions covering all details and aspects of the stimulus material. The main disadvantage of this method is, of course, the danger of suggestion. The witness prompted by "leading questions" is a familiar figure in the courtroom.

Stern (1938) found many factors affecting the observer's reports. The first distortions and omissions seem to occur during the original perception of the picture or episode itself. The observer tends to blot out details peripheral to the main theme. There is much that he doesn't see at all. As time elapses, his report becomes less and less accurate, and the distortions more serious, especially if the witness is subjected to a cross-examination. As long as he is permitted to give a spontaneous narrative he can pick and choose among the details of the original event and report only those which stand out clearest and presumably most accurately in his memory. Under cross-examination, however, he is forced to make definite statements about items which lie only on the dim margin of remembrance. In such circumstances he is liable to be guided by the form and innuendo of the examiner's question.

Stern found likewise that the event to be reported must stand alone in the subject's mind if reasonably accurate reporting is to be obtained. If he confuses the scene with other similar experiences, the report becomes a sorry mixture. Stern remarks, and the point has great importance in rumor, that "there are countless people in whose consciousness the past has but little temporal organization." Something that happened at a certain time becomes hopelessly confused with other things that happened at other times. Anyone who has tried to give an orderly chronological description of his childhood memories can testify to the blurring that occurs in the time frame of memory.

Testimony, Stern found, does particular violence to odd, unfamiliar features in the stimulus. Either they are reinterpreted to conform to what the subject is accustomed to, or else their unusualness is greatly exaggerated and made a central feature of the report.

In the verbal reporting, additional sources of distortion are brought into play. Subjects do not have unlimited vocabularies. They employ clichés and verbal conventions to express their frequently incomplete and unordered memory images. When words are used, more definite form is given to the recall than the unverbalized recall itself possesses. Words sculpture our thoughts and commit us to ideas which are uncertain until uttered.

Finally, Stern discovered that differences among subjects in intelligence and in habits of oral expression markedly affect the report. One subject is inclined to give a simple enumeration of disconnected features in his experience; an-

TESTIMONY

other spins a yarn in which explanation and evaluation are all mixed up with the report itself. On the whole, there seems to be no consistent difference between the accuracy of men's and women's reports. Children, however, are so inaccurate and so readily influenced by suggestion (because their store of experience is neither adequate nor well enough assimilated to hold a firm structure) that virtually no confidence can be placed in their accounts. Stern's demonstration of the unreliability of child testimony was responsible for changes in German law that restricted the extent to which such testimony was admissible in court.

Following Stern's work many comparable investigations were made.[2] Some dealt with the suggestive influence of cross-questioning,[3] some with the effects of various intervals of time elapsed upon the accuracy of report,[4] others with age and sex factors. All of them found serious limitations to eyewitness testimony, especially in conditions where excitement existed during the original perception or in the process of narration. Normal defects of perception, retention, and verbal report are serious enough, but emotional states greatly magnify them.

Figure 2 presents a typical testimony stimulus employed by Freyd (1921) in his attempt to devise a picture test for accuracy of reporting. This *Aussage* test was part of a battery designed for the purpose of gauging journalistic aptitude. Freyd's subjects were allowed to look at the picture for one minute and were then tested on a large number of details, such as the license number of the automobile, the number and route of the streetcar, the time of day indicated on the jeweler's clock.

[2] A review of the work done until 1909 may be found in G. M. Whipple (1909).
[3] For example, E. Claparède (1906).
[4] For example, M. Borst (1904).

TESTIMONY AND RECALL

Experiments such as these all show clearly how unreliable eyewitness accounts usually are. Even firsthand reports are

Fig. 2. A test for ability to report.

so faulty that they seldom can be trusted in detail. Rumor, being once, twice, or a thousand times removed from eyewitness testimony, is just so much more invalid. No wonder, then, that in most courts hearsay evidence is strictly ruled out.

PERCEIVING, REMEMBERING, REPORTING

The three psychological steps in testimony are *perceiving, remembering, reporting*. The same three steps make up rumor transmission, excepting that in the latter case the steps are endlessly repeated throughout each

PERCEIVING, REMEMBERING, REPORTING

link in the chain, and perceiving is reduced, in all links but the first, to a mere matter of listening to hearsay.

Strictly speaking, the three steps cannot be rigidly separated. What we perceive is already influenced by what we remember concerning relevant experiences in the past and is sometimes influenced also by what we intend to report. Remembering depends upon the perception but also upon the words with which the situation is held in mind. Report is a function of both the preceding stages but also of the social situation in which the report is made. Its form depends upon our available vocabulary and upon our purpose in speaking.

As this complex process unfolds itself, progressing from initial perception to final report, many fascinating transformations occur as the original sensory impressions, past memories, and emotions inextricably fuse. Selective forgetting and subjective distortion inevitably change the values of nearly all events in the outer world.

The story is told most completely by Bartlett (1932), whose numerous experimental approaches bring him close to the basic phenomena of rumor. This investigator demonstrates in many ways the creative or constructive character of memory. No recollection, he proves, lasts as a mere trace, like an image fixed upon a sensitive film, reproducible whenever needed. On the contrary, memories start to change immediately following a perception. Indeed, the original perception itself is no mere aggregate of sensory components, for it is always fused from its beginning with relevant previous experience. Habit, emotion, cultural conventions play their part. The most crucial role of all is played by attitudes and expectations. It is they that make remembering a *constructive* rather than merely a reproductive function of the mind.

Bartlett's central concept is "effort after meaning" (a concept we have employed in previous pages). In his words, "It is fitting to speak of every human cognitive reaction —perceiving, imaging, thinking, and reasoning—as an effort after meaning." [5] Bartlett here calls attention to the tendency of the mind to reshape all experience into neat, meaningful, useful categories. If these categories are sometimes fanciful and unfounded, it makes no difference. Memories must fit into the "schemata" by which a person regulates his life. However false from an "outside" point of view, a memory is always the result of the individual's effort to make economical sense out of his experiences.

Most of Bartlett's experiments were conducted on individual subjects in the Cambridge Psychological Laboratory. Each was shown a picture or given a story to read. At varying intervals of time they were asked to reproduce as accurately as they could what they had seen or heard. Sometimes the recalls were elicited a few minutes after exposure, sometimes after an interval of months, occasionally after the passage of years.

In all cases, Bartlett found extensive omissions from the material. Details dropped out to a marked degree. There was a marked tendency for any picture or story to gravitate in memory toward what was familiar to the subject in his own life, consonant with his own culture, and above all, to what had some special emotional significance for him. In their effort after meaning, the subjects would condense or fill in so as to achieve a better "Gestalt," a better closure— a simpler, more significant configuration.

Bartlett found that elaboration (increase in complexity) was relatively rare. In general, people skeletonize their memories rather than elaborate them. The same trend, as

[5] F. C. Bartlett (1932), p. 44.

PERCEIVING, REMEMBERING, REPORTING 57

we shall later see, holds for rumors. They are seldom elaborated; more often they are extremely simplified versions of the original event. One exception occurs, however, when the memory of some single feature becomes greatly "sharpened," leading to an elaboration of that one feature at the expense of others, which tend to fade out. Bartlett gives as an example the illustration of a geometrical figure containing seven circles.

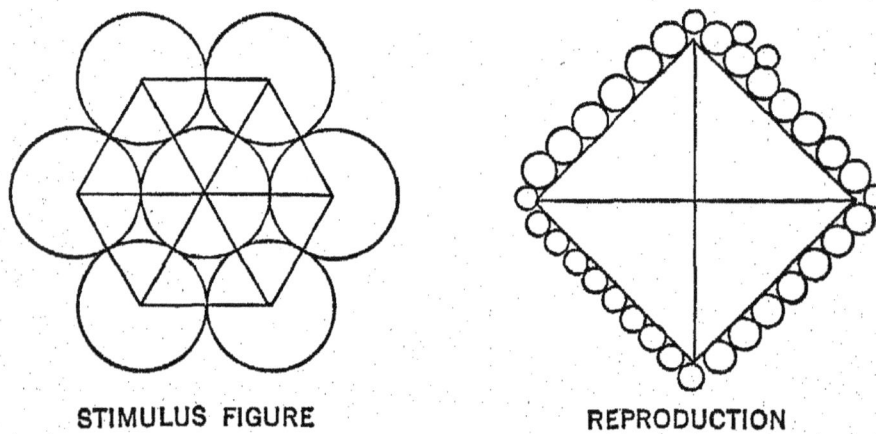

    STIMULUS FIGURE   REPRODUCTION

Fig. 3. Circles become sharpened at the expense of other features.

The reproduction in Figure 3 diminishes emphasis upon the angular features and elaborates the circles. The subject who drew the reproduction from memory was fairly well satisfied with his attempt but remarked, "There ought to be more circles in it."

In his experiments in story telling Bartlett approached more closely to the problem of rumor. Even the same individual retelling the same story at intervals of a few days or weeks continuously lost details. The final versions were always shorter than the original version, and hardly ever recognizable. Especially faulty were names, dates, numbers. Again and again it appeared that the transformation of material in recall follows the course of an individual's personal interest, this course being established in his first perception. He obtains a "general idea" from the story that accords with

Fig. 4. How the owl became a cat—a visual rumor.

his own biases, and as time goes on fits the story more and more closely to this preconception.

Bartlett repeated his experiments using a chain of subjects (serial reproduction) instead of individuals. Here he is approaching very closely the conditions for true rumor, except that successive versions of the story were written and read rather than being spoken and heard. The important result is that all the same types of change occur as are found in the decay of individual memory, though to a magnified

INDIVIDUAL vs. SOCIAL MEMORY

and accelerated degree. Those restraints that might hold an individual within bounds (because, after all, he has seen the original object) do not operate in serial transmission.

In Figure 4, reproduced from Bartlett, we see the serial transmission of a drawing (from person to person).

Starting with a drawing of an owl, we end up with a cat. It was sufficient for one member of the series to make a basic mistake in identification. Henceforth the errors snowballed under the influence of the new directive idea. In successive reproductions by the same individual, on the other hand, we may confidently expect an original directive idea determined by the first perception to persist to the end. The *form* of the owl might change, but the *idea* of an owl would remain.

INDIVIDUAL vs. SOCIAL MEMORY

The courses of individual memory and of "social memory" are in most respects parallel. The same pattern of distortion exists in both. And this is not surprising since "social memory" is a matter of successive individual minds handling the same essential material.

Suppose the question is asked, "Which is more accurate, individual or social memory?" The answer would, on the whole, be in favor of individual memory. To a considerable degree the original perception constrains the individual to keep his transformations within bounds. Usually with the aid of imagery and verbal labels, he holds onto the essential features of the original perception, and may likewise do a considerable bit of rehearsing between the time of the presentation and the report. Social memory, on the other hand, has no comparable anchorage. A new listener has no remaining image against which to check his conceptions and, however unlikely he may regard some of the details that he hears, he has little choice but to accept them at their face value.

Yet individual memory may be *less* accurate if an individual misperceives and continually rehearses and reinforces his error. Such distortion is especially serious if the errors are in accordance with the subject's salient interests, past habits, or prejudices. Of course, the same danger exists in social memory, especially if the group is homogeneous and shares the same biases and preconceptions. Still, it often happens that by shifting from individual to individual the story is prevented from being too closely tailored to one individual's interests, and the resulting product may actually be more accurate.

It is a characteristic of social memories that they usually become highly *conventionalized*. Since a number of individuals are involved, the meaning that emerges is likely to be what is *common* to the group in question. The idiosyncrasies of one respondent are apt to be omitted by the next, and thus the story is whittled down to a core understandable to all. Rumors are therefore usually more standardized, more acculturated, and have more of a common denominator than do individual memories. For the same reason they are more likely to acquire a moral tone characteristic of the culture.

4 AN EXPERIMENTAL APPROACH

WHENEVER possible, psychologists, like other scientists, prefer to investigate a problem under the restricted and controlled conditions of an experiment. They want to discover what essential changes take place when certain known influences are operating. They like, if possible, to vary these influences systematically in order to discover the contribution that each one makes to the phenomenon in question. But many mental phenomena resist the experimental approach. How could we experiment systematically, for example, with such common phenomena as falling in love, mystical experience, the thrill of receiving an unexpected legacy; with grief, or with irritation at one's mother-in-law?

How do matters stand with rumor? The experimentalist would like to plant a rumor and trace each link in its chain of transmission, discovering not only every successive version of the tale but analyzing exhaustively the interest systems and mental contexts of each rumor agent. Although the first step, the planting of rumors in the social soil around us, is easy enough, it soon becomes impossible to follow the chain in detail. The best we can do is to pick up later and random versions as the story we launched circumnavigates back to us.

During the tense period of waiting for Japan's surrender, when conditions for rumor spreading were optimal, a wag in Washington conducted such an incomplete experiment.

The story as told by John C. Metcalfe in the *New York Herald Tribune* (August 18, 1945) follows: [1]

RUMOR DELIBERATELY PLANTED

Perhaps the most fantastic false rumor of the entire "death watch over Japan" was born in a deliberately planted story which two newsmen concocted in Washington and which within six hours bounced back with high alarm from Naval sources in San Diego.

The false rumor was created two nights before the official surrender in a Washington café at midnight. It was based on the Hitlerian theory that "the bigger the lie, the more people will believe it."

"Just for the fun of testing this theory," one of the reporters said later, "we dreamed up a story so fantastic that it even staggered our own imaginations."

The story was that Emperor Hirohito, accompanied by a heavily-armed squadron of Japanese Kamikaze suicide planes, had flown to Guam for a rendezvous with General of the Army Douglas MacArthur, Allied Supreme Commander in the Pacific and Far East, and Fleet Admiral Chester W. Nimitz. The story went on to say that these two American officers and the Emperor then boarded a huge American transport plane and accompanied by a powerful bomber squadron were flying to Washington. The climax of this incredible tale was that the Emperor was coming to the White House to sign the surrender terms in the presence of President Truman, the Cabinet and the American military and naval command.

To plant this false rumor with hope of devastating effect, one of the reporters phoned an officer of the Navy Department who he believed would be sure to spread the story. Then the newsmen went home for the night to await the anticipated repercussion.

The reaction was not long in arriving, but even the reporters were amazed at what took place.

Six hours later a girl reporter on the staff of another publication phoned one of the two instigators of the rumor and in a high state of alarm confided that she had just received a phone call from her husband, a naval officer stationed in San Diego, and went on to repeat breathlessly the full account of the planted story.

To what other distant points this hair-raising tale may have spread must be left to speculation in light of the account of the official surrender. But the false rumor for a brief time bounced merrily about the White House.

Some of the other tales spun about reports that Emperor Hirohito had flown to Moscow to sign

---

[1] Reprinted by permission of the *New York Herald Tribune*.

the surrender terms in the Kremlin; that the Japanese had discovered the secret of the atomic bomb and were stalling for time to prepare for its use in a great surprise attack on the American Navy; that the Emperor had arrived in San Francisco and would broadcast to the American people; that Admiral Nimitz and other high naval officials were discussing terms with the Japanese at a secret meeting place near Tokyo.

Then, too, there were scores of false rumors regarding the delivery of messages in Washington, in Bern and in Tokyo; of secret American-Japanese conferences in Guam, in Okinawa, in Manila and in Pearl Harbor. And to top all of them, the nation was momentarily set afire with false belief in the fake surrender flash that the United Press carried, and, officials said, was instigated by a prankster whose identity is still under investigation by the Federal Bureau of Investigation and half a dozen other government and private detective units.

Accepting this account at its face value, we note first the speed with which rumor seems to travel, especially in times of tense expectancy. We are struck too by the home-stretch or "goal gradient" phenomenon—the nearer the realization of a hope seems to be, the more fertile is the soil for anticipatory rumors (see p. 47). In the account we note also the amazing fecundity of rumor when ambiguity and importance are at a maximum.

The prankster who planted this story did conduct an experiment (an incomplete and loose experiment) on rumor. But the results tell us nothing about the successive links in the chain, or about the specific distortions that the original story underwent. Perhaps we can improve upon the prankster's technique by shifting to the psychological laboratory.

THE LABORATORY APPROACH

THE laboratory approach to rumor has its roots in the experimental work on memory and testimony described in the preceding chapter. The basic procedure of these experiments is to confront a subject with a standard stimulus situation with which his later reproductions can be compared. The course of transformation in his successive reports is noted. This basic procedure can be varied in any number of ways, some of which were described in the preceding chapter. For our purposes, the most essential variation of the testimony experiment is to have the report transmitted through separate individuals—the "method of serial reproduction"; by so doing we can explore the social factor in rumor transmission.

Laboratory control can be achieved, we admit, only at the expense of oversimplification. By forcing serial reproduction into an artificial setting we sacrifice the spontaneity and naturalness of the rumor situation. In place of the deeplying motivation that normally sustains rumor spreading, we find that the "go" of the laboratory rumor depends upon the subject's willingness to cooperate with the experimenter. In the experimental situation hostility, fear, and ego gratification find only limited expression. The influence of personal friendship between teller and listener (i.e., the peculiar rapport that ordinarily exists in rumor spreading) is also lost. Outside the laboratory, the narrator tends, as a rule, to add color (pathos, humor, or excitement) to his story for his listener's benefit. In the laboratory, the atmosphere makes for caution and intended precision of report. The teller, feeling that his reputation for accuracy is at stake, does his best to transmit in the report exactly what he hears. When students are used as subjects, the school atmosphere, with its emphasis on accuracy of observation and fidelity of report, tends still further to make successive stories more colorless and impersonal than actual rumors ever are.

There are additional differences between real-life rumors

and those that we study in the laboratory. In ordinary life the listener can chat with his informer and, if he wishes, cross-question him (though, in fact he seldom does so), whereas in experiments this doubtful aid is denied the listener. In real situations, days, weeks, or months may elapse between the hearing and telling of a rumor, whereas in the laboratory, the report is customarily asked for immediately. Also, in order to make the process uniform, the experimenter ordinarily instructs the listeners to report as accurately as possible. In ordinary rumor spreading there is no critical examiner on hand to see whether the tale is rightly repeated. Most important of all, as pointed out above, the conditions of motivation are quite different. In the experiment the subject strives for accuracy. His own fears, hates, hopes are not aroused. He is not the spontaneous rumor agent that he is in ordinary life.

It will be noted that nearly all of these differentiating conditions may be expected to enhance the accuracy of the report in the experimental situation and to yield far less distortion and projection than in real-life rumoring. Yet in spite of all these limitations and constraints, laboratory experiment succeeds fairly well in eliciting all the basic phenomena of rumor spreading. "Indoor" rumors may not be as lively, as emotionally toned, or as extreme, as "outdoor" rumors, but they are cut from the same psychological cloth.

STANDARD PROCEDURE

Out of a college class or forum audience, a group of people—usually six or seven—are selected (ordinarily volunteers being used). They are asked to leave the room. It is customary not to tell them that the experiment pertains to rumor, though if such suspicion exists no harm is done, for studies show that the distortions that occur are but slightly affected by such knowledge.[2] They are told only that they must listen carefully to what they will hear when they return to the room and repeat what they have heard "as exactly as possible."

When the subjects have left the room, a slide depicting some detailed situation is thrown on the screen and some member of the audience is assigned the task of describing it (while looking at it) to the first subject. He is requested to include approximately twenty details in his description.[3]

After the initial description of the picture a member of the group of subjects is called back into the room and is placed in a position where he cannot see the picture on the projection screen although everyone else in the room can see it. (If no alcove or other architectural feature of the room provides a shielded location near the door where the subjects enter, some movable screen should be placed in an appropriate position before the experiment commences.)

The first subject listens to the "eyewitness" account given him by the selected member of the audience or by the experimenter.

A second subject is called into the room, taking his position beside the first subject. Both are unable to see the screen. The first subject then repeats as accurately as he can

[2] See C. Kirkpatrick (1932).
[3] There is an alternative procedure useful for certain experimental purposes. The experimenter himself may read to the subject a *standardized* description of the scene. By this method the stimulus situation is interpreted in a constant manner at the start of each experiment whereas the initial descriptions made by members of the audience vary widely.
It seems to make little difference which method is used, since in any case the picture itself serves as a standard of comparison. By allowing the first verbal description to vary we may count it as the "first reproduction" and demonstrate how selective and how inaccurate a perception is even when it is reported by a witness who is at the time looking *directly* at the scene.

what he has heard about the scene (still visible to the audience on the screen). The first subject then takes a seat where he can observe the balance of the experiment.

A third subject then takes his position next to the second and listens to his report.

Fig. 5. Battle scene used in rumor experiments.

The procedure continues in the same manner until the last subject has repeated the story he has heard, and taken his seat (usually amidst laughter) to compare his final version with the original on the screen.

Figures 5, 6, 7, and 8 present the principal stimuli employed in our experiments. There is no reason why other material (e.g., Figure 2, p. 54) should not be used with equally good results, provided only that the picture is rich in detail and possesses some central theme by which the amount and direction of distortion can be gauged. Accompanying each of the illustrations is a series of "terminal reports" which represent an exact record of what the final subjects *said* the picture contained in various experiments in which the picture was used. By comparing these terminal reports with the original picture we see how far distortion and loss of detail may proceed even in the brief course of six or seven word-of-mouth transmissions.

Terminal Reports (Fig. 5)

A church is on fire, there is a cross. I don't remember the next part.

* * *

There is a church steeple. There are four Negroes working. The church has a clock. It is ten minutes past two.

* * *

My impression of the picture is a war scene with airplanes overhead. There is a partly demolished house in the middle. There is a Negro rifleman on one side and several other items.

* * *

In Italy. Knocked down church. Bombers dropping bombs.

* * *

In the foreground a battle is going on. A large black man is throwing a hand grenade. There is a Red Cross building, and a wounded man lying there. In the background there is a building with a clock which says ten minutes to two.

* * *

Bombs. A plane and a red cross. (Children serving as subjects.)

* * *

A Negro throwing a hand grenade at church. There are planes fighting. A lot of wrecked houses and ambulances.

* * *

STANDARD PROCEDURE 69

French battleground. Looks as though there had been fighting; woman standing in front.

* * *

There's a battle in a churchyard. Statue of a Negro. Planes overhead. Two men wounded.

* * *

The scene is in France, 50 miles from Cherbourg and at a distance from Paris, and in this scene is an ambulance and also a Negro soldier.

* * *

Terminal Reports (Fig. 6)

This is a street scene on the low side of town. A couple of boys, a Negro boy and a white boy, are playing ball. There is a policeman. Across the street is a movie theater playing a Gene Autry picture. Upstairs is a bowling alley. Near the bowling alley is a blank wall with a sign, "No ball playing." There is a window with three flower pots, one falling out. At another window a man is smoking something, and whatever it is is falling out of his mouth.

* * *

A street scene. There are lots of streets coming together. Stores have signs about various bargains. There are unattractive clothes in one store. A fat woman is walking down the street. A cat is eating out of a garbage can. There is a fruit vendor selling cantaloupes at five cents, apples, and fruit of various varieties.

* * *

Fig. 6. Street scene used in rumor experiments.

A duck and a car and a dog and a plane. (Children serving as subjects.)

* * *

This is a street scene. There is a pushcart full of fruit, a little boy stealing fruit, and an officer remonstrating with him, or someone scolding him. In the background is a doctor's house with a sign out that says Smith.

* * *

Terminal Reports (Fig. 7)

This takes place on a street corner. Something is happening. There is a Negro with a razor, a man with a beard, two women reading newspapers, not particularly interested in what is happening.

* * *

Fig. 7. Subway scene used in rumor experiments.

This is a picture of a typical subway scene. In the picture three people are standing. The subway has the usual characteristics. There are ads, one of them for McGinnis for Congress. Sitting down are a man and a woman. Two other men, one a Negro, are discussing the coming election. The Negro is waving a razor. In another part of the car a woman is standing, holding a baby. You also see that in the subway.

* * *

Scene is a streetcar or subway. There is a Negro man and a laborer with a razor in his hand. Sitting down are a lady sleeping, an old man with a beard, a priest. There are signs: a camp sign and a sign to vote for somebody.

* * *

Picture of a trolley car with seven people. There is a woman with a baby. There are some colored people. Someone is flashing a razor blade.

* * *

There's a train and a man smoking. (Children serving as subjects.)

* * *

Trolley car. Tough boy in it. Man in front of him. There's a lady. Plate on it saying where it is going. Mountains outside window.

* * *

On subway train. Seven people. Two standing, one colored and a lady with a baby in her arms. Two people pointing at something. Two signs—some kind of soap, $99^{44}/_{100}\%$ pure.

* * *

This is a subway train in New York headed for Portland Street. There is a Jewish woman and a Negro who has a razor in his hand. The woman has a baby or a dog. The train is going to Deyer Street, and nothing much happened.

Terminal Reports (Fig. 8)

This is a gathering of people. A group of people are interested in some incident. The center of interest is a Negro youth with clothes disarranged, shoes off, and other evidence of having been maltreated. Close to him is a police officer trying to handle the situation. It is not clear whether the police officer has arrested the Negro or is trying to protect him. In the inner circle is another Negro apparently attempting to get away from the gathering.

* * *

Fig. 8. Riot scene used in rumor experiments.

International News Photo

A picture of the Detroit riot. There is a police officer with a club. Somebody wants to take it away from him.

* * *

A Negro and a white man outside a public building. One is running away. There are between seventy and eighty people.

* * *

The scene takes place during the race riots in Detroit. There are two buildings in the background. A rather tall policeman is standing over a Negro. I don't know whether he is helping him or not.

* * *

Subjects. In the thirty-odd experiments the results of which we report in the following chapters the procedure just described was used with a wide variety of groups, including college undergraduates, trainees in the Army Specialist Training Program, members of a community forum, patients in an Army hospital, members of a teachers' round table, and police officials in a training course. In addition to these adult subjects, children in a private school were used, in each grade from the fifth through the ninth.[4]

Audience Effect. It will be noted that most of the experiments were conducted in the presence of a sizable audience (20 to 300 spectators). The subjects' reports were thus given in the presence of their classmates or fellow trainees, with whom they shared some social, economic, or professional interest. There were no evidences of stage fright, probably because of the homogeneity of the groups, and because reliance on volunteers eliminated people markedly subject to self-consciousness. Yet it is obvious that some social influence operated. The terminal protocols were shorter and

---

[4] We acknowledge the kind assistance of Miss Katherine Taylor, principal of Shady Hill School, Cambridge, Mass., and of Miss Hope Wiswall, who helped conduct the experiments with children.

on the whole less accurate when obtained with an audience than when obtained from subjects making their reports only to the experimenter.

It is commonly found in studies of social influence that people grow cautious and conservative when they feel themselves to be under observation.[5]

To throw light upon the audience influence we conducted some comparison experiments with no observers present except the experimenter. The protocols, one of which is presented on page 77, clearly show that the presence of an audience results in briefer reports—the product of conservatism and caution. Reporters tend to play safe and to tell only the items of which they feel reasonably sure. At the same time the distraction and self-consciousness induced by the audience tend to reduce the accuracy of the reporting even while it makes for meagerness.

It is true that rumor spreaders in everyday life seldom tell their tales with an audience keeping check. But, granted that slightly greater accuracy is to be expected without an audience, still the nature and course of rumor distortion, which are the subjects of present interest to us, are not appreciably different under the two conditions.

Didactic Value. The reason that most of our experiments were conducted with an audience is that they are useful, vivid demonstrations of the psychology of rumor for audiences of all types. The experiments never fail to reveal the essential features of the rumor process. They are guaranteed to disappoint neither lecturer nor audience.

A single experiment requires approximately fifteen minutes and makes an admirable prelude to a lecture or discussion concerning the topics of testimony or rumor.

[5] J. F. Dashiell (1935).

5 RESULTS OF THE EXPERIMENTS: LEVELING AND SHARPENING [1]

As a rumor travels, it tends to grow shorter, more concise, more easily grasped and told. In successive versions fewer words are used and fewer details are mentioned. The complete terminal reports (i.e., the sixth or seventh reproduction) accompanying Figures 5, 6, 7, and 8, show in every case how the initial descriptions, containing twenty or more details, shrink to a striking brevity, an average of about five details.

The number of details retained declines most sharply at the beginning of the series of reproductions. The number continues to decline, more slowly, throughout the experiment. Figure 9 shows the percentage of the initial details retained in each successive reproduction.

The curve, based on eleven experiments, shows that about 70 percent of the details are eliminated in the course of five or six mouth-to-mouth transmissions even when there is virtually no time lapse. The rate of loss follows a continuous downward trend, a larger percentage of details dropping out in the early reproductions.

The rapid rate of leveling must be due, in large part, to the fact that successive reporters in serial reproduction, not having seen the original stimulus, have no lingering trace of it to retard the rate of loss. Nor have they time for

---

[1] An abbreviated account of the results reported in this and in subsequent chapters was published by the authors in an article entitled, "The Basic Psychology of Rumor" (1945).

"mental rehearsal," which would enable them to pass on to the next listener a more complete description. The rapidity of leveling is also due in part, as we have said, to the audience effect in our experimental design. Conscious of a group

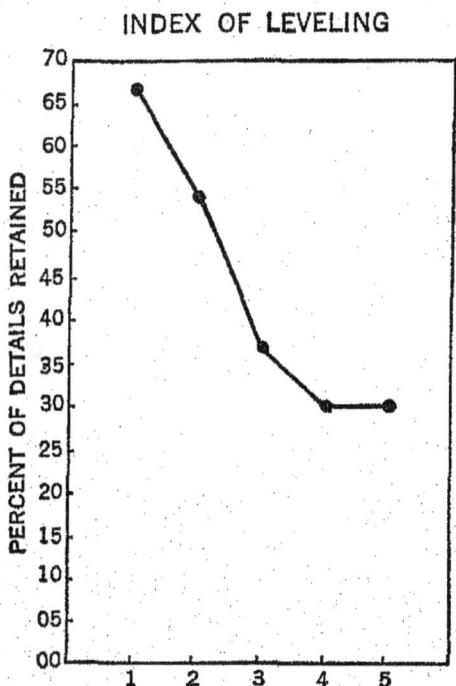

Fig. 9. Percentage of details originally given which are retained in each successive reproduction.

of critical listeners (who have the original picture constantly before them), the reporter, feeling himself to be on trial for accuracy, tries to avoid mistakes by omitting items of which he is not sure.

The existence of this audience effect is easily seen by comparing the following Protocol A (obtained under the audience condition) with Protocol B (obtained from subjects without an audience). Both protocols are based on Figure 5.

LEVELING AND SHARPENING

PROTOCOL A

(with audience)

Description from the Screen: There are four men in the picture, one standing and one kneeling. In the left-hand corner there is a church, below the church a signpost with two directions. One of the four men is a Negro in the center part of the picture, below him is a man kneeling with a rifle in his hand. On the right is a Red Cross wagon. The Negro is standing on a wall with a hand grenade in his left hand. There is a clock showing ten minutes to two on the church steeple, also a cross on the church steeple. There is a plane over to the left of the church steeple. There is a Negro standing on a stone wall. There are two men by the Red Cross truck over on the right side. There is a man with his head against the wall, and a man with binoculars looking into the church. By his side seems to be a cannon ball.

First Reproduction: There is a picture on the screen. In the picture there are four men, one a Negro standing on a stone wall with a hand grenade in his hand. There are two men by a Red Cross wagon. There is a church on the right-hand side of the picture with a cross on the steeple. The clock shows ten minutes to two. There is a signpost by the church and an airplane in the sky.

Second Reproduction: There are four colored men, one with a hand grenade in his hand. On the right there is a church with a cross on top of the steeple. The clock says ten minutes to two. There is also a signpost.

Third Reproduction: There are four colored men working, one holding a hand grenade. There is a church steeple with a cross on it. The time is ten minutes past two. There are also signs along the side of the road.

Fourth Reproduction: There are four Negroes working, one holding a hand grenade. There is a church with a cross on the steeple. The time is ten minutes past two. There are signs along the road.

Fifth Reproduction: There are four Negroes working. There is a church with a steeple and clock. It is ten past two.

Sixth Reproduction: There is a church steeple. There are four Negroes working. The church has a clock. It is ten minutes past two.

PROTOCOL B

(without audience)

Description from the Screen: There is a battle scene. In the foreground is a group of soldiers, one of whom is looking through binoculars toward a church in the background. A soldier is firing a rifle to the right. A Negro, throwing a grenade, is standing on a wall over which the soldiers are firing. He is gesturing toward the enemy troops returning the fire from behind the church. In the right background is a Red Cross ambulance with two men running forward. In the right foreground a man is lying in evident pain. Near the enemy there is another man dead. This is in France and a sign locates Cherbourg $50\frac{1}{2}$ kilometers to the left and Paris $20\frac{1}{2}$ kilometers to the right. The wall they are firing through was part of a store. The store had a sign "Pain et Vin." In the air airplanes are firing and bombs are dropping, shells bursting. In the countryside there are gutted houses, a church and broken-down trees. On the steeple of the church there is a clock reading ten minutes to two. The enemy in the background are dressed in uniforms of dark color, vaguely resembling the German. The man in the foreground with the binoculars is a first lieutenant with one shoulder strap.

First Reproduction: Evidently this is a battle scene. In the foreground are three men, one a second lieutenant with a bar on his shoulders, looking through binoculars at the enemy who are on the left background. Another man is lying next to him firing over the wall of the wreckage of an old shop of some

LEVELING AND SHARPENING

sort. A sign says "Pain et Vin." In the background is a church, in front of which the enemy are fighting, wearing dark or black uniforms. The clock on the steeple says ten minutes to two. All around are gutted buildings. Airplanes are up in the sky, dropping bombs. In the background is a Red Cross ambulance with two men running from it. In the right foreground is a man lying on the ground evidently in great pain. Another man is lying in front of the enemy, I don't know exactly where. I imagine toward the middle of the picture. There is a Negro standing on the wall beckoning toward the enemy, beckoning the men to attack the enemy.

Second Reproduction: There is a battle scene. A man supposed to be a lieutenant with a bar on his shoulders is directing the battle. He is in the left foreground. There is another soldier lying down shooting at the enemy who is in the background. The soldier is shooting over a stone wall which seems the remnant of some shop, probably some sort of tavern because there is a sign, "Pain et Vin," which means bread and wine. On the other side of the picture there is a church and a steeple and the clock says ten minutes to two. On that side there is an ambulance and two men running away from it. There is a general carnage among gutted ruins and everything is shot up. There is a Negro in the picture who is supposed to be urging the men to attack.

Third Reproduction: This is a battle scene. The scene is one of general ruin, evidently a village shot up pretty badly. In the left foreground is a lieutenant in charge. There is a soldier lying down and shooting over the stone wall of the ruins of a restaurant. There is a church steeple on which a clock says ten minutes to two. There is also an ambulance with a couple of fellows running away from it. In the distance is the enemy. Somewhere in the foreground there are a lot of fellows, one of them a lieutenant because you can see the bar on his shoulders. A Negro in the picture is apparently trying to urge the men on to fight.

Fourth Reproduction: This is a picture of a town badly shelled and wrecked—a war scene. In the left foreground is a lieutenant. We know he is a lieutenant because of the bar on his uniform. Below the lieutenant a soldier is firing over a wall. I forget what he was firing at. The enemy obviously. The building over which he was firing was the remnant of a French restaurant and had something about bread and wine on the sign. There is a Negro soldier somewhere in the picture, probably in the middle, urging the soldiers to fight. There was a clock which said ten minutes to two in the distance in the right background.

Fifth Reproduction: This is the scene of a war-torn town, pretty badly demolished. Down in the lower left-hand corner there is a lieutenant who is a lieutenant because he is wearing bars. Below him in a prone position is a soldier firing a rifle. He is firing over some sort of a wall. This wall is probably from a French restaurant because it says something about bread and wine. In the middle foreground is a colored soldier giving orders. In the upper right-hand corner, a clock registers ten minutes to two.

Distracted by the audience and conscious that its members are aware of their mistakes, the subjects in Protocol A become more brief, more hurried, more "safe," in their reporting (see also p. 74). Without an audience, the subjects in Protocol B do a better job of reporting. But though the rate of leveling is speeded up with an audience, the phenomenon itself is universal.

LIMITS OF LEVELING

LEVELING never proceeds to the point of total obliteration. The stabilization of the last part of the curve in Figure 9 is a finding of some consequence. It indi-

LIMITS OF LEVELING

cates (1) that a short concise statement is likely to be faithfully reproduced, (2) that when the report has become brief, the subject has very little detail to select from and the possibilities of further distortion grow fewer, (3) that the assignment becomes so easy that a virtually rote memory serves to hold the material in mind. In all cases, the terminal and the anteterminal reports are more similar than any two preceding reports.

In Protocol C (based on Figure 7), for example, the rote type of persistence is demonstrated even though the terminal (sixth) report, as compared with the fifth report, shows some additional leveling and some invention (the appearance of a "blade").

PROTOCOL C
(illustrating the growing rote effect)

Description from the Screen: The scene is on a streetcar or a train. There are eight persons in the car. On the left-hand side there is a man reading a paper, next to him an elderly lady with a shopping bag in her right hand. A couple of seats away there is a woman with a baby in her hands, then there is an elderly gentleman with a beard, and a fat man sleeping. A Negro and a white man are standing in the car. The Negro has regular clothes on—a zoot suit, the white man is a war worker. They are having an argument. There is a razor in the white man's hand. There are four ads in the car: one for "Lucky Strikes"; one for "Gosling Soap, $99^{44}/_{100}\%$ pure," with a goose in it; one saying, "Spend your vacation at Camp Idlewild, hotel comfort, restricted clientele"; and "Elect McGinnis Alderman."

First Reproduction: This scene is on a streetcar or a train. There are seven adults and one child. There is a woman sitting in one seat holding a baby and there is an elderly chubby man sleeping. Two of the adults are a colored man in a zoot suit and a white man having an argument. The white man has a razor in his hand. There are four ads, one is for "Lucky Strikes," one for some soap, one for some sort of a hotel.

Second Reproduction: This is a streetcar with seven adults in it. There is an elderly woman with a child in her lap. Someone is having an argument and has a razor in his hand. There are four colored persons on the streetcar. There are four advertisements, one is a "Lucky Strikes" sign.

Third Reproduction: This seems to be a trolley car with seven adults on it. There is an elderly woman with a child on her lap. Someone is having an argument and has a razor in his hand. There are four colored persons on the car. There are four ads, one a "Lucky Strikes" sign.

Fourth Reproduction: The picture is about a trolley car with seven persons on it. There are four colored persons. There is a lady with a baby. Somebody is flashing a razor. There are also some advertising signs.

Fifth Reproduction: This is a trolley car with seven persons on it. There is a woman with a baby. Somebody is flashing a razor. There are some signs and some colored people.

Sixth Reproduction: Picture of a trolley car with seven people. There is a woman with a baby. There are some colored people. Someone is flashing a razor blade.

It appears that the subjects tended to rely on rote memory so far as they were able. Under instructions to repeat what they had heard "as accurately as possible," rote retention provided the safest and most foolproof method of carrying out the assignment. Undoubtedly the reliance on rote is more conspicuous in our experiments than in ordinary rumor spreading, where accuracy is not the aim, where time interval interferes with rote retention, and where strong interests prevent literal memory. There are, however, two special conditions where rote likewise plays a part in ordinary rumor spreading. If the individual is motivated by no

LIMITS OF LEVELING

stronger desire than to make conversation, he may find himself idly repeating what he has recently heard in the form in which he heard it. Or, if a rumor has become so crisp and brief, so sloganized, that it requires no effort to retain it in the literal form in which it was heard, rote memory seems to be involved. For example:

The Jews are evading the draft.
The CIO is Communist-controlled.
Wallace believes in a pint of milk for every Hottentot.

The importance of rote has been recognized by the writers of advertisements. They endeavor to make their slogans brief, concise, and rhythmic—easy to remember:

>Lucky Strikes mean fine tobacco.
>Smoke Chesterfields—they satisfy.
>Duz does everything.

and so on, *ad nauseam*.

Similarly, many legends and superstitions have been abbreviated to such an aphoristic point that it is almost impossible to forget them:

>Stuff a cold and starve a fever.
>An apple a day keeps the doctor away.
>A red sky at night, the sailor's delight.
>Spare the rod and spoil the child.

Leveling does not mean random omission of details. Some are more likely to be affected than others. Among items especially liable to leveling Bartlett lists proper names and titles. Proper names (unless well known) have little meaning or interest for the subject. They do not help him in his "pursuit of meaning" and are therefore omitted. Our own results are in agreement with Bartlett's in showing that names are among the most unstable elements of a story and especially subject to leveling. In virtually all our experiments names of places and persons either dropped out or were distorted beyond recognition. The reader will perceive this effect in virtually all our protocols.

Although the rapid and complete leveling out of names is the rule, there are exceptions. If the subjects' interest or training predisposes them to pay especial attention to proper names, these may be retained throughout an entire series of reproductions. Protocol D (based on Figure 5) was obtained from a group of ASTP students. It will be noted that the names of the cities appearing on the signposts and their distance from the scene of action are retained throughout the entire series of reports even though most of the other details drop out. In Army life geographical data—names of places and distances—play an important part. Survival may depend upon correct reporting of geographical data. But even this professional anchorage does not prevent the distances from becoming confused and erroneous.

PROTOCOL D

(illustrating the effect of military interests on retention)

Description from the Screen: The scene is laid in France during wartime. Several men in uniform are obvious. Two of them are firing, one is on his back, wounded, with a bandage around his knee. There is a Negro soldier standing, ready to throw a hand grenade. Behind them there is a destroyed building with one doorway. There is a sign at the crossroads, reading "Cherbourg 21½ km., Paris 50 km." There is also a sign reading "Pain et Vin." There are shells at the sides of the wrecked building. Behind the building there is a church with a big roof hole. The church has a steeple, with the clock showing ten minutes to two. There are two airplanes behind the church,

LIMITS OF LEVELING 85

as there are explosions to be seen. There is an ambulance at the extreme right, with men coming out with shells. Sign, "Bread and Wine."

First Reproduction: The scene is laid in France. There are two soldiers in a trench. Close behind them, is another, wounded. Nearby there is a wrecked house. A Negro soldier is throwing a grenade. There are signs reading "50 miles to Cherbourg and 21 miles to Paris." There is a church with a steeple, showing ten minutes to two. The designation of shells bursting indicates that there is a battle going on. There is an ambulance somewhere in the picture. There is a sign "Bread and Wine."

Second Reproduction: The scene is in France. There is a trench with two men, one firing. A soldier is on his back, wounded. There is a signpost—"Paris 50 miles and Cherbourg 21 miles." There is an ambulance in the picture. There is a house or a barn behind a Negro soldier throwing a grenade. Behind the house is a church. On the steeple the time reads ten minutes to two. Behind the church there are some airplanes.

Third Reproduction: The scene is in France. There are two soldiers in a trench and a wounded soldier. There is an ambulance in the picture, and a house in the background, also a church with a steeple; the time is . . . I don't remember. There is a signpost "Cherbourg 21 miles, Paris 50 miles." There is a Negro soldier in the picture.

Fourth Reproduction: The scene takes place in France, 21 miles from Cherbourg, 50 miles from Paris. This information is given by a signpost. There are two soldiers in the picture and also a Negro soldier. In the distance there is a church, and also a house. There is an ambulance nearby.

Fifth Reproduction: The scene is in France, 21 miles from Cherbourg, 50 miles from Paris, as we can read on a signpost. There is a Negro soldier in the picture. There is a church nearby and also an ambulance.

Sixth Reproduction: The scene is in France, 21 miles from Cherbourg, and 50 miles from Paris as a signpost indicates.

There is a Negro soldier in the scene. An ambulance and a church are near by.

Seventh Reproduction: The scene is in France, 21 miles from Cherbourg, 50 miles from Paris. There is a Negro soldier in the scene, and also an ambulance.

Eighth Reproduction: The scene is in France, 50 miles from Cherbourg and at a distance from Paris, and in this scene is an ambulance and also a Negro soldier.

In this particular protocol the third subject forgot the exact time indicated on the steeple clock and apparently was unwilling to hazard a guess. In other experiments with trainees, however, the exact time reading on the church clock was, as a rule, faithfully reproduced in successive reports. Time and place have preferential value for the military profession.

The reader may have noted that as the protocols become briefer, items that are not leveled out are, of necessity, made relatively more salient. They are *sharpened*.

SHARPENING

SHARPENING may be defined as the selective perception, retention, and reporting of a limited number of details from a larger context. It is the reciprocal phenomenon of leveling; the one can never exist without the other. Although sharpening occurs in every protocol, the same items are not always emphasized. What is sharpened in one protocol may be leveled in another. Note, for example, what happens to the election sign depicted in Figure 7. In many protocols (see, for example, C, p. 81) there is no mention of the sign following the initial report. In the following protocol, however, McGinnis for Alderman (one of four

SHARPENING

signs) is not only retained but Mr. McGinnis acquires the exalted position of a candidate for Congress.

PROTOCOL E
(illustrating sharpening)

Description from the Screen: This is a picture of an elevated train stopping at Dyckman Street. Evidently an Avenue Express. It shows the interior of the train with five people seated and two standing. There are the usual advertising signs above the windows. One is about smoking a certain cigarette, one is a soap ad, another about some camp, another is a political ad for a certain McGinnis for Alderman. Seated is a man with a hat on and a newspaper. He is a funny, rounded man engrossed in his newspaper. Next to him is a woman with a shopping bag on her right arm, eyeglasses, and a funny hat. Then there is some empty space, and in front of it a Negro in a zoot suit, pork-pie hat and loud tie, talking with a defense worker wearing old clothes: overalls, high boots, sleeveless sweater, and cap. He seems to be a shipyard worker, has a razor in his left hand, and is evidently arguing with the Negro. Next person sitting is a woman with a small baby in her arms, watching the two men in their argument. She is commonly dressed and has long hair. Sitting next to her is a man in a cloak, a Jewish rabbi, reading a book, with a funny hat. He is wearing a long coat, not modern. Sitting next to him is a fat man, fast asleep, with his hands clasped.

First Reproduction: A picture of a subway train, stopping at Dyckman Street. It shows the interior of the subway car, about five people sitting, two standing. There are the usual ads, one for cigarettes; one for a political candidate, McGinnis. The people sitting are a fat man interested in his newspaper, next to him a woman, then an empty seat, then a Negro in a zoot suit having an argument with a defense worker carrying a razor. It seems to be a serious argument. Then a woman holding a baby, then a man who appears to be a Jewish rabbi; a fat man fast asleep. The two men are standing; a fat woman is watching the two men standing.

Second Reproduction: Scene is in a subway train at Dyckman Street. This is the interior of the car with five people sitting and two standing. There are the usual ads, one for cigarettes, one political for a candidate named McGinnis. People sitting are a fat man very interested in his newspaper, a woman, then an empty space, then a Negro and a defense worker. The Negro is wearing a zoot suit, and one of them is carrying a razor. They are having a serious argument standing. Then there is a woman and child and another man.

Third Reproduction: This is a scene inside a car at Dyckman Street. There are seven people in the car, five sitting and two standing. Among the signs is a political one for a man named McGinnis. People standing are a fat man and a woman with a baby. Sitting down are two men, then a space, then a woman and two defense workers having an argument. One is a colored man with a zoot suit who has a razor in his hand. The argument must be pretty heated.

Fourth Reproduction: Scene is in a subway car. Five people are seated and two standing. Signs and ads are along the top of the car. One is for McGinnis for Congress. There are a man sitting and a woman, and two defense workers. One of them is a Negro in a zoot suit who is waving a razor. A woman is standing with a baby in her arms. There is a fat man standing.

Fifth Reproduction: The scene is in a subway car, with five people sitting and two standing. In the car there are advertisements; one of the ads is for McGinnis for Congress. In the front of the car there are a man, a woman, and two defense workers, one a Negro with a razor, which he is waving in anger. One person is standing, woman holding baby. The man standing is a fat man.

Sixth Reproduction: This is a picture of a typical subway scene. In the picture three people are standing. The subway

SHARPENING

has the usual characteristics. There are ads, one of McGinnis for Congress. Sitting down are a man and a woman. Two other men, one a Negro, are discussing the coming election. The Negro is waving a razor. In another part a woman is standing, holding a baby. You also see that in the subway.

Sharpening often seizes upon *odd, perseverative wording,* which, having appeared early in the series, catches the attention of each successive listener and is often passed on in preference to other details intrinsically more important to the story. An instance of this effect is seen in Protocol F (based on Figure 6). Note that the statement is the first reproduction, "There is a boy stealing and a man remonstrating with him," is transmitted practically verbatim throughout the entire series. This quasi-literary word "remonstrate" somehow caught the attention of each successive listener and was passed on without change.

PROTOCOL F

(illustrating sharpening through retention of phraseology)

Description from the Screen: This is a street corner scene, corner 16th Avenue and Bartlett Street. In the foreground there is a pushcart with fruit. There is a boy who appears to be stealing a piece of fruit from the cart. The owner of the cart is speaking to him about taking the fruit. There is a Negro policeman coming down the street and a Negro boy coming around the corner. There is a sign over a store, "Levy and Son, Haberdashery." In the background there is a building on which is written, "Storage Warehouse," and "No ball playing here." On another corner there is a building which is apparently a theater, Loew's Palace, advertising a picture with Gene Autry. There is a doctor's office, with a sign, "Anthony Smith, M.D." From one of the windows a flower pot is falling. There is a store having a sale on the 25th of June. Dresses for sale are from $6.95. There are two animals in the picture: a cat climbing on a tin can and a dog. There is a hydrant in the foreground. In one of the windows there is a service flag with one star.

First Reproduction: This is a street scene. In the foreground there is a peddler's pushcart with vegetables. A little boy is stealing from it and a man is *remonstrating* with him. It takes place at the corner of 16th Street and Boulevard Street. Coming down the street is a Negro policeman and a little boy. In the scene there is a haberdashery store with the name "Levy." Also in the background there is a place labeled "Warehouse Storage," also a doctor's office, Anthony Smith, M.D. From one of the windows a flower pot is toppling. There is also a theater, Loew's Palace, which advertises Gene Autry in some picture. Also in the picture are a dog and a cat.

Second Reproduction: There is a street scene. In the foreground there is a man with a pushcart piled with vegetables. A little boy is stealing and the man *remonstrating* with the boy. In the background there is a store, Levy's Haberdashery. There is a movie house, Loew's Palace, playing a film with Gene Autry. There is a doctor's office with a sign, Somebody Smith, M.D. Also coming down the street there is a policeman and a colored man, or else a colored policeman. There is a cat and dog in the street.

Third Reproduction: It is a street scene. In the foreground is a pushcart loaded with fruit. There is a child stealing and a man *remonstrating* with him. In the background there is a store, Levy's Haberdashery, and a moving picture house, Loew's Palace, at which a picture with an actor by the name of Gene Aurich is playing. There is a doctor's office, name is Smith, M.D. There is a street down which are coming a policeman and a colored man or a colored policeman—the narrator was not sure. There are also a cat and a dog.

Fourth Reproduction: A street scene. There is a pushcart and a little boy stealing fruit, and a man *remonstrating* with him. There is a haberdashery and a movie theater. The film has

SHARPENING

an actor in it by the name of Gene Aurich. Also a doctor's office, the name is something or other Smith.

Fifth Reproduction: The picture represents a street scene with a pushcart with fruit, and a little boy stealing from it, and a man *remonstrating* with him. On the street there is a haberdashery and a moving picture house. The actor is named Gene Aurich. There is also a doctor's office; the name appears to be something Smith.

Sixth Reproduction: This represents a street scene. There is a pushcart with fruit on it; a boy is stealing from it, and a man *remonstrating* with him. In the background there is a doctor's office, the doctor's name is Smith. There is also another office.

Seventh Reproduction: I am told this is a street scene. There is a pushcart with fruit on it; a little boy is stealing from it, and a man *remonstrating* with him. In the background there is a doctor's office. The doctor's name is Smith. There is also another office.

Eighth Reproduction: There is a street scene. There is a pushcart full of fruit, a little boy stealing fruit, and an officer *remonstrating* with him, or someone scolding him. In the background is a doctor's house with a sign out that says Smith.

Sharpening may also take a *numerical* turn, items being sharpened by multiplication. For example, in Figure 5 the Negro, whose size and unusual appearance invite emphasis, becomes in Protocol A (p. 77) expanded from one Negro to four.

There is also *temporal* sharpening manifested in the tendency to describe events as occurring in the immediate present. What happens *here* and *now* is of principal interest and importance to the perceiver. In the few instances where the initial description is couched in the past tense, immediate reversal occurs and the scene is *contemporized* by the listener.

Obviously this effect cannot occur in rumors which deal specifically with some alleged past event. One cannot contemporize the rumor that "the *Queen Mary* sailed this morning with 10,000 troops aboard." Yet many stories gain in sharpening by being tied to present conditions. For example, a statement that Mr. X bought a chicken in the black market last week and paid $1.50 a pound for it may be (and usually is) rendered, "I hear they *are* charging $1.50 a pound on the black market for chicken." People are more interested in today than in last week, and the temptation therefore is to adapt the time of occurrence, when possible, to the present. As we shall see in Chapter 9, some venerable legends circulating in World War I were dusted off between 1941 and 1945 and made to apply to World War II.

Sharpening often takes place likewise when there is movement represented in the original story. In many protocols for Figure 5 the flying of airplanes and the bursting of bombs are frequently stressed in the telling. Similarly, the falling flowerpot in Figure 6 is often retained and accented. Not only is the detail of the falling flowerpot sharpened and retained but in Protocol G the "falling motif" is extended to the cigar which a man in the picture is smoking. This effect also illustrates the numerical sharpening previously mentioned.

PROTOCOL G (Fig. 6)

(illustrating sharpening of movement)

Description from the Screen: This is a street corner scene. In the background is a clothing store, Levy & Sons. It is the corner of 16th Avenue and Bartlett Street. In the right-hand corner in the foreground there are some garbage cans and a boy leaning on a post. A dog is on the edge of the street. In the rear foreground is a peanut vendor selling peanuts at five cents a bag. Across the street there is a Loew's theater with a bowling

SHARPENING

alley on top of it, and with Gene Autry playing. There is a big building that looks like a warehouse with a sign on it, "No ball playing." On top of the store there are three windows. One has a doctor's sign; one has three flowerpots, with *one falling out* of the window; in the third there is a service flag. A boy is swiping peanuts and the vendor is yelling at him. A Negro cop is coming down the street toward him. Across from the warehouse is a clothesline. From the bowling place a man with a cigar is hanging out of the window. One of the boys, leaning on the post, is a Negro.

First Reproduction: Scene is a street corner in not such a hot district of the city. One detail is that it is on 16th Avenue. On the corner are a few boys, a Negro, a Negro policeman. Also a couple of garbage cans, a cat or a dog on the curb scavenging in the cans. Also visible is a Loew theater, a bowling alley on the second floor; near it the large blank wall of a warehouse with sign, "No ball playing." Across the space is a clothesline. Further in the background is a clothing store. The name is Debe (anyway there are two "e's" in it). On the top floor or one floor above there are windows. One has three flowerpots, with *one falling out.* In one of the other windows a man is visible smoking a cigar. *Either the cigar or the man is falling out.* At Loew's Theater a Gene Autry picture is playing.

Second Reproduction: The scene is a street corner on 16th Street or Avenue. It is not the best part in town. There is a group of fellows on the corner, one Negro seems to be a policeman. There are garbage cans on the corner, a dog or a cat scavenging. Across the street is a Loew theater with a Gene Autry picture playing. On the second floor is a bowling alley. Next to it is the blank wall of a storage house with a sign, "No ball playing." Further down is a clothing store, name has two "e's" in it. Above the store are several windows, in one there are three flowerpots, *one falling out.* In another window a man is smoking a cigar. *Either cigar or man is falling out of the window.*

Third Reproduction: Scene is a street scene in a low section of town. A couple of boys are playing on the sidewalk; there is a Negro boy and a Negro policeman. Across the street is a theater, Loew's Theater, at which a Gene Autry picture is playing. Upstairs is a bowling alley. Next to the bowling alley and theater is a blank wall with a sign on it which says, "No ball playing." Next to the blank wall is a clothing store, name with two "e's." Somewhere there is a window with three flowerpots, *one falling off* the window sill. At another window a man is smoking a cigar or cigarette. *One or both are about to fall out.*

Fourth Reproduction: This is a street scene in a low section of town. There are two boys playing on the street. A Negro and a Negro policeman. Across the street is a theater with a Gene Autry picture playing. Above the theater is a bowling alley. Next to the theater is a blank wall with a sign, "No ball playing." Next to the wall is a clothing store; name has two "e's." There is an open window with three flowerpots, *one falling out.* In another window is a man smoking a cigar or cigarette. Either *one or both are falling out of the man's mouth.*

Fifth Reproduction: Picture is of a street scene on one of the lower sides of town. On the street two kids are playing. There is a Negro officer and a Negro boy. Across the street is a theater with a picture playing featuring Gene Autry. Above the theater is a bowling alley. Next to the theater is a blank wall with a sign, "No ball playing allowed." Nearby is another building with an open window. There are three flowerpots by the window, *one falling down.* At another window a man is smoking. *Whatever he is smoking he is dropping.*

Sixth Reproduction: This is a street scene on the low side of town. A couple of boys, a Negro boy and a white boy, are playing ball. There is a policeman. Across the street is a movie theater playing a Gene Autry picture. Upstairs is a bowling alley. Near the bowling alley is a blank wall with a sign, "No ball playing." There is a window with three flowerpots, *one*

SHARPENING

falling out. At another window a man is smoking something, and *whatever it is, is falling out of his mouth.*

Sometimes sharpening is achieved by ascribing movement to objects which are really stationary. Thus the train in Figure 7 is clearly at a standstill in the subway station but is frequently described as moving.

The tendency to sharpen movement where it is present and to ascribe it to objects that are stationary is an instance of a well-known law of attention. Movement in the visual field (especially if most objects are at rest) almost always captures our attention. There is a good biological reason why this should be so. Moving objects are potentially menacing, promising, or otherwise of possible moment to us. It behooves us to watch them. It is because of this law of primary attention that in our experiments objects reported as moving catch the listener's attention and tend to be retained and reported.

Size makes for sharpening. Like movement, size is a primary determinant of attention.[2] The first reporter calls attention to the prominence of large objects, and each successive listener receives this emphatic impression. Since he has to rely solely on the report and cannot check against the original picture, he may, in his imagination, greatly exaggerate the relative prominence of the object. Sometimes he reports the fact in the same words that he hears; sometimes (as mentioned above) reduplication occurs, as when the large Negro

[2] The importance of size as a determinant of attention can be demonstrated by a simple experiment. A number of letters or numbers are evenly spaced on a slide. All the items are of equal size, except one, which is considerably larger than all the others. The slide is then shown to the subject for a very short time and he is asked to report what he has seen. He will invariably report the larger letter or number. All the other items have an equal but slighter chance of being seen.

in Figure 5 becomes "four Negroes." Likewise the descriptions of Figure 6 often retain a report on the "big warehouse" or the "large blank wall" throughout the series.

There are verbal as well as physical determinants of attention. Thus there is a pronounced tendency for *labels* to persist. In our experiments, the label is usually a specification of the locale and principal theme—the setting of the stage. Reports on Figure 5 are usually introduced by some version of the statement, "This is a battle scene," and this label persists throughout the series of reproductions. In the same figure the fact that the scene is located somewhere between Paris and Cherbourg is often retained, though the distances are invariably distorted. Figure 6 is introduced as a rule with some variation of the label, "This is a street corner scene." Descriptions of Figure 8 usually open with the statement, "This is a picture of a race riot."

To explain this type of sharpening we may invoke the desire of the subject to achieve some spatial and temporal orientation for the story to come. Such orientation, essential in ordinary life, seems needed even when imaginal material is dealt with. An additional factor making for preferential retention of spatial and temporal labels is the fact that they are generally mentioned at the beginning of the story. An item that comes first in any series is likely to be better remembered than subsequent items (primacy effect).

Current events favor sharpening. Figures 5 and 8 depict situations having a direct bearing on incidents contemporary with the experiment—a battle scene and the Detroit race riot. In the former case the fact that a battle in France was in progress was almost invariably reported. In the latter, the street skirmish is usually described as occurring in Detroit even though nothing in the picture itself gives an indication of its location. At the time of the experiment the Detroit riots were very much in the limelight of discussion and the subjects took it for granted that the picture of the incident had come from that city. By a sharpening of the contemporary aspect of this scene the ambiguity of the situation is diminished for the subject and he attains a firm point of reference in his pursuit of meaning.

Sharpening also occurs in relation to *familiar symbols*. For example, in Figure 5 the church and the cross are among the most frequently reported items. In our culture these common symbols convey much meaning and are known to all. The subject feels secure in reporting them because they are so familiar. Such symbols further play readily into the process of conventionalization that is such an important aspect of rumor development (see p. 156).

In Figure 8 the night stick, symbol of police authority, is usually prominent throughout the series of reports. In Figure 7 the razor, stereotyped symbol of Negro violence, is virtually always retained and sharpened. Occasionally in the process, the razor is reported as being "brandished" or "flashed," thus illustrating the additional process of sharpening through the ascription of movement.

Closure is a form of sharpening. It refers to the subject's urge to make his experiences as complete, coherent, and meaningful as possible. There are many examples of closure in our protocols. In the case of Figure 6 the signs contain many intentional incompletenesses and errors, which disappear in the process through closure. Thus, *Bow—* is always reported (if reported at all) as *Bowling Alley*. The name *Gene Antry* on the moving picture marquee, when reported, is always *Gene Autry*. *Lucky Rakes* usually become *Lucky Strikes*. These closures usually take place in the first report (description of the scene) and demonstrate what all proofreaders know—that it is hard to catch errors when one is very familiar with the correct and complete spelling.

The tendency to achieve closure may sometimes lead to amusing results, as in the case of the falling flowerpot in Figure 6. This oddity, we have said, catches the subjects' attention and is usually reported. But in one protocol this "uncomfortable" situation is rectified and the flower pot is said to be "caught" in mid-air. This fanciful closure makes the reporter feel better, for the untoward motion is arrested.

Another possible form of closure is the introduction of explanations and rationalizations. This is less evident in our experimental material than in the rumors of everyday life. Sharpening through the addition of meaning was highly characteristic of war rumors where shortages, setbacks, discomfort, worry, were regularly "explained" through bogy tales of losses, or through ascriptions of blame to the "brass hats," "Jews," "OPA officials," or to "F.D.R." A large number of everyday rumors are nothing more than specious explanations or justifications of what we personally feel or suffer.

6 RESULTS OF THE EXPERIMENTS: ASSIMILATION

IN common speech we often make a sharp distinction between "intellectual" and "emotional" thinking. A certain writer, or artist, or composer, we say, "appeals to the reason," is "intellectualistic" or "cerebral." Another, we hold, "appeals to the emotions," is "intuitive" or "romantic." In the same way we sometimes label our own mental activities as either "rational" or "irrational," or sometimes as "cognitive" or "affective." Occasionally, too, the word "conative," meaning striving or willing, is employed as a contrast to "cognitive."

Such sharp contrasts, though used even by psychologists themselves, are inaccurate. No mental activity is ever purely cognitive, in the sense that it is at the same time devoid of motivating or emotional force. Memory is ordinarily regarded as a *cognitive* function, but it would be impossible to account for memory unless the individual were *motivated* to remember. The motive may be as intense as a political or racial hatred, or it may be as mild as a desire to please the experimenter by carrying out his instructions. In any event, cognitive processes (which include the intellectual changes in rumor) and motivational processes (which include the interest factor in rumor) are always blended and fused.

The subtle interpenetration of cognitive and emotional processes is evident in the changes which our stimulus material undergoes in the course of transmission. When we ask what it is that leads to the obliteration of some details and the pointing up of others, and what accounts for all the transpositions, importations, and other falsifications that mark the course of rumor, the answer is to be found in the process of *assimilation,* which has to do with the powerful attractive force exerted upon rumor by the intellectual and emotional context existing in the listener's mind.

Although we are not justified in sharply contrasting the intellectual and emotional aspects of assimilative change, we shall, in the interests of analysis, speak of assimilative tendencies that are *relatively* unemotional and of those that are *relatively* more emotional in character. But all the while we should keep in mind the truth that cognitive and emotional assimilation are in reality indistinguishably blended.

RELATIVELY UNEMOTIONAL ASSIMILATION

GESTALT psychologists have been the primary discoverers of a self-contained type of dynamic change in what they are pleased to call "memory traces." As soon as perception occurs, so the theory goes, stresses are set up which lead to mnemonic reorganization. In the initial act of perception not all of the physical "objective" characteristics of the stimulus are reproduced. From the outset perception is selective and tends to simplify the world around us. Memory continues and hastens the process. Unconstrained by the presence of the stimulus, memory accelerates the formation of "good Gestalten." The change is toward simplicity, symmetry, good configuration. The intellect, as Leibnitz was fond of pointing out, is self-active. It seems to want to hold its content in as pregnant a form as possible. For this reason economical processes are set up that bring about better configurations in memory than existed in the stimulus itself.[1]

Assimilation to Principal Theme. As pointed out on page 58, items become sharpened or leveled according to the demands of the leading motif of the story. They also become twisted in such a way as to render the story more coherent, plausible, and well rounded. For example, in Figure 5 the war theme is preserved and emphasized in all reports and made the focus for certain importations; thus in one report, an imaginary chaplain is introduced into the picture; a number of people are reported as being killed; the ambulance becomes a Red Cross station; demolished buildings are multiplied in the telling and the extent of devastation is exaggerated. All these reports, false though they are, fit and amplify the principal theme—a battle incident. If they were actually present in the picture, they would make a "better" Gestalt. Never are objects extraneous to the theme introduced—no apple pies, no ballet dancers, no baseball players. If imported, they would create a confused or "worse" Gestalt.[2]

---

[1] The basic experiments that have led to the discovery of the laws of configuration are summarized by Koffka (1935).
Some Gestalt psychologists argue that the course of memory change is affected relatively little by the association of new memory material with old. The changes that occur, they say, result principally from primitive or "autochthonous" brain processes. Critics, on the other hand, make the counterclaim that all changes in memory are essentially the result of associational processes—that is to say, of the adaptation of new material to preceding mental contexts or habits of thought. In our own discussion of assimilative distortions we remain neutral in this dispute and list under "assimilation" changes that are due either to primitive brain mechanisms or to association with pre-existing mental content.

[2] We find only a single exception to this statement. In one of the terminal reports (see p. 105) a mantelpiece is introduced into the picture! It crept in apparently as a result of the unusual sharpening of the clock in successive reproductions. The association *clock—mantelpiece* is a common one and was made "automatically" by the reporter. This particular distortion illustrates the assimilative force of linguistic habit (p. 104).

Besides importations we have other falsifications in the interest of supporting the principal theme. The picture shows that the Red Cross truck is loaded with *explosives*. Yet it is ordinarily reported as carrying *medical supplies* which is, of course, the way it "ought" to be. This assimilative error is sometimes present in the perceptual report itself. In this case the individual describing the picture from the screen does not "see straight." But more often, the false item of medical supplies creeps in as an assimilative error of memory.

The Negro in this same picture is nearly always described as a soldier, although his clothes indicate that he might be a civilian partisan. It is a "better" configuration to have a soldier in action on the battlefield than to have a civilian among regular soldiers.

The enemy troops attacking the church are sometimes designated as German although there is nothing in the picture to identify them as such. Since the signposts in the picture are in French, it seems natural to assume that the enemy must be German. Presently this inference is reported as fact.

Good Continuation. In the previous chapter it was pointed out how the tendency to reach a closure makes for sharpening. The subject attempts to complete what is incomplete in the stimulus field whether it be the original picture or the report heard. The sign, "Loew's Pa . . ." in Figure 6 is invariably read and reproduced as "Loew's Palace," and Gene *Antry* becomes Gene *Autry*.

All these, and many instances like them, are examples in Gestalt terms of "good continuations." They illustrate not only the sharpening process but the assimilation process as well, for they obviously exploit pre-existing knowledge in

UNEMOTIONAL ASSIMILATION 103

the interests of bringing about a more coherent, consistent mental configuration.

Assimilation by Condensation. It sometimes seems as though memory tries to burden itself as little as possible. Instead of remembering separate items, it may be more economical to fuse them into a single general category. Instead of a series of subway cards in Figure 7, each of which has its own identity, reports sometimes refer only to "a billboard," or perhaps to a "lot of advertising." In describing Figure 6 it is more convenient to refer to "all kinds of fruit" rather than to enumerate all the different items on the vendor's cart. Again, in descriptions of Figure 7 the occupants of the car are typically described by some such summary phrase as "several people sitting and standing in the car."

As a result of this tendency, that which is similar and common to many items is stressed while individual differences and characteristics are lost. Assimilation by condensation helps to account for *stereotyping*, which is a result of undue simplification in the interests of economizing mental effort. Rumor does not go in for subtle differentiations. It is content to speak of "a big fat man," "a mob," "a Jew," "a Jap."

Assimilation to Expectation. In addition to changes that help to fortify the principal theme, many items take a form that supports the agent's ordinary habits of thought. Things are perceived and remembered the way they usually are. Thus the drugstore in Figure 2 moves up to the corner of the two streets and becomes the familiar "corner drugstore." The Red Cross ambulance carries medical supplies rather than explosives (an example of assimilation to expectation as well as to the principal theme). The kilometers on the signposts in Figure 5 are invariably changed into miles to conform to our customary unit of linear measurement. Descriptions of Figure 7 often have it that the colored man and the defense worker are arguing about a vacant seat—a plausible source of trouble on crowded subway trains. Reports on Figure 8 usually describe the policeman in the act of arresting the Negro, although a few reports point out the more apparent possibility that the officer may be protecting the colored man. Police are better known for their arrests than for their protection. In short, when an actual perceptual fact is in conflict with expectation, expectation may prove a stronger determinant of perception and memory than the situation itself.

Perhaps the most spectacular of all our assimilative distortions is the finding that in more than half the experiments the razor in Figure 7 moves (in the telling) from the white man's hand to the black man's. This result, which we shall discuss more fully on page 111, is a clear instance of assimilation to stereotyped expectancy. Negroes are "supposed" to carry razors, white men not.

Assimilation to Linguistic Habits. Expectancy is often merely a matter of fitting perceived and remembered material to pre-existing verbal clichés. For example, the colored man in Figure 7 is described as a "zoot-suiter" or "zoot-suit sharpie." Such sloganizing helps not only to sharpen the image but to stereotype the person. The qualities of the man are suggested and held in mind by this reference to his clothes, and because he is a "zoot-suiter," the razor is more readily located in his hands.

We have already referred to one odd distortion, clearly due to linguistic habit, occurring in connection with Figure 5. The clock on the church tower gets displaced to a "mantel-

MOTIVATED ASSIMILATION

piece." Even in the setting of a war scene it appears that the habit of linguistic association was too strong for one reporter. Here are the relevant portions of the protocol:

Sixth Reproduction: This is a picture of a battlefield. There is a chapel with a clock which says ten minutes to two. A sign down below gives the direction to Paris, and Paris is 150 miles and Cherbourg is 21 miles away. People are being killed on the battlefield.

Seventh Reproduction: This is a picture of a battlefield. There is a chaplain,[3] and a clock on the mantelpiece says ten minutes to two. There is a sign, so many miles to Cherbourg.

The powerful effect that words have in arousing images in the listener and fixing for him the categories in which he must think of the event is, of course, a major step in the conventionalization of rumor. Many rumors are carried almost exclusively in terms of verbal stereotypes. Over and over again they include sloganized and often prejudicial phrases such as "draft dodger," "Japanese spy," "brass hat," "dumb Swede," "long-haired professor," and the like.

MORE HIGHLY MOTIVATED ASSIMILATION

THE conditions of our experiment, as we have already pointed out, did not give full play to emotional tendencies underlying ordinary gossip, rumor, and scandal. Such tendencies, however, are deep in human nature and sometimes express themselves even under laboratory conditions.

Assimilation to Interest in Clothes (Women). For Figure 6 we have the following protocol taken from a group of

[3] This change seems to be an assimilation to theme, facilitated also by a verbal misunderstanding of the word "chapel" (see p. 122).

college women. The interest in bargains and clothes persists throughout. In none of the male groups were clothes as prominently mentioned.

PROTOCOL H

(illustrating assimilation to a special interest)

Description from the Screen: The picture shows a scene at 16th Avenue and Bartlett Street. The main thing is a big sign, "Levy & Sons, Haberdashery." There are two store windows. *In one window it says "Sale Today," and there are three terrible-looking dresses. In the other window there is a sign, "Bargains."* A man is standing by a fruit cart yelling at a boy trying to steal some fruit. There are cantaloupes at five cents apiece, pears, other fruit. In the foreground there is a Negro right by the fruit cart. A colored policeman is coming up the street. The colored boy is standing by the sign, 16th Avenue and Bartlett Street. There is a dog standing in the street, and a cat trying to pull garbage out of a can. There is a theater, Loew's Palace, with Gene Autry playing in something or other. It is not open; nobody is in the box office. There is laundry strung across the street, and there is a bowling alley on top of the movie theater. There is a warehouse on the other side of the street. Walking by the warehouse is a big fat woman with an umbrella.

First Reproduction: The picture is a scene in a large city. There are lots of stores around, and many signs in the stores. The main street corner is at 16th Avenue and Bartlett Street. *There are many stores, a couple labeled "Sales" and "Bargains."* There is a store called "Levy Brothers." In front of the store is a fruit wagon selling peanuts, cantaloupes, pears, and apples. The slices of cantaloupe are five cents apiece. There is a fat lady walking down the street, and a garbage pail with a cat rummaging in it. In the background is a Loew's theater, with Gene Autry playing, unoccupied. *There is a store with bargains, in which the dresses are not very nice.*

MOTIVATED ASSIMILATION 107

Second Reproduction: A large city with a great number of signs. *Many stores have bargain signs and sale signs. One has very unattractive dresses.* One sign is 16th Avenue and Bartlett Street. There is a Loew's theater with Gene Autry playing, now vacant. There is a garbage pail, and a cat rummaging through the garbage pail. A fat woman is walking down the street. There is a fruit vendor along the way, selling peanuts, cantaloupes, apples, and watermelon at five cents a slice.

Third Reproduction: It is a picture of a city with large streets. There are lots of signs and lots of stores. *Many stores have bargains. In one store the dresses are very unattractive.* There is a Loew theater where Gene Autry was playing, now vacant. A sign says 7th Avenue and Bartlett Street. A fat woman is walking down the street. A cat is eating out of a garbage can. A fruit vendor is selling pears, apples, cantaloupe, and watermelon at five cents a slice.

Fourth Reproduction: It is a picture of a city with many streets in it. *There are quite a few stores with bargain signs. In one store there are especially unattractive clothes.* There is a Loew theater in which Gene Autry was playing, which is now closed. There is a fat woman, and a cat eating out of a garbage pail. There is a fruit vendor selling pears, apples, slices of cantaloupe at five cents a piece.

Fifth Reproduction: This is a picture of a street scene. *There are a lot of stores and various signs about bargain sales. There are particularly unattractive clothes in one store.* There is a fat woman walking down the street, a cat eating out of a garbage pail. There is a fruit vendor selling apples and cantaloupes at five cents a piece.

Sixth Reproduction: A street scene. There are a lot of streets coming together. *Stores have signs about various bargains. There are unattractive clothes in one store.* A fat woman is walking down the street. A cat is eating out of a garbage can. There is a fruit vendor selling cantaloupes at five cents, apples and fruit of various varieties.

Assimilation to Occupational Interest. Our military subjects may again serve as an example. Reporting on Figure 5 these groups characteristically maintained a special interest in the time of day, and in the reading of the signpost for distances and direction. Occupational training had made them sensitive to both.

With a group of subjects who were patients in a military hospital it was noted that in all descriptions of military scenes, the soldiers were designated merely as "men." In all civilian groups, on the other hand, these same characters were "soldiers." This small detail shows the assimilative powers of an unconsciously assumed frame of reference. To the patients, isolated from civilian life, all soldiers are "men" because all men in their immediate environment are soldiers; to civilians, men are not soldiers, unless specifically designated as such.

Assimilation to Self-interest. Most rumors circulate because people have an ax to grind or a nest to feather or a ghost to lay. In short, they circulate because of some form of self-interest.

We illustrate the point with reference to Figure 8, which was used with a group of police officers as subjects. In the resulting protocol, we note how the entire reproduction centers around the police officer (with whom the subjects undoubtedly felt keen sympathy or "identification"). The night stick, a symbol of his power, is greatly sharpened and becomes the main object of the controversy. The tale as a whole is protective of, and partial to, the policeman.

MOTIVATED ASSIMILATION

PROTOCOL I

(illustrating assimilation to the self-interest of police officers)

Description from the Screen: This is an excerpt from a motion picture that appeared in a national magazine. The scene is Detroit during the colored-white riot. *There is a crowd around a police officer with a riot stick in his right hand* and a Negro sitting on the ground, holding onto his leg. On the right a boy is running away. On the left, *facing the officer is a man who looks hostile but is afraid to go nearer because of the riot stick.* The crowd comprises approximately 100 people.

First Reproduction: The picture on the screen is an excerpt from a motion picture taken at the time of the Detroit riot. *In the picture a police officer with a stick in his right hand is standing over a man on the ground.* On the right is a small boy, on the left is a *man who wants to interfere but is afraid of the policeman's stick.*

Second Reproduction: This is an excerpt from a movie taken at the time of the Detroit riot. *There is an officer with a stick in his hand* and a man on the ground. There is a small boy and a *man who wants to interfere but is afraid.*

Third Reproduction: Picture was taken during the Detroit riot. There is a man in the picture, also a police officer. *The man has a stick in his hand and wants to interfere* but does not for some reason.[4] There is also a child.

Fourth Reproduction: This is a picture of the Detroit riot showing a policeman and a civilian. *The policeman has a billy in his hand, and the man wants to take it away from him.*

Fifth Reproduction: A picture of the Detroit riot. *There is a police officer with a club. Somebody wants to take it away from him.*

[4] Note the falsification which becomes rectified in the following reproductions by virtue of assimilation to expectation.

110   ASSIMILATION

A protocol based on the same picture, taken from a group of subjects who were not policemen (in this particular case, a group of teachers) follows. It illustrates how in a different occupational group the focus of interest and direction of sympathy is quite different.

PROTOCOL J

(illustrating direction of sympathy in a different occupational group)

Description from the Screen: First thing, there are signs of race war. There seems to be a group of rather aggressive people. In the center there is a man who looks like a Negro. Over him there is a person holding a club, holding it in his left hand. Then there is a very aggressive individual, with clenched fist and wide-open mouth and threatening expression. At the extreme left is another Negro trying to escape. The attitude of the group is extremely menacing. The poor victim in the middle seems to be without shoes.

First Reproduction: This seems to represent a problem of race, headed Race War. The center is occupied by a Negro in a sorry position. He is most abject, has no shoes, is in the center of a very aggressive crowd, carrying clubs or rolled-up newspapers. Standing in the back is a policeman supported by the group. On the other side is a Negro attempting to escape.

Second Reproduction: This incident concerns racial affairs. Apparently there is a Negro in the midst of a crowd, worse for wear and without shoes, surrounded by menacing people. Next to him is a police officer supported by the group. It is not clear whether the Negro is under arrest. Over on the other side there is a Negro trying to escape. There is great excitement.

Third Reproduction: You and I are walking and come to a group of people. Something is wrong. In the center is a Negro who has been in a fracas. His shoes are missing. Standing beside him is a policeman who looks worried. Don't know whether the Negro is under arrest. On the side another Negro involved is trying to make his escape.

N *Fourth Reproduction:*[5] This is a gathering of people. A group of people are interested in some incident. The center of interest is a Negro youth with clothes disarranged, shoes off, and other evidence of having been maltreated. Close to him is a police officer trying to handle the situation. It is not clear whether the police officer has arrested the Negro or is trying to protect him. In the inner circle is another Negro apparently attempting to get away from the gathering.

Assimilation to Prejudice. Hard as it is in an experimental situation to obtain distortions that arise from hatred, we nevertheless have in our material a certain opportunity to trace the hostile complex of racial attitudes. Figure 7 proved particularly interesting for this purpose.

In over half of the experiments with this picture, at some stage in the series of reports the Negro (instead of the white man) is said to hold the razor in his hand. Several times he was reported as *brandishing* it wildly or as *threatening* the white man with it. Sometimes the razor migrated from the white man to the Negro fairly early in the series of reproductions, sometimes at the very end.

Whether this ominous distortion reflected hatred and fear of Negroes we cannot definitely say. In some cases these deeper emotions may be the assimilative factor at work, though the falsification might well occur even among subjects who have no active anti-Negro bias. There is so much unthinking acceptance of the widespread cultural stereotype of the Negro as hot-tempered and addicted to the use of razors as weapons that the report may mean nothing more

[5] The letter N in Protocols J, K, and L designates the reproductions of Negro subjects.

than an assimilation to verbal clichés and conventional expectation. Hence distortion in this case does not *necessarily* mean assimilation to hostility. Much so-called prejudice is a mere matter of conforming to current folkways.

In connection with this same figure the reports of our Negro subjects sometimes betrayed a deeply motivated type of distortion. It was their desire (because it was to their interest as members of the race) to de-emphasize the racial caricature.

PROTOCOL K

(illustrating assimilation to racial self-interest)

Description from the Screen: The scene is in an express car headed for Cortlandt Park, just passing Dyckman Street station. There is a man sitting and reading a paper. There is a woman next to him. There are also three other people sitting there: a woman with a baby, a man with a beard, and a man with a bald head. In the foreground two men are standing, a Negro in a zoot suit and another man in work clothes. They are having a disagreement, perhaps about the vacant seat beside them. The boy in overalls seems to have a weapon in his hand which looks like a razor. Three of the people sitting are watching the young men, wondering what the outcome will be. The Negro in the zoot suit is not agitated, the man in work clothes is all worked up, pointing with his hand at a sign above; he seems to be doing all the talking at the moment. There are several signs overhead. One sign advertises, "Smoke Luckies," the second sign is an advertisement for Gosling Soap, with a picture of a duck. The next sign is an ad for a camp, "Spend your vacation at Camp Idlewild." The last sign is a political ad, "Elect McGinnis Alderman."

First Reproduction: There is an express train marked Cortlandt Park passing Dyckman Street. A man with a bald head is reading a paper, a woman with a baby is beside him, and three other people. There is a vacant seat. Two young people,

MOTIVATED ASSIMILATION 113

a Negro in a zoot suit and another young man in work clothes, with a razor, are looking at the signs. There is a sign, "Smoke Luckies," another ad for some soap, and another about Camp Idlewild. There is an election sign for some office.

N *Second Reproduction:* The picture is in an express train. There are a man, woman, and child and other people in it. There is a character in a zoot suit, possibly a Negro. There is a picture in the car advertising cigarettes and soap, and something about a razor, I don't know what. An accident has taken place.

N *Third Reproduction:* The picture takes place in a train. There is a man, woman, and child. One man seems to be in a zoot suit. They are not sure whether or not he is a colored person. There is somebody selling cigarettes and soap. There has been an accident, something about a razor in it.

Fourth Reproduction: The scene takes place in a train. There is a man, woman, and child, and a man in a zoot suit. They are not sure whether the man is colored or not. There has been an accident with a razor in it.

Fifth Reproduction: The scene takes place on a train. There is a man, woman, and child, and a man in a zoot suit. I am not sure whether he is the same man or not. There has been an accident, no details given.

From these protocols it will be seen that the Negro reporters, though instructed to repeat what they had heard as accurately as possible, tended (1) to suppress the fact that the character in the picture was colored, or at least to mention the fact as casually as possible; (2) to de-emphasize undesirable characteristics of the member of the colored race. Such phrases as "sharp clothes," for example, were avoided. No Negro spontaneously removed the razor from the white man's hand to place it in a colored man's hand.

One Negro subject transmitting a description of Figure 5 omitted the fact that the central character of the picture about to throw a hand grenade is a Negro (Protocol L). He may have felt that to include a racial reference (even though not disparaging) is to invite prejudice and encourage stereotyping.

PROTOCOL L

(further illustrating assimilation to racial self-interest)

Description from the Screen: This is a battle scene. The four main characters are soldiers leading an attack on a group sheltered in a church. There is a colored soldier about to hurl a grenade. There are two men kneeling in the foreground, one firing, one looking through glasses. The fourth main figure is a man wounded in the arm and lying on the ground. This is a spot $21\frac{1}{2}$ kilometers from Paris and 50 kilometers from Cherbourg. In the background is an ambulance with several attendants running toward the battle scene. The church itself, within which the enemy group has taken shelter, is a typical old church with a high spire, with a clock that reads 10 minutes to 3 (discussion from audience which points out that time is 10 minutes to 2). The attacking soldiers, who are unidentified, are taking shelter behind a stone wall. At the corner there is a sign which reads, "Pain et Vin." In the air there are two airplanes which are fighting with one another. In the background bombs are bursting.

N *First Reproduction:* The picture represents a battle scene. The enemy is taking shelter in a church with a tower and a clock in it, with the hands pointing to 10 minutes to 2. There are bombs bursting in the background and two airplanes above. The attacking force has had one man wounded. It is fighting from behind a stone wall. There is a sign indicating $21\frac{1}{2}$ miles from Cherbourg and 50 miles from Paris.

Second Reproduction: The picture is supposed to represent a battle scene. The enemy is taking shelter in a church, with a tower and a clock showing 10 minutes to 2. There are airplanes in the background and bombs bursting, too. There is

MOTIVATED ASSIMILATION 115

also a road sign which says 50 miles to Paris and 21 miles to Cherbourg.

Third Reproduction: The picture is a battle scene. There is a church in the background with a clock which shows 10 minutes to 2. There is an airplane and a bomb bursting. A road sign says 150 miles to Paris and 21 miles to Cherbourg.

Further reproductions show the usual features of these protocols.

In reporting on the Detroit riot scene (Fig. 8) one Negro respondent construes the ambiguous situation in favor of the Negro who occupies the center of the scene. The statement that the Negro had been in a "fracas" becomes an assertion that he has been "maltreated."

Thus, even under laboratory conditions we find assimilation in terms of deep-lying emotional needs. The rumor tends to fit into, and support, the occupational interests, class or racial memberships, or personal prejudices of the reporter. True, the presence of emotional distortion encountered in our experiments is far, far less than in the rumors of everyday life. Yet the mechanisms are the same, and in spite of our laboratory limitations, we have probably succeeded in calling attention to all the basic forms of assimilative distortion that occur.

7 RESULTS OF THE EXPERIMENTS: CONCLUDED

MOST rumors start as a report of an actual episode—that is to say, with someone's perceptual experience of an event which he deems of sufficient interest and importance to communicate to others. Usually the subject matter (the principal theme) of the report persists to the end: an anti-Semitic story remains anti-Semitic, and a horror tale continues as a horror tale. The resistance of the central theme to change was noted by Hartgenbusch (1933) in his experiments in which both sentence material and short stories were successively reproduced by subjects of different age levels and educational backgrounds. No matter what the material was or who the subjects were, the principal theme was always the least changeable of all items. Likewise, inspection of our terminal reports shows that in most cases, the subject matter, though skeletonized and badly distorted, bears some relation to the original incident.

SHIFT OF THEME

THERE are a few exceptions. Once in a while peripheral details may become sharpened at the expense of the principal theme, a new theme resulting. Thus, in Protocol G, the reports are at first centered around the boy *stealing* fruit from a vendor's cart. Later, however, the central theme shifts to *playing* and *falling:* there are boys playing ball, there is a sign, "No *ball playing,*" there is a

SHIFT OF THEME

picture *playing* at the movie theater. A flowerpot is *falling* out of a window, and the cigar which a man at another window is smoking is also *falling* out.

In the following protocol based on Figure 7, the advertisement calling for the election of McGinnis, one of several posters, is sharpened out of all proportion. The terminal report has it that there is a commotion in the car, with people shouting, "Elect McGinnis Alderman."[1] The original central theme—the quarrel between the war worker and the Negro—has completely disappeared. Yet even in this case one cannot say that the final report is a complete "tissue of lies." A kernel of fact from the original scene is preserved: a subway, a rabbi, a woman, and a reference to McGinnis vaguely reflect matters of fact.

PROTOCOL M

(illustrating shift of theme)

Description from the Screen: The scene takes place on a New York subway going to Van Cortlandt Park or Street. There are seven people—five sitting and two standing. An old gentleman in a hat is reading the Boston *Globe*. There is a woman in a hat. There is a rabbi reading a little book. There is a bald man next to him. A woman in a polka-dot dress is holding a baby. There are two people standing—a Negro and a white man. The Negro has a zoot suit on. The white man is a worker and has a razor in his hand. They seem to be having an argument, of which the other people are quite oblivious. There are several advertising signs: "Come to Camp Idlewild"; "Elect McGinnis Alderman, Honest, Safe, Reliable, Man of the People." There is also a sign for Gosling Soap. The train is an express.

[1] The extraordinary sharpening of the election sign in this instance also reflects assimilation to local interest. The subjects in this experiment were college students, among whose instructors was a Mr. McGinnies. The familiar name attracted attention and led to this dramatic example of sharpening.

First Reproduction: The scene is in a New York subway train going to Van Cortlandt Park. It is an express. There are seven people—five sitting and two standing. There is a lady in a polka-dot dress, a rabbi reading a book, a man reading the Boston *Globe,* a man looking over the shoulder of a lady. There are two people standing up—a white man and a Negro. The white man has a razor. They are arguing but nobody is paying attention. There are two or three signs. One is "Elect McGinnis Alderman or Mayor"; another is about some kind of soap.

Second Reproduction: There is a train going to Van Cortlandt Park. On it five people are sitting and two are standing. There is a lady in a polka-dot dress, a rabbi, a lady or a man reading a Boston *Globe.* Someone is looking over her shoulder. Two people are standing up—one is a white man, the other a Negro. The white man has a razor in his hand. There are two advertisements: one says "Elect McGinnis Alderman" or to some other office. There is also another sign.

Third Reproduction: There is a subway train going to Van something. In it is a man standing up and also a man sitting down reading the Boston *Globe,* and a rabbi. There is a woman in a polka-dot dress. There are signs in the subway, one of which says "Elect McGinnis Alderman."

Fourth Reproduction: This is a subway train going to Van something. There is a crowd on the train and also a rabbi. There is some kind of commotion going on, and people are shouting "Elect McGinnis for Alderman" or something. A woman is sitting down doing something I don't remember.

Fifth Reproduction: There is a subway train going to Van something. There is a crowd in the train and a rabbi in the train. There is some kind of commotion and people are shouting, "Elect McGinnis for Alderman." There is also a woman in the train sitting and doing something.

Another case, based on Figure 7, is still more extreme and shows two shifts of theme in the course of the protocol.

In the original description the scene centers around a disagreement between the Negro and the white worker. In the first reproduction the focus shifts to the signs in the car. The two protagonists are no longer represented as quarreling, but are both described as looking at signs. In the second reproduction a fictitious accident is introduced which persists to the end of the series. Even in this fantasy, however, the orientational fact is correct, namely, that the imaginary episode takes place in a subway.

Although they occur only in a minority of the cases, such thematic shifts are among the most striking results of our experiments. Where they occur, they seem to be due to the sharpening of minor details. Once a new theme has resulted, it begins to influence and, as far as possible, to assimilate to itself all the individual details that remain in the story.

INVENTIONS AND ELABORATIONS

There are few cases where we can speak of outright invention in the sense that an item cannot be explained as a distortion of detail present in the preceding reproduction. In other words, inventions are nearly always instances of assimilation. Fanciful details appropriate to the central theme may be supplied by the narrator. We recall, for example, how in Figure 5 a chaplain is fitted into the war scene. In the protocol just read, one narrator supplied an election crowd milling about in the subway car to round out the story of McGinnis's candidacy. In reporting on Figure 8 one subject (Protocol J) supplies clubs and rolled-up newspapers for the mob. Not only is it "reasonable" to expect mob members to carry clubs but this invention was hastened through assimilation to the policeman's night stick, which is correctly reported in the story. If one weapon is present, why not others?

In the case of our own experiments we find relatively little of what is ordinarily called *elaboration*. The stories grow shorter and shorter, not longer and longer. Bartlett too finds this same constricting tendency in his individual memory experiments, but speculates that in serial reproduction one might expect expansion and elaboration.[2] We do not find such to be the case. Our serial reproductions demonstrate remarkable sharpening and leveling, more even than Bartlett found in his experiments on individuals. As we have already explained, some of this effect is traceable to the presence of an audience, and some of the experimental instructions (to be "as accurate as possible"). Yet, rumor collections from everyday life (see p. 83) also show that rumors become extremely brief, and even aphoristic as they circulate. The degree of abbreviation will, of course, depend to some extent on the nature of the rumor. A horror tale is unlikely to become sloganized, since an enumeration of gruesome details lends point to the story. On the other hand, a hostility rumor such as "The Jews are evading the draft' probably has been whittled down to a short catchy sentence, after starting in a circumstantial manner with the case of Sam X, or from some fallacious statistics.

Once in a while curious *reversals to truth* occur in the course of rumor transmission. On rare occasions we find that a cautious or skeptical person in a rumor chain may insert qualifications or interpretations that retard a rumor in its precipitous course of distortion. For example, the subject whose report appears as the fourth reproduction in Protocol J exerts a wholesome influence. What the fourth subject

[2] Bartlett (1932), p. 165.

says is actually a truer interpretation than that given in the previous reproduction. Referring to the ambiguous situation depicted in this slide the subject said, "It is not clear whether the police officer has arrested the Negro or is trying to protect him." In expressing his own bewilderment he accidentally reverts to the only interpretation which the picture itself justifies. Other subjects, too, occasionally are careful to point out that their information is unreliable. Qualifying phrases such as "I don't know . . . ," "My impression is . . . ," "I am told . . . ," are sometimes used. It is necessary to emphasize, however, that such qualifications are the exception rather than the rule, even under the caution-inspiring conditions of the experiment. They are even less frequent in real-life rumors.

EFFORT AFTER MEANING

In order to explain the course of inventions, we shall have to revert again to the concept of "effort after meaning." In ordinary rumor we find a marked tendency for the agent to attribute *causes* to events, *motives* to characters, a *raison d'être* to the episode in question. In our experiments the instructions emphatically discouraged such rationalized explanations. Accordingly we have many protocols that dwindle into sheer childlike enumeration of unconnected items. Enumeration is the path of caution. But even so, most of our reports retain a story quality. Plausible inferences are made by one rumor agent and, when passed on, are accepted uncritically by his listener. Though the meaning of the scene in Figure 8 is in reality ambiguous, subjects supply interpretations of various sorts: the Negro has been a victim of mob violence; he is being arrested; he is being protected by the white officer.

VERBAL MISUNDERSTANDINGS

A LESSER, but still important, source of invention and falsification comes about through verbal misunderstandings. When a person does not see the initial incident, and when he has no prior knowledge as to its nature, he becomes exclusively dependent upon his own auditory impressions for his understanding. The auditory apparatus is faulty in many people, but even those with normally acute hearing often mishear, or misinterpret, words for which they have no supporting mental context. Consider the following reproductions taken from a protocol based on Figure 7:

Fourth Reproduction: Picture is of a subway or streetcar. There is a Negro in it and a laborer with a razor. They are going along a street. There are signs outside: *vote for somebody and for some camp.* On the right side there is a woman asleep, a man with a beard, and a priest.

Fifth Reproduction: Picture is of a streetcar or subway. There is—somebody or other—a Negro and a laborer with a razor. On the right side of the car there is a lady asleep, a man with a beard, *campaign* signs to vote for somebody, a priest.

Sixth Reproduction: Scene is a streetcar or subway. There is a Negro man and a laborer with a razor in his hand. Sitting down are a lady sleeping, an old man with a beard, a priest. There are signs: a *camp sign* and a sign to vote for somebody.

In the fourth reproduction *signs, vote, camp* are separate concepts. In the fifth a condensation occurs to a single idea, represented by *campaign signs.* Verbal misunderstanding restores *camp* to a separate place in the story. This curious incident demonstrates the impossibility of reasoning from the final version of a rumor what the intermediate steps have

VERBAL MISUNDERSTANDINGS

been. A legend we hear may at one time have contained items not now present, and the version we hear now may, in fact, be more correct than some of the versions that intervened.

Occasionally, the damage is more serious, as in the following protocol, based on Figure 6. The subjects were students in the fifth grade. (The disconnected enumeration and absence of a story quality are typical of subjects of this age.) In the first reproduction, we read, "A *doctor* lives up in one of the windows." In the second reproduction, we find, "A duck in one of the windows." Subsequent reporters have, of course, no means of spotting the mistake, and the misunderstanding is retained until the end of the series. Similarly the "plant" mentioned in the fifth reproduction is transformed into a "plane" by the sixth reporter, probably as a result of verbal misunderstanding.

PROTOCOL N

(illustrating enumerative tendency in children's reports and verbal misunderstanding)

First Reproduction: There is a cart and a boy is trying to get something out of it. A sidewalk. A cat. Trash cans. A *doctor* lives up in one of the windows. There is a flowerpot falling out. Some other flowerpots. A clothesline. Two boys.

Second Reproduction: Cart. Two boys. One of the boys is trying to get something out of the cart. A house. A *duck* in one of the windows. Flowerpot falling out of one of the windows. Clothesline. Sidewalk. Some other flowerpots.

Third Reproduction: Car. Boy trying to get something out of the car. A *duck*. Some flowerpots on the sidewalk.

Fourth Reproduction: A *duck*. A car. A dog. A plant.

Fifth Reproduction: A *duck* and a car. A dog. A plant.

Sixth Reproduction: A *duck* and a car and a dog and a *plane*.

TIME AND PLACE ERRORS

MANY rumors describe events alleged to have taken place at a definite point in space and time, but our experiments show that descriptions of *specific* time and place as well as proper names are among the items most subject to distortion in a series of reports.

Errors are less serious in the descriptions of the general *geographical* setting of a scene. Identifications of the general setting of the incident ("a street scene," "a French battle scene," "a subway scene") are usually retained throughout the entire series of reproductions without serious distortion. Such statements provide the most basic spatial orientation for each successive listener. Without some such anchorage it would be especially difficult for the listener to structure the ambiguous situation with which he is dealing. To some extent such statements are successfully retained also because they are generally given at the beginning of a description. Learning experiments show that items at the beginning (and end) of a series are favored in retention. As a result of these factors—the subject's need to achieve orientation in an ambiguous situation and the effect of primacy—the general setting of the scene is seldom omitted or seriously distorted.

Specific details of locality, on the other hand, are usually short-lived and often suffer serious mutilations in the course of transmission. Take, for example, Figure 7. The names of the station and the destination of the express train, both clearly indicated by signs, never survive intact to the end of the series. Either they are omitted early in the series or become distorted beyond recognition. Similarly, the names of the streets depicted in Figure 6 are seldom reproduced correctly. If the names of these localities had been better known

TIME AND PLACE ERRORS

to the subjects, the loss would have been less serious. The names of the French cities in Figure 5—Paris and Cherbourg—were often remembered and were subject to no distortion. The names of these cities were familiar to most subjects, not only in terms of their past experience but also in terms of newspaper discussion then current. The two distances indicated on the signpost, however, are seldom reproduced faithfully. The two numbers—50 and 21½—are frequently reversed as between the cities, and the figures become falsified. There is also the tendency to round off numbers, 21½ becoming 20.

Names of persons, like names of places, are extremely unstable items, especially if they are unfamiliar to the subject. Most of these names drop out early in the series, but before being leveled out they usually have become hopelessly garbled.

An interesting example of the transformation of persons' names is seen in Protocol G, based on Figure 6. At first the name of the haberdashery is correctly given as Levy and Sons. In the course of the successive reports it becomes first changed to Debe, and then to "a name with two 'e's' in it." This distortion was undoubtedly facilitated by some kind of auditory misunderstanding. Proper names when casually heard lack the familiar anchorage of most common nouns, and are therefore especially susceptible to distortion.

Table 2 shows what happens to proper names in the course of word-of-mouth transmission. We note that even in the original descriptions 8 percent of the names are given incorrectly. This fact proves once again that even eyewitness perception is not always reliable. It is subject to the same type of distortions and assimilative changes as is memory; somewhat less so, to be sure, because of the constraining influence of the stimulus. When we come to the fifth reproduction, only 18 percent of the proper names are mentioned correctly, 5 percent are mentioned but are in error, and all the rest are leveled out.

TABLE 2

PERCENTAGE OF PROPER NAMES MENTIONED IN SUCCESSIVE DESCRIPTIONS

(The total number of proper names contained in the original descriptions constitutes the 100-percent level. The entries in the table are percentages computed to that base.)

Reproduction number	Percent correctly given	Percent incorrectly given	Percent leveled out
Original description	92	8	0
1	51	18	31
2	43	16	41
3	30	17	53
4	23	13	64
5	18	5	77

Like the names of places and people, specific details of *time* are usually leveled out or distorted. Except by a military group (see p. 84) the time indicated on the church tower in Figure 5 is never correctly reported for more than one or two reproductions. Similarly, the time indicated on the station clock in Figure 7 fares little better. The exact hour at which the incident occurs is not essential to the story and is therefore easily omitted or falsified without seriously affecting the coherence of the story. Temporal distortion is enhanced by the tendency of the reports to be almost without exception in the present tense. A picture which has caught a fleeting historical incident is considered by the observer timeless. In talking about the picture, the subject contemporizes it. The story is told as if happening *now*.

CHILDREN'S REPORTS

In several respects the reports of children differ markedly from those of adults.

Leveling Is More Striking. Younger children retain fewer items in their successive reports than do older children, and far fewer than adults. Although our number of cases is small in each grade of school, a count of the items mentioned in the terminal reports reveals the following averages:

Grade	Items
4th	3.0
5th	3.5
6th	6.0
7th	5.5
Junior high school	8.5
Adults	9.0

The increase in ability to retain items with age is, of course, a well-known phenomenon. Standard intelligence tests, for example, expect a child of three to repeat three digits correctly after one hearing, a child of ten, six digits. McGeoch (1928) studying the ability of children to *compose* a narrative based on an event which they have witnessed, finds that the richness of the report increases steadily with age. Under the conditions of his experiment, the average fourteen-year-old reproduced 28.5 items correctly in his report compared with 18.2 items for nine-year-olds. Leveling, therefore, is clearly, in part, a result of incomplete maturation of memory capacity.

The Report Is Enumerative. The following record taken for Figure 5 from fifth-grade children shows the disjointed nature of reporting at this level.

PROTOCOL O

(illustrating the enumerative tendency and rapid leveling in children's reporting)

Description from the Screen: There is a man, a Red Cross truck, a gun, three signs, a church. There are some planes, some antiaircraft, some bombs, and a lot of wrecked stone wall. There are mountains in the distance. A man is lying down. There is a man standing up looking through binoculars. There is an old broken fence post and one pretty shabby tree and a few bushes. There is a colored man. A battle is going on. There are enemy planes which are dropping bombs trying to wound the people in the town. The Red Cross truck is trying to take care of the wounded.

First Reproduction: A Red Cross truck. A shaggy tree. A colored man. A man lying down. A man looking through binoculars. Old broken-down stone wall. Planes overhead. Bombs. A gun.

Second Reproduction: Red Cross truck. Bombs. A plane. Stone wall.

Third Reproduction: Red Cross truck. Bombs. A plane and a stone wall.

Fourth Reproduction: Red Cross. Some bombs. A plane.

Fifth Reproduction: Bombs and a plane and the Red Cross.

Sixth Reproduction: Bombs. A plane and a red cross.

The account is helter-skelter, with no indication of an attempt to tell a coherent story. In the junior high school years the situation is slightly better, as Protocol P shows.

CHILDREN'S REPORTS 129

PROTOCOL P

(illustrating reports at 13-14 years of age)

Description from the Screen: Scene of battle. Ten minutes of two by clock in church steeple. There's a statue of a Negro slave. One man wounded. One lying beside him with binoculars. One shooting over a wall. Sign, "Paris $21\frac{1}{2}$ kilometers"; and "Cherbourg 50 kilometers." In background an ambulance with two hospital men. Church has hole in ceiling. Planks standing against ruins of a building. Statue, or not—not sure. Stone wall near by. Two planes in the distance above church—a small and a large one. Explosions in back of church.

First Reproduction: Takes place on battlefield. Statue of Negro slave near. Church near. Two airplanes above—a small and a large one. Shots near by. About ten by clock in the steeple. Wall near church. One man wounded with man lying beside him using his binoculars.

Second Reproduction: Battlefield. Statue of Negro slave. One wounded soldier with man beside, using his binoculars. Wall near church. Two planes—a little and a big. Shots going off. It's ten o'clock.

Third Reproduction: Battlefield. Statue of Negro slave. Two men lying on battlefield wounded. One using the other's binoculars. It's ten o'clock. Planes going over. A wall and a church on the other side.

Fourth Reproduction: Battlefield and statue of Negro. Two men lying on field wounded, using each other's binoculars. Ten o'clock. Planes going over. There's a church.

Fifth Reproduction: Battlefield. Statue of a Negro. Two men wounded, lying, using each other's binoculars. It's ten o'clock. There are planes and a churchyard.

Sixth Reproduction: There's a battle in a churchyard. Statue of a Negro. Planes overhead. Two men wounded.

It may well be that the instructions given to the children to report "as accurately as possible" facilitated an enumerative attitude toward the task. It is well known, however, that in describing pictures young children will simply enumerate objects. Only at the age of twelve do they normally tend to weave them into an interpretative story. Under the conditions of our experiment, where stress is laid on accuracy of report, enumeration persists even at higher age levels (thirteen and fourteen). This enumerative bent seems to show that children do not feel compelled to understand, to rationalize, to interpret and unify an experience as much as an adult does.

Since children take many episodes in life as frankly beyond them, they do not feel the need to fit all that they encounter into adequate categories of meaning. For this reason, we find few assimilative changes in their reports. Leveling occurs, bringing the report in line with the juvenile memory span at various ages, and a reciprocal sharpening of retained items takes place. But neither the associative nor the emotional type of assimilation plays any large part in the process of distortion.

Racial Factor Is De-emphasized. With the stimulus material used in these experiments we had a good opportunity to learn how children respond to the racial aspect of the scenes. Without qualification we report that children tend to *de-emphasize* the racial angle. In several protocols the racial characteristics of people were omitted altogether—in this respect these protocols were similar to those of Negro respondents (see p. 113). Combing all protocols of children and of adults, we find that 83 percent of adults' reproductions mentioned the racial identity of the people depicted in the scenes, as against only 43 percent of the children's.

If racial items were retained at all by children, they were

CHILDREN'S REPORTS 131

mentioned as one of several enumerated characteristics. *In no case do we find any assimilation to a disparaging attitude.* For instance, in none of the protocols for Figure 7 was the razor transferred from the white worker to the Negro, though it did so in more than fifty percent of the reproductions by adult subjects.

The following protocol, typical of the children's reports on this figure, shows the unemotional quality of the youngsters' handling of the racial theme, and its quick disappearance.

PROTOCOL Q
(illustrating children's handling of racial theme)

Description from the Screen: There's a trolley car with a lot of people sitting down. A little boy with cap on back of his head is talking to a Negro man. There's a woman sitting down. Out of window there is a picket fence. A little old lady's sitting down. The black man's telling something interesting to the boy. A lady with glasses and a cuckoo hat is behind them. Signs up on wall. Sign saying where trolley is going. Mountains outside. Man asleep on the seat. There are five people sitting down, two standing up. The little boy looks as though he is tough.

First Reproduction: It's a side view of a trolley car. There's a tough boy with a cap on back of his head talking to Negro man. There's a lady with a cuckoo hat. There are signs up. Also signs saying where it is going. There are mountains outside. Five people standing up.

Second Reproduction: View of inside of trolley car. Tough little boy with cap on head sitting talking to Negro man. There are five people standing up. There's a lady with a cuckoo hat. Signs where trolley car is going. There are mountains through window.

Third Reproduction: Inside of trolley car. Tough boy with cap on head; man sitting beside him. Lady with cute hat and man behind her. Mountains outside. Sign where trolley car is going.

Fourth Reproduction: Inside of trolley car. Tough boy sitting in seat. Beside him is a woman with a cute hat on. Out of window, mountains. Signs where trolley is going.

Fifth Reproduction: Inside of trolley car. Tough boy. Beside him is a man. Beside is a woman with a crew hat on. Outside are mountains. Signs where trolley car is going.

Sixth Reproduction: Trolley car. Tough boy in it. Man in front of him. There's a lady. Plate on it saying where it is going. Mountains outside of window.

Note the absence of stereotyped phrases in the description of the Negro. He is simply described as a "black man." There is no mention of a "zoot suit," or "sharp clothes," so frequently found in the protocols of adult subjects. The Negro is "telling something interesting" to the white "boy," whereas adults always describe the two as quarreling. This absence of emotion is characteristic of all the children's reports.

The lack of racial emphasis may be explained partly by the fact that the children who served as subjects in this experiment were students at a school whose deliberate policy it is to promote friendliness between racial and religious groups. The school has colored students and likewise some colored teachers who instruct both white and Negro children. Hence the children's relative lack of response to the racial element may also reflect their equalitarian school background. But apart from liberal policies of this particular school, it is a well-known fact that children are *not* sensitive to racial differences until they are forced upon them by incidents or by parental and cultural snobbery. There is, for example, the case of seven-year-old Johnny, who asked his mother if he might bring Tommy home to lunch some day.

The mother, knowing that many Negroes attended her son's school, asked, "Is Tommy white or colored?" The boy replied, "I don't know. I forgot to look, but I'll look next time I see him." Such innocence of race consciousness does not last for long in our society.

8 THE BASIC PATTERN OF DISTORTION

IN presenting in such detail the results of laboratory rumor spreading, have we wandered away from the garden variety of everyday rumor that is our main concern? To show that such is not the case let us take a run-of-the-mill rumor and see how many of our principal concepts of analysis can be applied to it.

We choose a trifling rumor incident and select it almost at random from the wartime crop of stories current in a rural Maine community in the summer of 1945, shortly before Japan's surrender.

A Chinese teacher on a solitary vacation drove his car into the community and asked his way to a hilltop from which he could obtain the pleasant view pictured in a tourist guide issued by the Chamber of Commerce in a neighboring town. Someone showed him the way, but within an hour the community was buzzing with the story that *a Japanese spy had ascended the hill to take pictures of the region.*

The simple, unadorned facts that constitute the "kernel of truth" in this rumor were never reported but were from the outset distorted in the three directions now familiar to us. They were *leveled, sharpened,* and *assimilated.* Let us consider each type of change in order.

(1) *Leveling.* Omitted from the rumor are many details which are essential for a true understanding of the incident: the courteous and timid, but withal honest, approach of the

THE BASIC PATTERN OF DISTORTION

visitor to the native of whom he inquired his way; the fact that the visitor's precise nationality was unknown although he was certainly Oriental. Likewise not mentioned was the fact that the visitor had allowed himself to be readily identified by people along the way; and the truth that no one had seen a camera in his possession.

These omissions are scarcely attributable to the unreliability of people's memory. Rather they are systematic omissions. They dropped out because if told, they would tend to negate the preferred interpretation: "a Japanese spy is among us." We do not know to what extent the omissions are due to a misperception of the situation by the native who first talked with the stranger, and to what extent the details kept dropping out as the story spread from person to person. It is probable that the eyewitness himself did not perceive all the relevant evidence because the sight of an Oriental had immediately activated his long-standing biases and preconceptions. Perceiving and remembering are parts of a single process. As Bartlett puts the matter: "Inextricably mingled with perceiving are imagining, valuing, and the beginning of judgment."[1]

(2) *Sharpening*. When some details are dropped, those that are preserved necessarily gain in emphasis and importance. Sharpening, as we have seen, is the reciprocal of leveling. Having accepted their special interpretation of the Chinese scholar's visit, the rumor agents accentuated certain features while minimizing others. The sharpening of

---

[1] Bartlett (1932), p. 31.

Bysow (1928) has characterized the start of a rumor by distinguishing three stages: (1) The event is perceived with interest by one or several persons. Their interest originates in the social importance of the event. (2) The event is edited and evaluated by the perceiver. (3) Having been edited, the rumor is started. Bysow's analysis is acceptable provided we do not assume any time lapse between stages (1) and (2).

selected details accounts for the overdrawn dramatic quality of the final story. What in the original situation was Oriental became specified as Japanese; what was merely a "man" became a special kind of man, a "spy." The harmless holiday pursuit of viewing the scenery became the much sharper, sinister purpose of espionage. The truth that the visitor *had* a picture in his hand became sharpened into the act of "taking pictures." The objective fact that no pictures of any possible value to the enemy could be taken from that particular rural location was overlooked. There were no industrial or military installations visible from that hill. Furthermore, the war was known to be in its last stages and spy activity, especially in remote regions, was, objectively considered, most improbable. Yet, such were the wartime emotions and suspicions that the sharpening occurred, putting point on the incident, making it crisp, understandable, and portentous. Here was something worth telling, worthy of rumination and respect.

(3) *Assimilation.* Leveling and sharpening, of course, do not occur haphazardly but take place in essential conformity with the past experience and present attitudes of the rumor spreaders. In the Maine countryside resident natives have had little contact with Orientals. Like most Occidentals they are unable to distinguish a Chinese person from a Japanese. They had only one available rubric for Orientals, firmly implanted in their minds by wartime news and stories: the "Japanese spy." No other category was available for the classification of this unusual visitation. A Chinese-teacher-on-a-holiday was a concept that could not arise in the minds of most farmers, for they did not know that some American universities employ Chinese scholars on their staffs and that these scholars, like other teachers, are entitled to summer

THE BASIC PATTERN OF DISTORTION 137

holidays. The novel situation was perforce *assimilated* in terms of the most available frames of reference.

"To take pictures of the region" is another clear instance of assimilation. The visitor carried no camera, yet as a result of the government's campaign for "security of information," as a result of prohibitions against cameras in strategic war areas and lurid movies dealing with espionage, the rumor agents were provided with a plausible motive for the strange visitor. The association of ideas is crude: a yellow man—a Jap—a spy—photographic espionage. One idea led to the other with almost mechanical inevitability until the final conclusion emerged.

Such mechanical association of ideas accounts, in part, for the story that spread, but an unmistakable dynamic factor was also present. In this remote Maine community the war was profoundly felt. Nearly every house had its son in the service. Hatred for the Japanese was intense, desire to defend America deep, and suspicion of foreigners a long-standing cultural characteristic of the region. To these inveterate attitudes the perception of the event was assimilated, and from these attitudes came the impetus to concoct the rumor. Wartime created the conditions that brought these dynamic factors into play. The event had potential *importance* to the people. It also had considerable *ambiguity*, for they lacked correct information regarding the visitor's nationality and purpose.

The three-pronged process of leveling, sharpening, and assimilation reflects the rumor agents' "effort after meaning." The facts of the situation, but dimly understood, did not provide the meaning that the strange visitation required. Hence a single directive idea took hold—the *spy motif*—and in accordance with it, discordant details were leveled out, incidents sharpened to fit the chosen theme, and the episode as a whole assimilated to the pre-existing structure of feeling and thought characteristic of the members of the group among whom the rumor spread.

UNIVERSALITY OF THE THREE-PART PATTERN OF DISTORTION

SOME years ago Wulf (1922) undertook a study of the changes which an individual's memory undergoes in time. The stimulus materials used by Wulf consisted of simple asymmetrical figures, a sample of which is given in Figure 10.

These designs were presented one at a time to the subjects in the experiment. Approximately thirty seconds later the subjects were required to reproduce the figure as accurately as they could. A day later the subjects were required to repeat the reproduction, again after one week, and finally after an interval of two weeks to two months. Thus he accumulated a large amount of material to study the fate of "memory traces," the changes they undergo in time.

If the old mechanical theory of memory (an impression on wax) were correct, Wulf maintained, the reproductions should become merely blurred as time went on. Instead, he discovered that the drawings showed a tendency to take on "better," "simpler," more "meaningful" form. Such changes go in the same direction regardless of the length of interval between stimulation and recall. Writing in German, Wulf expressed this tendency as one in which the retained trace tended to achieve *Prägnanz* (a more perfect and essential form). He believed there are three factors leading to progressive pregnance of the figures: (1) *normalizing*, a process essentially equivalent to our concept of "leveling," (2) *emphasizing or pointing*, which corresponds to our "sharpening," (3) *autonomous changes* which are inherent in the

THREE-PART PATTERN OF DISTORTION

trace pattern itself. This third category includes certain of the changes which we have described as "assimilation."

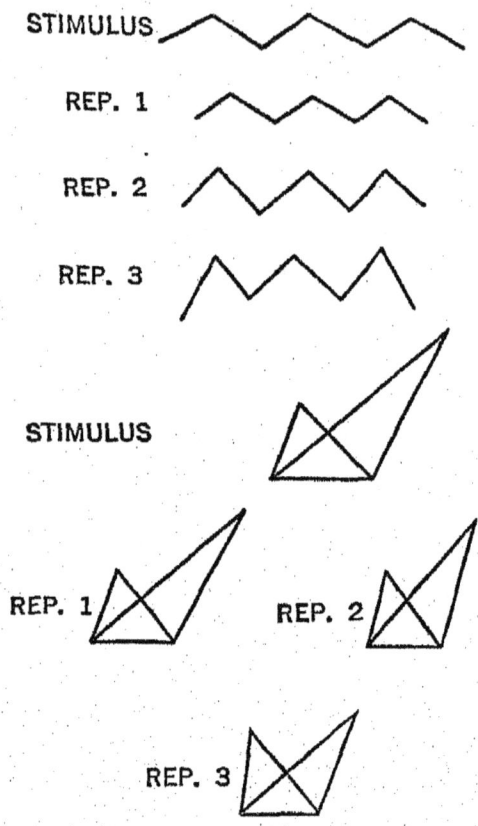

Fig. 10. Stimulus figures and successive reproductions—after Wulf. The upper portion illustrates "emphasizing" or "pointing" (sharpening); the lower portion illustrates "normalizing" (leveling). Both types of change show the tendency of memory traces to achieve *Prägnanz* (better configuration).

Wulf's line of interpretation follows Gestalt psychology, tending to regard the mind as a self-active agent which, when left to itself, produces more quintessential and sharper patterns. Bartlett sums up the tendency by saying that the

140   THE BASIC PATTERN OF DISTORTION

memory of an item is usually more coherent and more consequential than its original form.[2]

Later Gibson (1929) repeated the essential features of Wulf's experiments and in the main confirmed his results. Gibson's figures were even less familiar than Wulf's.

He presented his stimuli on a "memory drum" so that each figure appeared to the observer for 1½ seconds and was then followed by the next. The series of stimuli was pre-

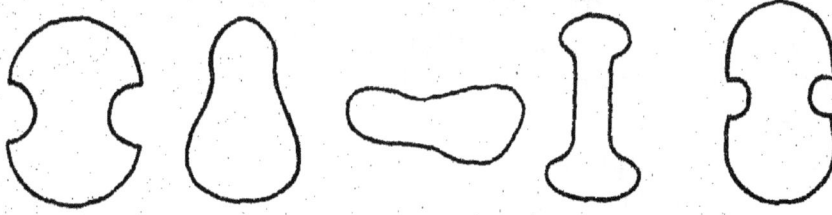

"STIMULUS"   "TORSO"   "FOOTPRINT" "DUMBBELL" "VIOLIN"

Fig. 11. Stimulus figure and sample reproductions by various subjects—after Gibson.

sented several times, and at the end of each series the subject was required to draw as many figures as he remembered in any order he wished. Although the original figures were unnamed, the subject was asked to tell what the object was that he had drawn. By forcing the subject in this manner to call on his linguistic habits it was found that the shape of the reproduction was strikingly altered to conform to the label. One subject drew a "torso," one a "footprint," and a third a "dumbbell." No doubt this object assimilation was started even during the initial act of perception, although the subject did not audibly name the object until he had drawn it. Successive reproductions five weeks and a year later showed how important an anchorage effect the verbal label exerts upon the form of the retention and the report.

[2] Bartlett (1932), p. 127.

THREE-PART PATTERN OF DISTORTION 141

In his interpretation of the results Gibson emphasized more than did Wulf the crucial part played by associational assimilation. Not only do figures tend to take on symmetry and good continuation, as Wulf said, but even more strikingly do they tend to resemble familiar objects and to be influenced by the process of naming.

In an analogous experiment Allport (1930) used as subjects 350 children of school age. To them he presented two designs which were more closed and more geometrical in appearance than those of Wulf and Gibson. After looking at the stimuli for ten seconds the children were required to draw these designs immediately from memory. Without warning, the experimenter returned in two weeks and again in four months and requested the children to draw again what they had seen on the card. The designs were those employed in the Stanford-Binet scale for measuring intelligence.

In the typical series of reproductions presented in Figure 12 we note how, with the passage of time, the impression tends toward simplicity and symmetry. Unequal proportions of the sides in the truncated pyramid is one detail that early becomes leveled out. The center stalk in the Greek key seems in Reproduction 2 to be fighting a losing battle for retention. It disappears completely in Reproduction 3, while the key itself becomes inverted. The final form is relatively hard, compact, a mere skeleton of its former self. It is leveled and sharpened; it is also assimilated to whatever tendencies exist in the mind to prefer symmetry, balance, pregnant form.[3]

[3] Whether these tendencies are due to primordial brain mechanisms, or to associational trends based on previous experience or on certain predispositions arising, for example, from the bilateral symmetry of the body, are questions that need not be debated here. For a fuller discussion of the problem, see Allport (1930).

142 THE BASIC PATTERN OF DISTORTION

Next we cite an experiment that demonstrates the striking effects of assimilation to language habits. Carmichael, Hogan, and Walter (1932) presented a series of drawings showing twelve simple geometrical forms to their subjects.

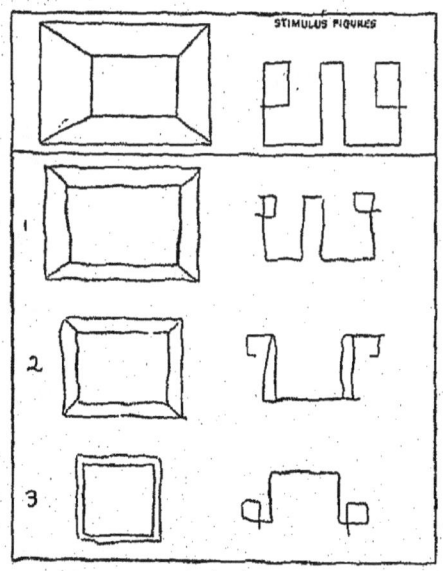

Fig. 12. Stimulus figure and successive reproductions—after Allport. The three successive drawings were obtained from the same child: Number 1 immediately after presentation of the stimulus; Number 2 after two weeks; Number 3 after four months.

Each of these drawings was so constructed that it resembled at least two actual objects. For different groups of subjects different names accompanied the presentation of the stimulus figures. The subjects were then asked to draw as many of the figures as accurately as they could from memory. The reproductions obtained from the subjects showed that the figures they remembered conformed to the names which had been attached to them. Figure 13, showing one of the stimulus figures, associated words, and typical

THREE-PART PATTERN OF DISTORTION

reproductions, illustrates this influence of verbal labels on memory for visual forms. Here we find a neat demonstration of the fact that we perceive and remember not what comes to us through our sense organs alone but likewise what our linguistic and cultural habits and past experiences predispose us to perceive and remember.

STIMULUS　　　　EYEGLASSES　　　　DUMBBELL

Fig. 13. Stimulus figure and reproductions by two subjects—after Carmichael, Hogan, and Walter. For one subject the stimulus was accompanied by the verbal label "eyeglasses," for the other, "dumbbell."

Now let us refer back to Bartlett's experiments described in Chapter 3. Summarizing his results respecting the changes that occur in successive reproductions of stories by the same individual, Bartlett reports three main lines of distortion. The reader will recognize them as another independent confirmation of the existence of leveling, assimilation, and sharpening:[4]

(1) "The story is considerably shortened, mainly by omissions." [Leveling]
(2) "The phraseology becomes more modern." [A special case of assimilation]
(3) "The story has become more coherent and consequential than in its original form." [Sharpening]

In his studies of multi-individual (serial) reproduction, Bartlett reports the same three processes, though he does

[4] These quotations are taken from F. C. Bartlett's *Remembering*, by permission of the Cambridge University Press, publishers.

not employ our terminology. "It appears," he writes, "that under conditions of the experiment the following are the main types of transformation likely to occur: [5]

> (1) "There will be more general simplification, due to the omission of material that appears irrelevant, to the construction gradually of a more coherent whole, and to the changing of the familiar into some more familiar counterpart." [Leveling and assimilation]
>
> (2) "There will be persistent rationalization, both of a whole story and its details, until a form is reached which can be readily dealt with by all the subjects belonging to the special social group concerned. This may result in considerable elaboration." [Assimilation and sharpening]
>
> (3) "There will be a tendency for certain incidents to become dominant so that all others are grouped around them." [Sharpening]

These varied experiments have been cited to prove that investigators, though using various kinds of stimulus material and different procedures, have repeatedly discovered the same fundamental three-pronged process underlying the course of individual and social memory change.

The dominant prong in the process seems to be assimilation, for in all these experiments it is evident that past experience, linguistic habit, cultural forms of thought, and personal motives and attitudes set the stage for the pattern of distortion that occurs and determine just what shall be leveled out and what sharpened.

Now let us look still further afield at certain findings in the study of personality based upon the use of so-called

[5] Bartlett (1932), p. 138.

THREE-PART PATTERN OF DISTORTION 145

projective techniques. In these studies the individual is confronted with an unstructured, ambiguous stimulus. Through the type of meaning that he gives to the stimulus material, he reveals, often in spite of himself, the pattern of his own mental structure. Thus, in the Rorschach test, he is shown a series of ink blots and asked, "What might this be?" In reporting, for example, that it "looks like a threatening lion" the subject is obviously disregarding (leveling out) many amorphous features. He is engendering a sharper meaning than exists in the ink blot itself. He is assimilating the blot to his own interests, experiences, and perhaps to his fears. In the ambiguous blot he sees what his mental predispositions make him *expect* to see. Because the perception becomes embedded in his personal life, his report often tells more about himself than about the stimulus. The entire usefulness of the projective technique depends on the disposition of the individual to *assimilate* his perception to the pre-existing structure of his mental life and to report the *fused* result.

Projective techniques can be used with a variety of stimulus materials—so long as they allow the subject to impart his own meaning and interpretation to them. By one method, the subject is asked to listen to a faint recorded sound of a human voice. Actually the sound consists only of scarcely audible vowel sequences. Asked what words he hears, the subject may report, "It sounds like 'be careful, be careful, be careful'." Or perhaps, "You must do it, Why don't you do it? Go to work." He interprets what he hears according to his own interests and personal conflicts.

Still another type of projective method is the Thematic Apperception Test. The subject is given a picture to view which contains at least one person of like sex (and preferably similar age) to the subject. In interpreting the picture (telling a story based on it) he frequently gives a straight autobiographical report, without realizing the fact. He does so because he identifies himself with the like-sexed character and then tells his own worries and hopes only slightly disguised to fit the picture.

This discussion of projective methods for studying personality suggests that rumor itself could be an excellent personality test. What does a person do with the story he hears? So long as it has some ambiguity (is not constrained by rigid and readily available evidence), and so long as it has some potential importance in his life, he reacts to it much as does the subject in the projective test situation. From the pigments of his own mental life he selects the colors with which he adorns the tale. And little does he know that he may be telling far more about his own nature than about the incident he is pretending to report.

CREATIVE EMBEDDING

The resemblance between rumor and memory for designs, or memory as tested in the retelling of stories or in projective performances, is now clear. But the generalization with which we are dealing extends still further.

All mental life is a process of subjectifying the world that lies outside. To be sure, in order to survive we adapt ourselves more or less suitably to the geographical and physical environment; but chiefly we live according to our own theories and evaluations of the surrounding world. What we perceive we invariably embed in our own personalities, and we then explain it to ourselves and to others in accordance with our pre-existing intellectual and emotional nature.

Consider the case of the artist—for the artist is expressly allowed to do what we all do unwittingly. He turns his attention to a specific situation—an aspect of nature, perhaps, or a human foible. What he perceives he deliberately subjectifies and weights with inner interpretation. Finally he projects it outwardly in painting or literature. Artists are expected to *level* our irrelevancies, to *sharpen* the features they wish to accent, and in so doing to *assimilate* the whole to their own standards of judgment, which, needless to say, are partly determined by cultural standards, and partly by their own natures.

Whether we possess talent or not, we are all, psychologically speaking, artists. The world we perceive and the world we express are invariably affected by what we are.

Viewed from this standpoint rumor is a homely work of art. It represents the embedding of a percept into the mental context and into the mental mechanisms that comprise our own nature. What is seen or heard *must* be simplified in accordance with the economizing process of memory; it *must* be imbued with meaning because of our intellectual drive to seek meaning and avoid mental confusion; the meaning acquired will of necessity conform to the interpretations of nature and of human behavior which we are accustomed to make. The process of embedding the rumor that we hear into our own lives cannot but affect the character of the rumor that we tell.

IS A RUMOR NEVER TRUE?

WE are now in a position to consider a question that is frequently asked, "Is a rumor invariably false?" Can we never, under any circumstances, believe a rumor?

148 THE BASIC PATTERN OF DISTORTION

There is obviously a semantic issue in this question. If rumor is defined as anything we hear at second hand, then it is entirely possible that some of the reports that come to us may be accurate enough to be credible. But when such a report does turn out to be trustworthy we usually find that secure standards of evidence have been available to persons in the "rumor" chain. They are speaking of events that they know at first hand or have had opportunities and a disposition to verify along the way. Shall we call such a tested report rumor?

In the preface we proposed as the most serviceable definition that rumor be considered a proposition for belief of topical reference, without secure standards of evidence being present. Such a definition has the advantage of helping to distinguish rumor sharply from news. If this definition is accepted, we may say: So great are the distortions that come from the embedding process (that is, from leveling, sharpening, and assimilation to personal sentiments) that it is never under any circumstances safe to accept rumor as a valid guide for belief or conduct.

Our experiments have shown how undependable are even the second- and third-hand reproductions obtained under relatively auspicious laboratory conditions. Everyday rumors probably suffer even more drastic deterioration.

But may it not be that every rumor, however defined, has its kernel of truth, and for this reason should not be totally repudiated? The truth about the kernel is simply this: nearly every rumor starts with a percept of some sort; assuming that the percept conforms to outer reality, then there is certainly a core of dependability in the eyewitness report. Further, as we have seen, the principal theme of a rumor is the factor most resistant to change, and we can, therefore, generally believe that the story we hear has *something* to do

EXAGGERATION 149

with the incident that it purports to treat. Yet the kernel of objective information becomes so embedded in the rumor agents' subjective mental life that the product cannot safely serve as a practical guide to action. The Japanese spy rumor recorded at the beginning of the chapter was wholly untrustworthy for practical purposes. It had so misshaped the kernel of truth that the latter was no longer recognizable.

There are, of course, borderline cases where we may not be able to say whether a given tidbit should or should not be called a rumor. A standard of evidence is hard to define, particularly if it rests on some trustworthy core of subjective knowledge. A group of atomic scientists discussing some atomic fact are not, according to our definition, spreading a rumor, for they all possess in their own minds closely knit standards by which to test the credibility of what they hear. And yet, reports made under even such favored conditions may not be entirely free from the embedding process. Usually, however, scientists are on their guard, for they know, better than most people, that when once a fact slips into the matrix of their hopes, desires, and preconceptions it becomes untrustworthy.

EXAGGERATION

EVERYONE knows that rumors exaggerate. Our analysis takes care of this notorious tendency with the aid of the concept of sharpening. The essence of a story, or what some listener takes to be its essence, is brought out through accentuation. The point of any rumor is to convey a unified impression of something deemed important. How better to convey this impression than through the rhetorical device of hyperbole? If a man is attacked by a vicious person, why not say that he is attacked by a maniac? Or, if the ele-

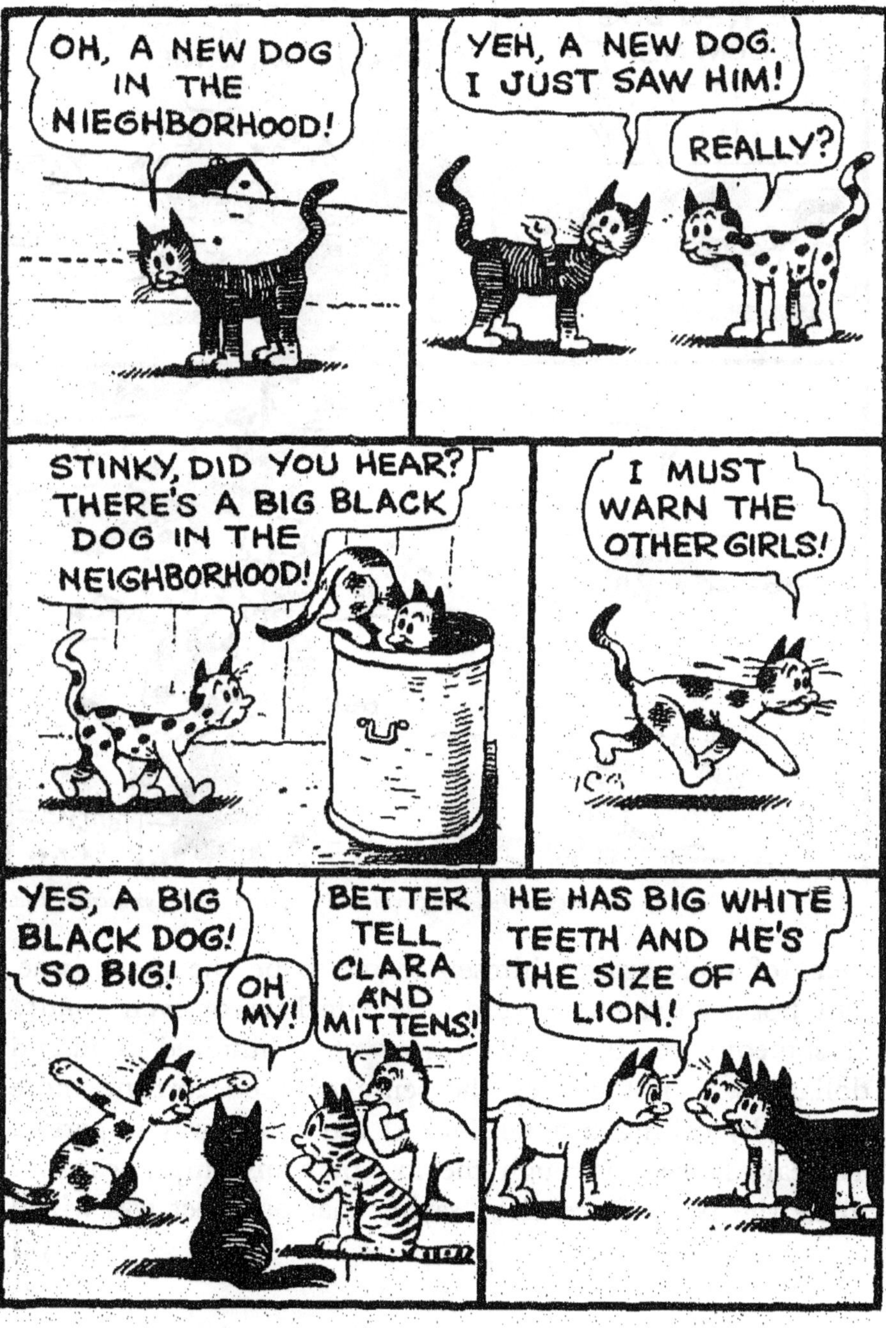

By BUD FISHER
Like Exaggeration

Reprinted by permission of the Bell Syndicate, Inc.

ment of odds against himself seems to be the main issue, why not say that there were *three* attackers, or even a *mob*? If someone receives a fat legacy of a hundred thousand dollars, why not convey the sense of good fortune more clearly by calling it a million? If our safety was imperiled at Pearl Harbor through the loss of many ships, why not make the point forceful by saying that our fleet was wiped out entirely? The emotional significance of the statement—that is, its essential purpose—is the same whether the numbers be accurate or exaggerated. But the expressive value of a statement is greater if it is transposed from a moderate register to high C.

A common form of exaggeration is magnification of numbers. In our experiments we found how the prominence of the Negro in Figure 5 was occasionally conveyed by such statements as "four Negroes," or the seven people in the subway scene (Figure 7) become the usual subway *crowd*. Seldom indeed does the numerical count of any item in a rumor dwindle in the telling. If plural items are regarded as worthy of retention at all, they are regarded as worthy of multiplication.

Exaggeration takes other forms as well. The motives implied in a story are generally highlighted to a point where the leading character is a creature of passion. The innocent Chinese sightseer became a sinister spy. The new neighbor whose child cries inopportunely is a veritable brute; the soldiers from a nearby Army camp, probably no better and no worse than most men, are said to be bent on rape and plunder.

Whatever is essential to the story tends to become sharpened. But, oddly enough, there are also occasionally incidental exaggerations that grow to the point where they take over the center of the stage, even to the extent of leveling out the original theme entirely. In one experiment, based on Figure 2, it was reported that an onlooker was "slightly stooped." This report impressed successive narrators and was stressed in the telling, with the result that the final version lost track entirely of the accident, and told a story only of a man who was stooping over and holding another man on his back! In this way original themes may become entirely altered by the casual exaggeration of originally subsidiary items.

ELABORATION

IT is often assumed that rumors become embroidered in the telling, or that they become enlarged like a rolling snowball. This is a misconception. Though we certainly find many insertions of reasons and circumstantial detail, they seem to occur only in the interest of sharpening. Elaboration which serves neither the purpose of coherency nor emphasis on the main point of the story seldom occurs—never in our experimental situations.

Bartlett, too, fails to find irrelevant elaboration in his studies of memory reproductions, written and drawn. He wonders, however, whether in word-of-mouth transmissions there may not be more tendency to add a fanciful superstructure.[6] Perhaps he has in mind the undoubted fact that a good raconteur adds digressions to maintain suspense and imports auxiliary witticisms in order to pad out his story. But this padding is seldom found in the over-all course of rumor. Even if one verbal artist inflates its content, the normal trend is ever downward. In the main, rumors shrink, becoming brief, crisp, often aphoristic (see p. 83). The elaboration that takes place, paradoxical though it is, is really in the interest of simplicity, dealing as it does with accentuation of the main theme. Figure 3, taken from Bartlett's work, shows elaboration of a sort in the changing of the circles, but the reporter in his reproduction was merely *pointing up* the essential simplicity of his own conception.

There is perhaps one condition under which true elabora-

[6] Bartlett (1932), p. 165.

tion occurs, though no special study has yet been made of the possibility. We sometimes note that after an event of very great emotional strain, say a serious accident or a family crisis, there is set up a strong perseverative tendency. People deeply involved in the incident mull it over, talk about it endlessly, explore in fantasy all possible consequences. To each newcomer they add more details, relevant and not so relevant. They tell what they thought, retrace all their steps, and elaborate upon underlying conditions, producing more and more rationalizations along the way. Strong emotional perseveration may, therefore, be the ground for true elaboration in persons immediately involved in a calamity. But it is still true that *subsequent* tellers will tend to sharpen and level the rumor in such a way that its course becomes one of condensation rather than elaboration.

In this connection special study should be made of the development of legends. A saga is by no means short. Long northern winter nights discouraged brevity, and put a premium on verbal padding. The phenomenon here is probably a special one: a central character or group of characters becomes a focal point for the confluence of many related rumors. The legend becomes part of an ethos. It serves as more than a single "proposition for belief of topical reference," and so transcends the category of simple rumor. Yet even in folklore we know that there is a tendency for separate fragments to follow rumor's aphoristic course. George Washington and the cherry tree is a brief enough tale; so too Newton and the apple. Though there may be special reasons for elaboration of legends, the tendency toward pithiness is by no means absent.

It is probable that cultural differences exist in the tendency to abbreviate or to elaborate a tale. Bartlett mentions the fact that Hindu subjects in his experiments were disposed to amplify and embroider a tale more than his Anglo-Saxon subjects. It is likewise said that Chinese rumors grow in their dimensions as well as in sharpness. Hence the crispness that we have observed both in our experiments and in our collections of rumor may, to a degree, be the product of the Americans' love of terseness.

CONDENSATION

Our memories are too unstable to retain each particular event inviolate in identity, filed away, as it were, for future reference. The "storehouse" theory of memory has long since been discarded.

What usually happens is that an event once experienced becomes blended with previous similar events, so that they form a generalized memory. Everyone has had the shock of discovering that he has confused two different people in memory, or that a single recollection of childhood turns out to be a fusion of entirely distinct episodes. Dreams are most notorious for their condensation: many bits of experience unrelated in reality become subtly blended into a fantastic tale whose originality consists chiefly of a rampage of associations oddly reassembled.

In his experiments Bartlett discovered that no single subject failed to confuse and to blend what were originally entirely separate stimuli.[7] In our own experiments multiple stimuli were not employed, but we have noted the fusions of varied experiences that occur in the process of assimilation (see p. 103).

The moral for everyday rumor is that the story we hear may in reality be a blend of several similar episodes. In particular *stereotypes* may be viewed as a species of con-

[7] Bartlett (1932), p. 103.

densation. Diverse experiences with members of a racial, religious, or other social group may become blended into an uncomplimentary generalization that is indiscriminately applied to all members of the group in question. A rumor starting "There was a Jew . . ." almost defines the theme that will follow. A pre-existing stereotype is aroused, which in turn represents nothing more than a condensation of ideas implanted by many previous uncomplimentary rumors and legends.

A special form of condensation is seen in the peculiar attractive power that certain types of characters have for certain types of stories. If a bawdy tale wants telling, it may attach itself to the bosomy Mae West. Mr. Anthony, Cal Coolidge, Baron Munchausen, Till Eulenspiegel, and many other characters past and present have served as lightning rods for current shafts of wit. The explanation is that a story assimilated to a well-known character gains in definiteness and added meaning. The storyteller will adopt almost any device to sharpen the point of his tale by making it concrete and personal.

CONVENTIONALIZATION

ALTHOUGH each of us has his own private stereotypes, most of them are derived from our social environment. As rumor circulates, it is inevitably divested of its idiosyncratic embellishments. Common words are used to convey common meanings. Unfamiliar vocabulary, subtle verbal twists, individuality of interpretation all are deleted. When diverse personalities spread a tale, only the least common denominator can survive. The story sinks in verbal simplicity to the level of the least educated, and verbally least gifted, member in the chain of transmission.

An instance of the downward assimilation of linguistic categories is seen in the following incident. The mistress of a diplomatic household was planning to entertain a foreign diplomat. She told the maid that she wanted everything "just right, because the Swedish minister is coming to dinner." In recounting the event to a friend, the maid reported, "Goodness, they had the minister to dinner and didn't even take the cigarettes off the table." The mistress knew at least two kinds of "ministers," the maid only one. Her assimilation of what she heard followed the only linguistic pattern available to her.

The maid in this story not only altered the meaning of her mistress' statement by fitting it into her own homespun verbal categories, but she added a moral interpretation in terms of her own standards of value which, of course, were the same as those of her own social group. Conventionalization often takes the form of ascribing praise or blame according to the standards prevailing in the group where the rumor circulates.

Bartlett discusses yet another important instance of conventionalization in the triple process of perception, retention, and report. One of his examples concerns a member of the Swazi tribe in Africa who visited England. Returning to his native country he told of the friendliness of the British traffic officers. Why should he have perceived and reported them as friendly? Because, as Bartlett explains, the Swazi greets his visitor with uplifted hand. Here was a familiar gesture, warm with friendliness in a foreign country. It was one of the few things the visitor saw that could be fitted immediately into his established social framework. It produced a quick impression and lasting effect.[8]

All rumors are liable to such cultural assimilation. Bart-

---

[8] Bartlett (1932), p. 248.

lett reports that the Hindu subjects in his experiments, besides being more given than British subjects to sharpening a tale through adornment and elaboration, also tended to insert a characteristic twist in its moral to accord with the customary course of Hindu fables.[9]

In various ways, therefore, culture contrives both to simplify and adorn a tale. Through its power to conventionalize, culture becomes one of the two major determinants of the basic pattern of distortion, the other being those inherent tendencies in individual perception, retention, and report to which up to now we have given the larger portion of our attention. In the following chapter we shall consider additional ways in which rumor is incorporated into the life of society.

[9] Bartlett (1932), pp. 138-146.

9 RUMOR IN SOCIETY

Up to now we have occupied ourselves largely with the mental processes of the individual rumor agent. But rumor, like every form of human discourse, is basically a social phenomenon. At one moment it makes for idle ripples of conversation; at another it unleashes floods of violence. Sometimes only a handful of people, but sometimes millions, are involved before a tale is finally exhausted and laid to rest. Not infrequently a specific rumor theme seems inexhaustible, and variants recur in successive periods of history. One variant may prove to be so useful that it crystallizes into an undying legend. But whether broad or narrow in coverage, brief or lasting in duration, peaceful or ravaging in its effect, rumor discourse exists in the tissue of every culture. To imagine society without it is impossible.

RUMOR AND HISTORY

The emperors of ancient Rome were plagued by rumor—so much so that they appointed public rumor wardens (*delatores* they were called) whose duty it was to mingle with the population and to report what they heard back to the imperial palace. The stories of the day were considered a good barometer of popular feeling. If necessary, the *delatores* could launch a counteroffensive with rumors of their own.[1] Psychological warfare is not new.

---

[1] Chadwick (1932).

The incident of the burning of Rome in A.D. 64 furnishes an interesting example. According to Chadwick's analysis of the evidence, the distressed populace accepted and spread the story that Nero, a none too popular sovereign, if he did not actually start the conflagration himself, at least reveled in the barbaric beauty of the flames and composed an ode in their honor. That the rumor was without foundation did not help Nero. In self-defense he himself started a counter-rumor to the effect that the Christians, who were even more disliked than he, had set fire to the city. This version proved to be an even better fit to the current prejudices and fears. It would be "just like" the despised Christians to do such a thing, and so upon these convenient scapegoats the mob vented its fury, forgetting for the time being its hostility toward Nero.

In this incident, assuming the facts to be as Chadwick reports them, we find the typical dynamics of rumor at work. The origin of the fire was unknown (ambiguity); its bearing on the lives of the people (importance) was of catastrophic proportions. They hungered both for an explanation and for the relief that fixing the blame would bring. Pre-existing hatred for their tyrannical ruler suggested a formula. Yet, fear of his power and long habits of obedience made them more than willing to deflect their vengeance toward a weaker scapegoat, the dimly understood and deeply distrusted cult of Christians. And so upon them, as upon defenseless minorities in all periods of history, the frustrated and infuriated populace wreaked its vengeance.

The incident has an additional point of interest. Although the rumor concerning Nero's culpability was temporarily rejected, it later came home to roost. Nero's composition of a musical ode to the conflagration became a historical legend and in time even attained the force of a proverb. Such

RUMOR AND HISTORY

a hard-hearted tyrant *would* fiddle while Rome burned. Whether he did so in fact is not relevant; the alleged conduct is a *symbolization* of his character. Crisp, incisive, and metaphorically true, the act is forever linked with his name. And since callousness in the face of large-scale human suffering is not an uncommon human failing, we find occasions without number to apply the well-pointed proverb which originally was derived merely from hostile slander.

Rumor sent Socrates to his death, claiming that he perverted the youth of Athens and incited them to rebellion. During the Middle Ages religious wars and crusades were sustained by exaggerated tales of miracles, malfeasance, and booty. A little later explorers spread over the world in pursuit of legendary wealth and bruited springs of eternal youth, or to obtain a glimpse of rumored sea monsters. The conditions of the papal court and the private lives of the pontiffs gave rise to a never-ending supply of stories, some of which no doubt helped prepare the ground for the Reformation.

How much of human history, we may reasonably ask, can be regarded as the reactions of important groups of people to current rumor? A great deal, we suspect, for until very recent times the inhabitants of the world had little to rely on other than rumored information. Newspapers, the telegraph, the radio are late inventions. Before their advent the public had to rely upon some traveler to bring with him word-of-mouth reports, upon some Paul Revere to announce approaching danger, or upon the town crier to tell his own version of the day's news. Only a few statesmen and a few monarchs received written and sealed dispatches, and their source was not necessarily rumor free. In our simple laboratory experiments we saw how fatal distortion ordinarily is in the fourth- or fifth-hand reports, and even in first-, second-, or third-hand as well. How inaccurate must have been the picture of the outer world to which the populace and even its leaders have responded throughout the course of history!

By contrast, our sources of evidence today are vastly more secure. Post, press, radio, telegraph, and dispatches by air, have lessened immeasurably our dependence on rumor. Scarcely anyone *needs* to be uninformed. It seems certain that the course of history henceforth will ground itself more securely upon matters of fact and less upon rumored belief.

Yet we cannot conclude that the net role of rumor in present-day life is less than in former times. The objective facts concerning wars, catastrophes, trials, explorations, public utterances, are known more accurately and more quickly than ever before, but as our horizons are broadened, the areas of ambiguity are correspondingly enlarged. The very fact that civil war in China, the birth of quintuplets, the private lives of actresses, are brought to our attention widens the realm of events to which our interest extends and wherein our information, though official in part, is yet inadequate and ambiguous. We still employ rumor to structure our enlarged environment. Furthermore, in spite of modern inventions our emotional and cognitive needs are no different from those of our ancestors. And we are fully as far as they from fashioning a coherent explanation for the unfathomed mysteries of our personal lives. Like them we often rely on legend.

RUMOR AND LEGEND

A LEGEND may be regarded as a solidified rumor. More exactly, it is an unusually persistent bit of hearsay which, after a prior history of distortion and transformation, ceases to change as it is transmitted from genera-

RUMOR AND LEGEND

tion to generation. As La Piere and Farnsworth (1936) say, "a legend is a rumor that has become part of the verbal heritage of a people." Linguistically the two terms are often used interchangeably.[2]

In order to become legendary, a rumor must treat issues that are of importance to successive generations. Topics pertaining to national origins and honor are such; so too topics of birth, marriage, death. Whatever has sweep and universal significance may become part of our folklore.[3]

---

[2] The Chinese designate both rumor and legend with the same basic term (*chuan*). And Van Langenhove's book, although entitled *The Growth of a Legend* (1916), actually deals only with atrocity rumors of World War I.

[3] Occasionally an age-old legend, having reached a stable form, may finally die out, leaving only a vestigial folk saying in its place. The following example, kindly provided by Miss Ying Liu, illustrates the process with an instance from Chinese folklore.

The current saying is that an Old Man from under the Moon is responsible for arranging marriages and signifies his choices by tying a bit of red (the bridal color) thread around the foot of the partners he selects. Although this lore is widely known, its origin is forgotten by the masses of people. Historically it seems to stem from a fuller story preserved only in rare records of legends current a thousand years ago. The earlier legend ran as follows:

Wei Koo of the Tang dynasty spent the night at an inn during his travels. There he saw an old man busy with a book under the moonlight. In answer to Wei Koo's question, the old man told him that the book contained the marriage matches of all the people in the world. Together they went into the city of Mee, and there encountered a blind woman carrying a baby girl, whom the old man designated as Koo's future wife. In anger Koo ordered his guards to kill the child. They struck the infant and ran away. Fourteen years later Koo was offered the hand of a very pretty daughter of an official of great prominence. Koo, loving her deeply, was curious concerning the fact that the charming bride always wore a pearl flower curled over her eyebrow. He learned that she was the baby girl who was struck by his own servant and that the ornament hid her scar. Koo felt thankful that his lovely wife had been spared, and became even more devoted to her. The inn where he first encountered the old man was called Engagement Inn ever after.

It appears that this legend out of the unknown past first assumed this well-structured form. But in the course of succeeding ages became further leveled and sharpened until nothing remained excepting the Old Man under the Moon and his marriage-making function. To this remnant somehow was assimilated the independent element of the red thread, the symbol of marriage ties.

Legends may survive also through their aptness in illustrating human character in its universal aspects. Nero's alleged fiddling not only characterizes him but all people like him. Sisyphus was cursed with the task of rolling a mighty stone uphill, only to see it repeatedly tumble to the bottom. The legend is applied today to unfortunate mortals who seem to suffer the same doom. The Christmas rose, in spite of ice and snow, is said to burst into bloom at midnight on Christmas Eve in northern countries; and well it might, to express the gladness felt by human hearts at that season.

Thus legends persist because they embody undying states of mind. They provide answers to the persistent riddles of life or, with fine if only metaphorical precision, deep human feelings. With the aid of legends, says Kimball Young, "the world takes on meaning and does not need to be constantly recast."[4] Young adds that the framework provided by a legend makes us feel secure in the continuity of our ideologies. The mighty sagas of the north supplied their listeners with a sense of stability, pride of ancestry, and a satisfying explanation of cosmic riddles. Like all legends they were interpretative tools for use during man's brief and confusing existence on earth.

Legends that deal with primal forces, cosmology, religious belief, are technically called *myths*. Expressing as they do a large part of the philosophy of life shared by a single cultural group, they are especially resistant to change. Though there are many versions of the story of creation, of the nature of afterlife, of the Messianic hope, each is persistent within its own cultural circle. What is passed on from generation to generation is always couched in concrete terms. Neither legends nor rumors contain abstract language even when

[4] K. Young (1936), p. 437.

they treat universal themes. The themes dealt with by myths are among the most *important* that man ever has to face, and the evidence pertaining to them is eternally *ambiguous*.

Since cosmic problems are age-old, it is *legend* rather than *rumor* that we normally find meeting the need. Yet there are briefer periods of ephemeral rumor that seem designed temporarily to assuage man's curiosity and religious hunger. Every so often rumors arise of the impending end of the world, of the coming of the Messiah, or supernatural cures at a certain shrine, or of visions in the sky. One recalls the story of the angel who appeared in the sky over Flanders trenches during World War I.

The leveling, sharpening, and assimilative changes that give rise to legends are most clearly seen in "historical" stories of the lives of national heroes. Accounts of the doings of King Arthur, of Frederick Barbarossa, of Joan of Arc, are a hopeless blur of fiction and fact in which the legend has gained the upper hand. No one, unless perhaps an occasional historian, extracts the kernel of truth, and no one seems to want to do so. The embedded form of the legend is taken as a satisfactory guide. "And why not?" asks the poetic soul. Does not Joan of Arc, for example, embody the ambitions and aspirations of large sectors of mankind? Is it not more important for a legend to symbolize a spiritual intention than for a prosaic critic to isolate the pure historical truth from the gradual assimilation and sharpening of this truth?

It does not take long for a historical personage to become a legendary character. In our own country prominent figures, especially those who died before the present generation was born, and who are celebrated in song or literature, take on a mythical cast. The story of John Smith and Princess Pocahontas rests on slim foundations of fact. In his original report of his voyage, Captain Smith hardly mentioned the princess. Sixteen years later, when he wrote his *General Historie*, he gave her the center of the stage. To what extent he himself dramatized his tale as the actual events grew dim in his memory we cannot say; but it is certain that subsequent writers and the romance-hungry public have preferred the spiced and sharpened version of the story.

Heard in childhood, the legend of George Washington and the cherry tree is remembered and warmly cherished. The reason lies in part in the simplicity and definiteness of its imagery, in part in the emotional identification of the young patriot with the virtuous father of his country. But the story is of doubtful authenticity. Its source appears to have been a clergyman who reported that he heard it from an aged lady who, as a distant relative, had sometimes visited the Washington family.[5] A thin foundation for a national legend!

But here again the poetic soul speaks up. "Why be so literal-minded?" he complains. "George Washington was an upright and admirable man. The story is in character. Let's allow it to symbolize our regard for the man and our understanding of his virtue. Don't be pedantic!"

METAPHORICAL SIGNIFICANCE OF RUMOR AND LEGEND

THE form of discourse in both legend and rumor is simple and declarative. A ship was lost with 1000 lives. Washington said, "I cut it with my little hatchet." Thor hurls his hammer to make the thunder. Such statements are allegedly statements of fact (i.e., propositions for belief of topical reference). Accordingly, when we talk about

[5] Nevins (1938); also Britt (1941).

the distortion of rumor, how it becomes deflected from the original evidence, we are using a literal criterion. We judge the content in comparison with the objective facts—with the "stimulus standard."

But does rumor *really* pretend to be designative and informative? The very form of its declarations would make it seem so. Yet on second look, the type of discourse represented in both legends and rumors often has a hidden mode of signification. It says *more* than it superficially seems to say, and the veiled signification may be the more important and the more valid. Were I to remark that the Jews own Wall Street, or that they evade the draft, or that they obtain cushion jobs in the Army, I am not, in spite of appearances, intending to tell you facts so much as I am notifying you of my distrust of the Jews. At bottom I am evaluating. Morris would call my discourse appraisive-poetic.[6] Or if I am repeating a cultural evaluation by telling a legend of creation, of a national hero, or a myth of afterlife, I am again not speaking altogether designatively or informatively, but in an appraisive-mythical manner.

Insofar as rumors pretend to be informative-designative, they are always, in part at least, erroneous. Since this pretense is always present, they are invariably a deceptive mode of discourse. But insofar as they are intended and taken as *appraisive*, they accurately signify the state of mind of the teller.

As rumors grow more and more aphoristic or more and more legendary, they acquire much of this appraisive or metaphorical character. That ostriches bury their heads in the sand is a false fable from the informative-designative point of view. Real ostriches don't. But it is true that many

[6] Morris (1946), pp. 134 ff.

human beings to whom this parable is applied hide their eyes from approaching danger. That Alaska is a region of unbroken cold is factually false. But if I wish to express a certain state of mind with an appropriate simile, I am not deterred by isotherms. I declare unabashed that "It's cold as Alaska."

Stefansson, the explorer, has much to say about the innumerable false beliefs that have developed in the course of time and have become the currency of civilized discourse in defiance of contrary evidence. These crystallizations of folklore he calls the "standardization of error."[7] But before we grow critical about such standardized error, we should decide to what extent error is really involved. Few people are interested in the fact that wolves travel in pairs or in small family groups. They aren't really concerned with zoological wolves at all. What they need in their discourse is a metaphor; a menacing stampede is the figure they seek. Wolf pack does nicely, whatever the scientific facts of the case may be.

Thus many people who tell rumors or recount legends are at least half aware that what they say should not be taken as literal truth, even though couched in the language of fact. They half realize that they are using a picturesque vehicle for conveying ideas. Literary artists do precisely this when with the aid of fiction they concretely represent a generalized truth. Rumor telling is sometimes a half-conscious fictionizing. Though the tale we tell may not be true if taken at its face value, we hold it to be true if taken symbolically. For example, *I* do not know whether the atomic bomb produces latent cancers and lingering death for miles around its target. When in the course of my rumor spread-

[7] Stefansson (1928).

ing I say that it does, I am signifying something broader and truer than the facts I narrate (perhaps half suspicious of them myself). I am saying, "What a dreadful thing is the atom bomb!" And who will doubt that I am wholly justified in this appraisive-poetic aspect of my statement?

Thus rumors and legends are high in *expressive* significance and should not be judged exclusively as the informative statements which they seem to be, but also as the appraisive statements which they usually are. In a free society we cherish the right of each person to tell how he feels, and if he prefers to use a rumor parable, why should he not do so?

The social problem of rumor arises from the peculiar fact that the listener usually receives it not in terms of the speaker's appraisive intentions, but rather as a designative statement of fact. Though the teller is revealing the emotional and cognitive complex against which he has assimilated an incident or bit of hearsay, the listener, if he is unwary, takes the statement as a deliverance of verifiable truth. In so doing he confuses expressive significance with objective denotation. It requires a good deal of insight to listen with the proper blend of appreciation and caution to rumor discourse.

THE CLASSIFICATION OF RUMORS

SINCE rumors and legends saturate our social relationships, it is reasonable to ask whether any principle of classification exists whereby we may order them. Or are the "propositions for belief of topical interest" potentially so numerous that the task of classification is entirely hopeless?

The answer to this question, as with similar questions

concerning the ordering of social and psychological phenomena, depends upon the interest of the analyst. For limited and special purposes it is quite possible to categorize rumors that are current at any given period of time, assuming, of course, that an adequate collection of these is at hand. There is, however, no exclusive validity for any one method of sorting. One student of the subject may be interested in (*a*) the speed, periodicity, or other temporal aspects of rumor spreading; another in (*b*) the subject matter with which the stories deal; a third in (*c*) the states of mind and probable motives underlying the current flow; a fourth in (*d*) the social effects, whether deleterious, beneficial, or indifferent. Other investigators may employ still other categories, seeking to separate (*e*) local rumors and widespread rumors; (*f*) new rumors and old; (*g*) plausible stories and implausible stories; (*h*) tales of long duration and tales of short duration. The rumor pie may be sliced in many ways.

We shall illustrate the first three principles of classification listed above.

a. The *temporal* criterion has been employed by a Russian sociologist, Bysow (1928). There is first, he says, the *creeping* rumor. It develops slowly and is whispered about with an air of secrecy until nearly everyone has heard it. Cassandra rumors predicting some misfortune are typical of this class; so, too, rumors about the sinister doings of international bankers, munitions makers, government officials, labor leaders. Hostility rumors are usually of this sort, their carriers forming an endless chain for their gradual dissemination.

Other rumors are *impetuous* in nature. They spread like wildfire because they deal with an immediate threat or immediate promise. Engulfing a community in an amazingly short period of time, they include rumors of violence, or

THE CLASSIFICATION OF RUMORS 171

accidents, catastrophes, or of great victory in wartime. Starting in a highly charged atmosphere, rumors of this class are likely to incite prompt and vigorous action because they are based on strong emotions of panic, rage, or sudden joy.

Finally, in Bysow's picturesque terminology, there are *diving* rumors. They are current for a while, then dive, as it were, under the surface to reappear sometime later when circumstances warrant their re-emergence. In spite of their psychological differences, World War I and World War II were similar with respect to rumor. Stories current from 1914 to 1918 seemed to submerge until the anxieties of 1939 to 1945 brought them again to the surface. There was, for instance, the tongue-and-the-stamp rumor. It ran as follows: An American prisoner of war (in a German camp in the first war; in a Japanese camp in the second) sent a letter to his family, containing no unusual information except a request to save the stamp on the letter. Since the soldier never had been a philatelist, the family was surprised and decided to investigate. Upon removing the stamp, they found writing on the envelope underneath informing them that the soldier's captors had cut off his tongue. This improbable morsel circulated in both wars in spite of two fatally contradictory facts: Prisoner-of-war letters did not carry stamps, and the removal of the tongue would almost certainly cause a person to bleed to death unless given expert surgical care.

The rumor that enemy troops have poisoned water wells recurs, it seems, in every war. So too the stories of enemy atrocities (cutting off the hands of children and the breasts of women). Whispering campaigns slandering successive presidents of the United States have a monotonous sameness (see p. 184).

Such "diving" rumors may be explained in two ways. Perhaps they linger dormant in the minds of certain individuals, who dig them up years later, maybe without recognition, when an environmental situation resembles that in which the rumor was first heard. Or perhaps the two rumors have no real continuity between them. Human needs in similar circumstances may well give rise to similar stories. It seems likely, for example, that well-poisoning represents a not improbable threat on the part of enemy agents in any time of war. Anxious people, wholly dependent on their water supply, may easily sharpen and dramatize their apprehension without suspecting that in so doing they are reenacting a familiar page of rumor history.

b. Analysis by *subject matter* is another principle of classification. Here the investigator simply counts the number of rumors that deal with a specified topic. In normal times, for example, we might seek the proportion of stories that deal with politics, illness, sex, foreign relations, minority groups. True, the range of topics is potentially so broad that such a method may run into difficulties, especially since different regions, occupational groups, and educational levels would almost certainly show marked variations.

In wartime, however, this method has greater utility, since then nearly all rumors are to some degree war-directed and widely circulated. The Canadian psychologist J. A. Irving (1943) found that wartime rumors in his country dealt with six principal themes: (1) horror, disgust, death; (2) waste and extravagance; (3) invasion, raids, threats to security; (4) anti-British sentiment; (5) intentions of the government regarding rationing, financing of the war, and conscription; (6) alleged incompetencies in the conduct of the war. Valuable as such a classification may be for the immediate purpose of morale-building and government public relations, the method at best tells *what* people are talking about. It does not reach into the motivation of the rumor spreaders or aid in uncovering any of the general laws of rumor.

c. In Chapter 1 we cited a more distinctly psychological principle of classification—one based on the *dominant type of motivational tension* reflected in a rumor. The reader recalls that the analysis of 1000 wartime stories current in 1942 indicated that nearly all seemed to express either hostility, fear, or wish. A few, to be sure, seemed to be nothing more than a reflection of a predominantly intellectual tension, a kind of curiosity. If the reader will glance back at Table 1 (pp. 12-13) he will see that these motivational mainsprings are employed as the primary categories of analysis, but that a content analysis showing what *objects* are hated, feared, desired, is likewise included. Thus these two principles of classification are combined.

To classify rumors in terms of their motivational mainsprings is probably much easier in wartime than in peacetime. But even in wartime the hate-fear-wish trichotomy is much oversimplified. Actually a fear rumor (e.g., concerning an enemy atrocity) may have elements of sexual interest, of adventure, and feelings of moral superiority to sustain it. The complex of motives to which a rumor is assimilated is a personal matter, and to find out why a given individual falls for a certain story would require a clinical study of that individual. Because of the diversity of motivational blends that may nourish a given rumor, any psychological classification will be inevitably oversimplified and crude.

FUSION OF PASSIONS AND ANTIPATHIES

WE conclude then that we must not expect to find any rumor correlated with only one emotion or with only one cognitive tendency. Assimilation does not work on a unit basis. Even a well-structured and apparently simple story may serve as explanation, justification, or relief for a mixture of feelings.

A convenient illustration is found in the common hostility rumors. They may mention only a single villain (although even if they do so, the underlying state of mind is usually complex). Often they assail directly or by implication more than one villain. A repulsive bit of doggerel, a slanderous rumor in rhyme, circulated during the election campaign of 1944, goes as follows. President Roosevelt is said to be addressing his wife:

> You kiss the niggers,
> I'll kiss the Jews;
> And we'll stay in the White House
> As long as we choose.

Three antipathies have fused. The hatred is tripronged.

One collection of anti-Semitic rumors reveals that the commonest type identifies Jews with Communists—a two-pronged hatred. Those who despise not only Jews but also Wall Street have no difficulty fusing their prejudices under the epithet "international banker"; and this particular label may serve to cover in certain cases additional phobias—of foreigners and of internationalism in any form. Perhaps the record for a fusion of antipathies was achieved by Hitler in his denunciation of the "Jewish international Communist pluto-democracies."

In Germany during World War I many atrocity stories were current describing the alleged treachery and inhumanity of the Belgian people against the German Army (many of the stories being identical with those circulating in Allied countries with the villains reversed). These stories commonly accused the Catholic clergy of being rabble-rousers

FUSION OF PASSIONS AND ANTIPATHIES 175

and instigators of the atrocities. Thus the dislike which many Protestant Germans traditionally felt for ultramontane Catholicism became fused with their anger against the Belgians for resisting the Germans (Van Langenhove, 1916). In World War II Nazi rumor often linked Catholic clergy with antifascist Social Democrats and Communists, whereas Russian stories sometimes accused Catholic priests of collaboration with the Nazis.

Fusion not only of hatreds but of fear, guilt, and economic bewilderment is found in the curious tales of the "Eleanor Clubs" circulating in large numbers in southern states in 1943. The theme of these stories was that large numbers of Negro women, especially domestic servants, were banded together under the spiritual sponsorship of Eleanor Roosevelt, their purpose being rebellion against the existing social order. Here the most obvious fusion is of antagonism against New Deal liberalism and traditional anti-Negro feeling. But the complex of motives goes even deeper.

There were many versions of the rumors pertaining to the Eleanor Clubs, which sometimes were called "Daughters of Eleanor," "Eleanor Angel Clubs," "Sisters of Eleanor," "Royal House of Eleanor" (Odum, 1943). These fanciful titles represent, of course, assimilation to stereotypes concerning the religiosity of the Negro or his supposed flair for pompous institutional names. It was widely told that the motto of these groups was, "Every white woman in her own kitchen in a year." A typical Eleanor story runs as follows: "A white woman was away for a while, and when she returned she found her colored maid sitting at her dresser combing her hair with her comb." Another represented the Negro servant as bathing in her employer's bathtub or as entertaining her friends in the parlor. One rumor had it that a white woman called her cook to come to prepare dinner for her guests. The cook turned the tables by demanding that her mistress be at her home by eight o'clock Sunday morning to fix breakfast for the cook's guests. One Negress was reported to have offered to pay a white woman to wash her clothes. Occasionally the stories hinted at coming violence, charging that the clubs were saving ice picks and butcher knives for a rebellion.

All these versions, besides reflecting anti-Roosevelt and anti-Negro feeling, show a distinct fear of *inversion of status*. The Negroes are represented not merely as nursing resentment beneath the surface but as being on the verge of revolt. They threaten to take over, to reverse the social scale. Why? Because the white rumor spreaders find their feelings of economic and social insecurity to some extent explained and relieved by these stories. Suffering a vague anxiety, they justify their jitters by pointing to Negro aggression, and derive a melancholy consolation from alerting one another to the menace.

But we must probe still further. A rumor of inversion of status admits in a circuitous way that a relationship other than the *status quo* between the races is conceivable. And according to the American creed the *status quo*, being essentially unjust, should not be permanent. Every American, as Myrdal (1944) points out, believes in and aspires to something higher than the present plane of race relations. At heart he agrees with Patrick Henry, the slave owner, who as long ago as 1772 wrote, "I will not, I cannot, justify it." At the same time most whites permit themselves only a squint-eyed insight into their moral dilemma. A century and a half after Patrick Henry the conflict still persists, for the Emancipation only nominally liberated the Negro. Were whites to face the issue squarely they would be torn asunder

FUSION OF PASSIONS AND ANTIPATHIES

by their conflicting loyalties: to the American creed and to their convenient belief in white supremacy.

Rather than face this pointed and irreconcilable conflict between two cherished loyalties, many white people twist and squirm and rationalize. The guilt-evasion rumor (see p. 41 f.) is eagerly seized upon as a means of escape. If, as the Eleanor Club stories hold, the Negro is overly aggressive, illegally plotting, vulgarly menacing, then he has no *right* to equal status. He must expect no more consideration than we give to trespassers, marauders, blackmailers. He must be kept in his place. If there are true instances of injustice, then our patience and indulgence more than make it up to him. After all he is only an unruly child (as the Eleanor stories show) and must be treated as such—kindly but firmly. By this devious mental maneuvering the bigot is able to escape his feelings of guilt.

Guilt evasion is likewise detectable in innumerable rumors detailing incidents of the Negro's criminal and disloyal tendencies. One wartime story had it that Negroes were not being drafted as rapidly as whites because authorities were afraid to let them get their hands on guns (Odum, 1943, p. 111). Even humorous yarns concerning Negro stupidity, gullibility, and laziness have the same functional significance; so too the myriad tales of Negro sexual aggression. All of these tend to allay the white man's sense of guilt, for what can we do with a black man who is disloyal, criminal, clownish, stupid, menacing, and immoral—except to keep him in his place just as we are now doing? The ideal of equality may be all right in theory, but it was never meant to apply to criminals, imbeciles, or black men.

The ultimate ally of anti-Negro prejudice is the sex rumor. Negroes are repeatedly represented as plotting to cross the color line and commit the sin of miscegenation. The stories invariably concern the relations between Negro men and white women, not the far more frequent liaisons of white man and Negro woman. There are stories of rape and attempted rape, or less lurid versions representing Negroes as approaching white women, following them on the streets, trying to hold their hands, and so on. One wartime story told that Negroes who were not drafted (the disloyalty theme) were saying to the white men who left for the war that Negroes would "take care" of the white women back home (the sex theme). Though especially common in the South, Negro sex rumors are frequent also in the North. In a New England city, known for its relatively peaceful race relations, a local story circulated to "explain" why the washroom in a certain restaurant had been boarded up. The reason alleged (wholly fictitious) was that two Negroes had taken a white woman into that particular washroom and raped her.

The motivational current here runs deep. All matters pertaining to sex in the American Puritan tradition are likely to have a high emotional charge, and for this reason, to spill over easily into other regions of strong passion. Sex, as a proposition for topical interest, is a never failing target for rumor. Like the matter of status it is also a source of heavy guilt feelings. To blame ourselves for our sexual sins (as for our sins against the American creed) is never agreeable. Better by far blame someone else for his real or imagined lapses. The resemblance between the sex and the minority-group rumor is close, projection in the interest of guilt evasion being common to both. This resemblance facilitates fusion. Why not escape guilt by heaping blame for sexual lapses upon the very persons who threaten our social position?

Deep inside, many people feel secure neither in their status nor in their economic future, nor in their own sexual morality. All of these matters are intimate and central in their lives. Such intense and pivotal interests cannot well be kept separate. A threat to one is a threat to the others. Hence the Negro scapegoat is seen not only as arrogant socially but as pressing upon us vocationally, and as sexually more potent and less inhibited than we. In him we perceive all the grabbing, climbing, and lewd behavior that we might indulge in if we let ourselves go. He is the sinner. Even if we are not blameless, yet his misdeeds (as recounted in rumor) are overt and worse than ours. We need not feel guilt at our peccadilloes.

While all this rationalizing is going on, we may, perversely enough, find the Negro's "animal" qualities darkly fascinating. If so, we must severely repress this satanic attraction, and through "reaction formation" (i.e., by turning against the fascination that we disapprove of) fight the devil even harder (McLean, 1946). We do so by adopting the most sacred of taboos, undeviating opposition to racial amalgamation. The very thought fills us with horror (or does it?). Were it violated, the way would be opened for a collapse of all our moral and economic standards. I would admit defeat at the hands of the black and evil stranger who, in my unconscious, I regard in part as my own unhallowed alter ego.

Complicated as this analysis of anti-Negro rumors is, it does not exaggerate the intricacy of the emotional and cognitive fusions that account for their appeal. It seems to be the rule for people to *personify* the forces of evil, and to center them in some visibly different, near-lying, *minority* group. The commonest, but by no means the only, "demons" today are the Communists, the Jews, and the Negroes. Since the blame ascribed to them is certainly in excess of their just deserts we technically call them "scapegoats" (see Harvard University, 1943).

RUMOR PUBLICS

EACH rumor has its own public. Financial rumors circulate principally among those whose fortunes can be affected by the ups and downs of the market. Rumors about changes in the draft law, in income tax rates, or about projected housing developments will spread mostly among those who are potentially affected. Children in school, all eager for a holiday, will seize greedily upon reports of a pending "teachers' meeting" or of necessary repairs on the school building. Occupational and social groups all have their peculiar susceptibilities. Physicians, clergymen, aviators, or stag parties will launch into tales that reflect the common interests of the group; so too will sewing clubs, bridge parties, friendship groups. A rumor public exists wherever there is a community of interest.

There are, however, striking individual differences in susceptibility to rumor. Not every American believes anti-Negro slander, even in regions where bigotry is most dense. Each village has inhabitants who are resistant to local gossip. Within a given community of interest, even under conditions of high ambiguity and importance, people become links in the chain of rumor only if they are *suggestible*.

To be suggestible is to accept a proposition for belief in the absence of evidence that might logically be demanded. Some people are accustomed to critical inspection of all that they hear. Trained in semantics, in social psychology, or for other reasons of a skeptical turn of mind, they wait like the proverbial Missourian for dependable evidence.

Suggestible people, on the other hand, are those whose mental life is either poorly structured or else overrigidly furnished with stereotypes and complexes. The first group

This sketch, drawn by Thomas Rowlandson (1756-1827), appears in his *Comparative Anatomy; resemblances between the countenances of Men and Beasts*. The artist did not name this sketch, and the reader is free to "assimilate" it to his own interests. Is it a rumor chain growing to an evil crescendo? Is it a representation of malicious gossip swirling around a young and innocent victim?

includes many poorly educated individuals. To them happenings in the physical and social environments are inherently mysterious; science is *terra incognita*. Cantril found that a large number of those who were frightened by the fanciful invasion of the earth by Martians reported in Orson Welles' imaginative broadcast were people who, upset by the unrest in Europe, by the depression, or by the breathtaking advances of science, felt that "anything might happen" (Cantril et al., 1940). They were so ill informed that it did not occur to them to check the radio report by inspecting the program schedule in the morning newspaper, by twisting the dial, or by verifying the "news" in some other equally simple way. They gave way to panic because their mental processes lacked critical anchorage. Their minds were "unstuck" and hence a prey to the fitful winds of communication.

Perhaps more often those who are suggestible toward rumor are people whose minds are in some respects "overstuck." Into their rigid compartments of explanation and prejudgment congenial rumors are greedily absorbed. Some of those who accepted the Martian story were pious people who were expecting the end of the world. Others were living in a state of insecurity induced by the depression and momentarily awaiting some catastrophe, not knowing of precisely what order. Evidence shows also that political slander is accepted most eagerly by those who distrust the administration in power (Allport and Lepkin, 1945). Stories about conditions inside Russia—a subject excelling in ambiguity and importance as well as in prejudice—provoke belief or rejection according to the political and social orientation of the listener. Hostility rumors circulate only among those predisposed to hate the victim of the story. Like propaganda, with which it is closely related, rumor activates and confirms pre-existing attitudes rather than forming new ones.[8]

One additional condition, the most obvious of all, must be met in order that a rumor may circulate. Susceptible individuals must be in touch with one another. Such closely knit groups as shipmates at sea, members of a combat unit, co-workers in a business office, the Friday bridge club, or the inhabitants of a small town all possess the requisite homogeneity and contact. Among them rumors fly fast. Yet even in a homogeneous population there are selective channels. In one army camp, for example, the rumor that all men over thirty-five years of age were to be discharged traveled like lightning—but almost exclusively among men over that age. In a business office, a dormitory, or a neighborhood, rumors will travel principally in the channels of *friendship*.

Rumor chains that result from social intimacy between tellers and listeners have been noted by Moreno (1934). This investigator's method of plotting the social geography of a community marks out the "psychological currents" along which gossip is likely to flow. This method, called "sociometry," asks people to name their best friends (perhaps by inquiring whom they would like to live with, to work with, to enjoy recreation with). The resulting network of relationships predicts the channel in which all forms of interpersonal communication, including rumor, are likely to travel.

Although friendly contact normally forges the rumor chain, there are circumstances where the barest of transient contacts suffice. To kill time in a Pullman car we may establish a linkage with a complete stranger, and across it may leap variegated gossipy chatter. Moreover, in times of emotional crisis people are prone to talk with any neighboring

[8] Cf. Lazarsfeld *et al.* (1945).

stranger about the crisis at hand. At a serious hotel fire the bystanders were heard to pass along the "information" that three, eight, ten, twenty guests were trapped in the upper floors. Thus rumor chains may be momentarily forged of boredom, or of emotion, as well as permanently forged through the ties of friendship.

An instructive study of rumor publics was made by the Office of War Information (1942). Two cities affected by war conditions were investigated—New Brunswick, New Jersey, and Portland, Maine. In both localities it was found that people who were rated by the interviewers as well informed showed a greater tendency to recount rumors than did those who were considered ill informed. To the well informed more issues seem important, worth thinking and talking about. The well informed are likely also to have greater verbal facility and to be accustomed to expressing their thoughts and feelings readily. Further, people who participate more widely in social life were found to be more rumor prone than those who were isolated. Working women, for example, heard and spread more stories than did housewives. Among those rated "socially active" 60 percent were found to be rumor agents, but among those who led comparatively secluded lives, only 30 percent.

This study requires a word of comment. Were the citizens whom the interviewers rated "well informed" really so? Had they known the full facts of an incident they would have been less, rather than more, rumor prone. What the finding means is that the wider the range of interest, the more possible occasions there are for rumor spreading. In Chapter 1 it was pointed out that news is counteractive only when it is complete and unambiguous. Well-informed citizens no doubt read extensively in newspapers and listen to many broadcasts, but their expanded social horizon may still be hazy. Distant events are often the least clearly understood, and for that reason most susceptible to the fanciful structure that rumor confers. It takes a great deal of informing before a person is well enough informed to resist rumors.

WHISPERING CAMPAIGNS

As we have remarked, intense feeling will cause the rumor spark to cross the communication gap between strangers. It is for this reason that in wartime, when there is a disaster, and at election time, gossip often overflows its normal channels. Being often of a purplish hue, perhaps libelous and obscene, it is communicated, literally or figuratively, through whispers.

Since politics is a subject upon which many people feel intensely, we are almost sure to encounter campaign whispers concerning candidates for election. The more heartily a candidate is disliked, the larger will be the barrage of rumors attacking his motives, his past life, his private morality, and future intentions.

From earliest times whispering campaigns have stained our presidential elections. Though the victims have been as different in personality as Andrew Jackson and Warren Harding, the topics of slander are usually the same: illicit sexual relations, brutal treatment of wives, drunkenness, and the alleged possession of Negro or Jewish blood. Jefferson was accused of atheism and immorality; Garfield was said to be on the verge of divorce; Arthur was carrying on adulterously with a society lady in Washington; Cleveland was supposed to get drunk every night and beat his wife; Harding had Negro blood; Al Smith was politically the Pope's mannequin (just because he happened to be a prominent Catholic lay-

WHISPERING CAMPAIGNS 185

man); Franklin D. Roosevelt was both Jewish and insane.[9]

Having assumed a Satanic character, the candidate we dislike becomes more worthy of our hatred and opposition. Before we heard the rumor we only *thought* he was diabolical, but now we *know* that he is. The dynamics resemble those of the anti-Negro slander. A wealthy man, for example, cannot quite justify his aversion to liberal reforms that, through higher taxes, would limit his wealth, for in his heart he may believe that social justice requires precisely just such limitation. But if the liberal candidate is said to be licentious, insane, Negroid, then his opposition, so it seems to him, is well directed. The feeling of antagonism spreads like a grease spot until it becomes impossible to identify the original center of the stain.

It has sometimes been remarked that whispering campaigns play less part in local elections than in national. If this observation is correct, the explanation would seem to be twofold. Ordinarily local campaigns arouse less passion, because the issues are seldom basic to one's economic self-interest. Secondly, the local candidate is relatively well known to his constituents and the region of ambiguity in his political and personal life is not so great as with national candidates, about whom "almost anything" might be true.

Commercial whispering campaigns are not unknown. Certain advertisers and public relations counsels, renowned for their adventuresomeness rather than for their ethics, were bound to discover them.[10] An agent, paid for the job, may from a convenient spot in a Pullman car, barber shop, or ball park, extol the merits of one product and slander its competitor. But it is doubtful whether such imaginative business practice pays. Psychologically its weakness lies in

[9] The dreary tale of these whispering campaigns is told by Adams (1932).
[10] See Littell and McCarthy (1936).

the fact that the listener does not regard the topic as important. Even though a germ of favoritism may be implanted in his mind for the product in question, he is not likely to repeat the tiresome tale to his friends. Money may hire a rumor agent but it cannot forge a rumor chain.

THE PRESS AND RUMOR

ALTHOUGH rumor travels primarily through spontaneous oral discourse, the part played by the printed word should not be underestimated. In countries where the press serves a totalitarian government it may become the fountainhead of rumors. It was so in Germany, Italy, and Japan. Rumor planting was one of the leading forms of Axis propaganda.[11]

Even in countries where the press is free, newspapers may inadvertently deal in rumors, perhaps by mistaking the authenticity of a "news release." More rarely the insertion of rumor may be deliberate. Irresponsible editors may rely, as did Hitler, on the shortness of the public's memory and upon its indisposition to check up on facts. The headline in a Hearst paper reads: "90% Professors Teach Communism, says Former Jurist." Few people would think of identifying any headline with rumor. But many headlines, by virtue of their sharpening and slanting (assimilation to the editor's prejudice) fit precisely the rumor formula. Seldes (1935) shows that the news story on which the headline just cited was based by no means justifies the sensational head.

---

[11] Hitler relied upon the forgetfulness of the public and believed that momentary tales, whether false or true, would incite partisan action without having a long-run boomerang effect. But human memory is not quite so short and human conduct not quite so specific as Hitler assumed. For a discussion of the shortsightedness and eventual failure of propaganda based on falsehoods and rumor, see Bartlett (1940).

Discrepancies between headline and story are not uncommon, the former revealing (like a rumor) the editor's or owner's bias, and the story serving, after a fashion, to protect him with its relatively greater truthfulness.

In a similar way the selective reporting that goes into an ordinary news story is sometimes a species of quasi-rumor. The printed account may indeed represent truth, but it cannot very well tell the whole truth, and fails frequently to present even a balanced truth. A somewhat distorted picture inevitably results, and when the reader recalls or retells the item he is likely to sharpen it still more in the direction in which it was first slanted. A content analysis of Boston newspapers at the time the Neutrality Act was before Congress in 1940 showed that most papers gave more space to speeches and arguments favoring their own editorial viewpoints. They tended, furthermore, to place at the beginning of a news article the facts and reported opinions favoring their editorial position, and toward the end of the article opposing facts and opinions. This sly editorial device served to level out in the reader's mind the disfavored view and to sharpen the favored (Allport and Faden, 1940).

Paris newspapers during the fall of 1945 were bedeviled by rumors reporting an illness of Stalin. The hearsay was featured by anti-Communist newspapers, which tended to sharpen it into an account of a crisis occurring in Russia. Pro-Communist papers, on the other hand, either ignored the news or denied both the illness and the crisis (Zerner, 1946).

Reporters are in an awkward psychological position. With the best will in the world their stories cannot always escape the course of typical rumor distortion. The reporter is seldom an eyewitness of an event himself, but arrives on the scene after a newsworthy happening has occurred. His sources of information may be twice or thrice removed from the eyewitness (whose own accuracy is none too great). The "news" has already become hearsay, and what the reporter writes and copywriter revises may slip still further down the precarious road of leveling, sharpening, and assimilation.

Seldes cites an example drawn from the Paris edition of the Chicago *Tribune*. An actress had committed suicide.

The Story	The Facts
Belgrade, Oct. 27—A few moments before she should have appeared on the stage at the Lioubliana Theater last night, Mme. Alla Behr, a Slovene actress, was found hanging dead in her dressing-room. The reason for the suicide is unknown.	After the first act. Not at Lioubliana but Klagenfurt. Her name, Ella Beer. Not Slovene, but Viennese. Not in dressing-room but hotel. The reason was known.

Seldes concludes, "In type there were exactly six and a half lines, containing exactly seven facts and of these seven, one, the suicide, was correct and all the others were wrong" (Seldes, 1935, p. 163).[12] In distortions of this type we cannot fix blame upon the motives of the reporter. As in our own experiments, in spite of every desire to give an accurate account, the reporter is at the mercy of the typical re-structuring and embedding process that haunts every serial reproduction.

For one or more of the reasons just mentioned, much that we see in our newspaper takes on some of the characteristics of rumor. Yet *in principle* the sharp opposition be-

---

[12] From *Freedom of the Press*, by George Seldes, copyright 1935, used by special permission of the publishers, The Bobbs-Merrill Company.

tween news and rumor remains inviolable. The former is characterized ideally by its conformity with secure standards of evidence, the latter by the absence of such conformity. But as clear as this theoretical distinction is between news and rumor, it is not always effective in the minds of the public. Some gullible souls seem to "believe everything" they read in the newspapers or hear on the radio. To them a piece based on hearsay is as true as a piece well documented. Other people, on the contrary, are so hypercritical that they "never believe anything in the newspapers." (Skeptics concerning radio newscasts are fewer.) Fooled once or twice, they have become chronic doubters. During World War I many false atrocity stories were printed. As a result, during World War II it was difficult for many Americans to believe that the macabre but authenticated reports of the concentration camps were based on secure evidence. Much that is entirely trustworthy in our news communications is pooh-poohed as propaganda. Should people become as rumor conscious in the future as they have become propaganda conscious in the past, reporters, headline writers, and editors will find it increasingly difficult to hold the public's confidence.

LABELED RUMOR

What is the effect of telling people that what they are hearing is only a rumor? Two experiments shed light on this question and show quite clearly that the public is not yet rumor conscious.

Kirkpatrick (1932) presented his college subjects with a series of statements which had allegedly been gleaned from the campus daily. Half the items were prefaced by the phrase "it is rumored . . . ," whereas half were presented as straight news. All items were fictitious. Analysis of the belief ratings given by the subjects showed that the precautionary phrase "it is rumored" served scarcely at all as a deterrent to belief.

More recently G. H. Smith (1947) used a set of fictitious "news" items, some favorable and some unfavorable to the Soviet Union. His subjects were students whose attitudes toward Russia had been measured by means of an attitude scale. The statements were presented under three different labels. Some were offered as authenticated *facts;* some as unverified *rumors;* some without any label at all. The subjects indicated the degree of their belief or disbelief in the statement by means of a scale ranging from rejection to unqualified acceptance.

Smith's results show that statements labeled *fact* were believed most readily, whereas items presented as *rumor* found least credence. Unlabeled items occupied an intermediate position. However, the *fact* label was more effective in shifting scores in the direction of belief than was the *rumor* label in making items less acceptable. In other words, the rumor label was found to be similar in its effects to no label at all. To tag a statement fact is to give it prestige and to induce submissive acceptance. But to tag a statement rumor merely places it in the category of undesignated discourse. People scarcely shy away from the epithet at all. Upon hearing something carrying a fact label the listener seems to be saying to himself, "Oh, a fact! Facts are true; I should believe them." On hearing the rumor designation, he hesitates a moment and concludes, "Well, rumors *may* be true," and if predisposed toward accepting the statement he gives it the benefit of the doubt.

In these experiments pre-existing attitude appears to be more important than any label, for, under all conditions of Smith's experiment, scores on the belief scale were correlated positively with scores on the attitude scales. Those favoring Russia are more inclined to believe both facts and rumors in Russia's favor; those opposing the U.S.S.R. are more disposed to believe facts and rumors unfavorable to Russia.

The relative ineffectiveness of the rumor label has important practical implications. It means that one cannot kill rumors merely by tagging them. More strenuous methods of refutation, including appeals to patriotism or to one's sense of shame, or perhaps basic instruction in the psychology of rumor, are required. It was these latter methods that the rumor clinics attempted to employ. It is important to note too that the label *fact* arouses positive idolatry in the hearer. Advertisers, who so widely use quasi-scientific blurbs, have already discovered this susceptibility. But unfortunately it is only the *symbol* that invokes the suggestibility; not everything labeled fact lives up to its label.

In order to gain in credibility rumors often masquerade as facts or cite high authority to support their cause. Many a tale begins, "My brother was talking with a man who ought to know . . . ," "The chief of police himself was saying . . . ," or "I have it on highest authority. . . ." Other devices too, such as mentioning specific cities or streets where an incident is said to have occurred, help to lend specious credibility. A concrete location for an event seems to imply that the event must, in fact, have occurred.

RUMOR AND HUMOR

SINCE every rumor is a "proposition for belief," it claims to state a fact or to describe an actual condition of affairs. But many stories that spread *like* rumors are frank products of imagination, intended to arouse not credulity but laughter. Yet they too may reflect a racial hatred, contain a political criticism, or relieve some other suppressed emotion. In the manner in which they circulate and in the function they serve, jokes and rumors are often surprisingly similar.

Here is a story that had wide currency in Europe's dictator-ridden countries. A citizen was walking beside a deep river when he suddenly heard the anguished cry of a drowning man. Jumping into the water, he safely fetched the man ashore. The rescued person proudly announced his identity. "I am Mussolini (Hitler, Stalin, depending on the country in which the story was told). You have saved my life. Ask anything you wish in return and it shall be yours." "I make only one request," replied the rescuer. "Do not tell anyone that it was I who saved you." Not a rumor—perhaps not too good a joke—yet men and women were sent into Siberian exile, German concentration camps, and Italian penal colonies for having told this story within earshot of an informer (Lyons, 1935).

The example illustrates the psychological affinity between humor and rumor. Both may serve as vehicles for the expression of private feelings, without the teller explicitly acknowledging the existence of these feelings. A person obsessed by sex will not admit this fact openly, perhaps not even to himself, but may break forth at the slightest provocation with pornographic jokes or gossip. (Some individuals incline more to jokes and others to scandal.)

When humor contains a distinct bite, as it does in the dictator story, it is technically called "tendency wit." Instead of saying, "I hate Negroes," people may tell jokes disparaging to the colored race. Others, to be sure, may thoughtlessly repeat the stories without themselves feeling, even unconsciously, the tendencious intent. But most jokes that disparage, ridicule, or humiliate their victim are in the long run sustained, just as rumors are sustained, by their value as emotional catharsis.

It is especially difficult to draw a line between hostility rumors that are wittily cast and tendencious anecdotes that are merely humorous. Their functional significance is almost identical, and both can be equally unfair and injurious to their victims. Such difference as exists lies entirely in the extent to which the tale is assumed to rest on verifiable evidence.

RUMORS AND RIOTS

WITHIN the social organism the bacilli of rumor are always active. Sometimes they move sluggishly in a nonvirulent fashion. Sometimes they burst into a fever of violent activity. The fever, unfortunately, burns most dangerously when the health of the social organism is least able to withstand its ravages. Wars, riots, epidemics, disasters, all damaging enough in themselves, become still more disastrous when the complications of rumor are added.

Internecine strife illustrates the close dependence of riot conditions upon rumor. In no case can we claim that hearsay is the sole or original cause of a riot, yet it seems always to play an important ancillary role. In fact, the evidence at hand is so convincing that we may advance it as a law of social psychology that *no riot ever occurs without rumors to incite, accompany, and intensify the violence.* Ordinarily four stages in the process are discernible.

1. For a period of time before an outbreak there are murmurs of unrest. These murmurs may take the form of stories featuring discrimination, insults, or misdeeds ascribed by

each group to its opponent. At this stage the rumors current do not differ from the usual run of hostile and accusatory stories. They sound like everyday gossip concerning the undesirable behavior of Negroes or Jews, or of employer greed or police brutality. But whenever the normal circulation is exceeded, or whenever the viciousness of the stories grows more acute, we may suspect a pre-riot condition. In themselves these tales will not lead to violence. They serve merely as a barometer of increasing social strain, indicating that unless the social wind shifts its direction, we may be headed for a storm. In the troubled summer of 1943, during which there were several race riots and near riots, the record shows a preceding period of intensified rumor spreading (Weckler and Hall, 1944).

2. Danger is indicated when the rumors assume a specifically threatening form. "Something is going to happen tonight by the river." "Be sure to come to the ball park after the game to see the fun." "They're going to catch that nigger tonight and whale the life out of him." Sometimes the stories may ascribe impending violence to the opposing camp: "The bastards have been saving up guns for a month." In the course of the Detroit disturbances in the early summer of 1943 it was rumored that carloads of armed Negroes were heading for Detroit from Chicago. This ominous message was even broadcast irresponsibly over the radio (Lee and Humphrey, 1943, p. 38). Inevitably it increased the prevailing panic.

It is at this stage when riotous outbursts are overtly predicted and threatened that the police should form their lines in order to prevent the threat from materializing. The time to prevent a riot is before it starts. One instance of excellent preventive policing occurred in Washington during the same disturbed summer of 1943. Rumor had it that large numbers

RUMORS AND RIOTS

of Negroes were planning an organized uprising, and that the occasion would be a Negro parade scheduled for a certain day. Such a rumor was calculated to bring out an opposing army of hostile whites. By taking a firm public stand in advance of the occasion, and providing adequate protection to the Negro marchers, the police of Washington were able to forestall the threatened clash (Weckler and Hall, 1944).

3. Often, though not invariably, the spark that ignites the powder keg is itself an inflammatory rumor. The serious Harlem riot in August, 1943, followed immediately upon rumored versions of an incident between a Negro soldier and a white policeman in a Harlem hotel lobby. In the altercation the policeman was wounded and the soldier sustained a shoulder injury. But rumor had it that the Negro soldier had been shot in the back and killed. Within a few minutes angry crowds gathered in front of the hotel, at the police station, and at the hospital to which the injured man had been taken. The mobs, hot and bored, long burdened with racial injustice, poverty, and overcrowding, went into action. Innumerable stores were looted and millions of dollars' worth of property destroyed. It should be noted that although a racial incident touched off the mobbish behavior, the resulting frenzy did not constitute a race riot. The depredations committed by Negroes were chiefly against Negro property. The violence seemed aimless and opportunistic, engendered of long-standing, insupportable frustration. The incident shows how planless and pointless mob violence may be when once it starts.

By contrast, the Detroit outbreak, more costly in casualties, was definitely a race riot. Its immediate occasion, following a long period of social strain (whose severity could have been gauged and combated had the pre-riot rumors been heeded) lay in wildly distorted versions of an incident on the Belle Isle beach. It was a hot summer Sunday afternoon—the time, we note in passing, when most riots break out. The precipitating incident as reported in the newspapers was a fist fight between a Negro and a white man. The incident was bruited with exaggeration up and down the beach and into the city itself. Its versions followed the assimilative predilections of each rumor agent, some being tailor-made for white ears, others for black ears. One version asserted that a Negro baby had been thrown from the bridge by white sailors; another that a white baby had been thrown from the bridge by Negroes. A white woman had been attacked on the bridge by colored men; white sailors had insulted colored girls; white girls had been accosted by Negroes while swimming (Lee and Humphrey, 1943). The sex motif, for reasons we have previously given, was bound to come in.

4. During the heat of a riot rumors fly faster than ever, but in this frantic period their character reflects acute fanaticism. Sometimes they are hallucinatory. Tortures, rapes, murders are recounted in a frenzied manner as if to justify the violence under way and to speed up the process of vengeance. Lee and Humphrey tell how at the peak of excitement the police in Detroit were flooded with calls reporting alleged incidents. One woman phoned that she had witnessed with her "own eyes" the killing of a white man by a mob of Negroes. When a squad car was dispatched to the scene of the reported crime, the police found a group of girls playing hopscotch and no evidence of violence. The fact that the caller claimed to have been an eyewitness suggests that rumor may, under extreme conditions of stress and excitement, be an outright pathological phenomenon.

Commenting on this point, Leighton writes: [13]

Psychiatrists observing patients who are emotionally unwell have long known that when they go into a state of panic they misinterpret ordinary events as horrible threats. The whistle of a distant train becomes a death scream, or two people seen talking together are instantly assumed to be plotting. More than this, it has been seen that patients in a panic can become hallucinated and see people coming to attack them who are not there at all, or may smell smoke and gas where none exists. It is more than probable that this happens to otherwise normal individuals when in a state of intense fear. . . .

In his own experience with Japanese-American evacuees from the West Coast, Leighton came into contact with many such hallucinatory rumors. During a strike at the resettlement center at Poston, Arizona, agitated demonstrators saw nonexisting machine guns and their crews. They saw imaginary hearses carrying away bodies at night. They believed that residents of the community were dying like flies because of heat, bad food, and inadequate medical attention. Babies were represented as perishing in overheated nurseries. Such tales are typical of the fourth stage of rumor in a situation of mob strife.

When rumors have reached stages 3 and 4 there is virtually nothing that the police or level-headed community leaders can do to stop them. It is the violence itself that must be checked, the wild stories being merely its verbal obbligato. But in stages 1 and 2 rumors may serve as a dependable warning to alert law-enforcement agencies, who without delay can and should take decisive steps toward controlling a disturbed population that is rapidly reaching a pitch of excitement and hostility where it can no longer control itself.

[13] Reprinted by permission from A. H. Leighton's *The Governing of Men* (Princeton University Press, 1945), p. 268.

If cast into a somewhat lower key this story of rumors and riots can be applied to many forms of social administration. In a business firm, in a factory, in a school, a prison, on shipboard—almost anywhere that people live together—rumors are an index of their state of mind. Tales of hostility directed against a subgroup indicate low morale within the unit. As these tales become more numerous, and especially as they acquire the element of threat or overtly forecast trouble, the administrator has fair warning of serious tension in his unit. Now is the time for him to take action.

SUMMARY

THROUGH the various sections of this chapter it has become increasingly apparent that rumor is woven deep into the fabric of society. Much of history, we have pointed out, has been determined by people's reactions to hearsay, and many of their beliefs are the product of age-old legends and myths.

The deceptive quality of rumor lies in the fact that although it is evaluative and incitive in significance, it usually masquerades as the provider of objective information. In reality its hidden expressive functions are more important than its alleged informative functions.

Attempting to classify rumors we discover that their elusiveness comes in part from the complex fusion of passions and antipathies that underlie them. Their functional significance in social life can be gauged only by probing into the deeper layers of personality and into the economy of the individual mental life. Certain large publics are susceptible to particular classes of hearsay. These rumor chains depend upon the suggestibility of the individuals who compose them. Whenever the excitement is intense, more and

SUMMARY

more people become involved in the chain. Wars, riots, elections tend to breed the sly type of rumor mongering known as whispering campaigns. In recent years we have learned what a close relationship exists between rumors and riots. It is certain that in order to control the latter, it is necessary to heed the former.

Since people do not ordinarily recognize a rumor when they encounter one, and since they are seldom deterred from believing it simply because it is clearly labeled, we are forced to conclude that the public is not adequately rumor conscious. It has built up little or no immunity.

The importance of hearsay in society cannot be expected to diminish unless several improbable conditions are met. News dissemination would have to become still more accurate and succeed better than it does in penetrating the minds of those it reaches. People who grope for an interpretation of the world they live in would have to find more satisfying explanations than they have now. There would have to be fewer passions of hate, fear, and wish to be justified and relieved in fantasy. Finally, a method would have to be found for remedying the distortion dynamics that afflict all retention and recall, however accurately intentioned the reporter may be.

Since these conditions are unlikely to be realized in the foreseeable future, about all the individual can do to acquire rumor immunity for himself is to become as familiar as possible with the psychological and social aspects of the phenomenon, and through continuous practice increase his skill in recognizing and in analyzing the daily installments of hearsay that reach his well-buffeted ears.

10 THE ANALYSIS OF RUMOR

In order to develop skill in rumor analysis one needs first familiarity with the principles set forth in the preceding chapters and secondly practice in applying them. It goes without saying that one requires likewise a wholesome (but not obsessive) degree of suspiciousness regarding messages that come to one's ears and eyes, as well as a disposition to check the messages against one's own relevant past experience, and wherever possible, against objective standards of evidence.

In the present chapter we invite the reader to examine selected samples of rumor discourse. The fact that some of the samples seem out-of-date is itself a demonstration of the *ephemeral* quality of rumor. "Propositions for belief" are likely to be short-lived simply because the panorama of human interest changes rapidly. Much may be learned, however, from a study of standard examples drawn from varied social atmospheres, even if some of them are dated.

The analysis of any given tale cannot be as perfect as we should like for the reason that the precise psychological and social conditions under which a rumor is told are known only in part and often through inference alone. Further, no single story can be expected to illustrate all the principles of rumor, although the basic formula should be detectable in every case. If the basic formula does not apply, we must conclude that the specimen under consideration is not, properly speaking, a rumor, or else that the formula itself is faulty. In fact, the validity of all of the principles presented in earlier chapters is testable by their success in explaining concrete examples of rumor. Should any of the principles presented be found persistently irrelevant or inept they should be discarded or revised.

To the examples that follow we append analytical comments, although we cannot in every case be certain that all comments are equally appropriate. A liberal amount of speculation must be allowed in an exercise of this order.

After the reader has followed our comments on the first two or three cases, he should try by himself to make the analysis before reading the authors' suggestions. At the end of the chapter he will find a series of unanalyzed cases which may serve as "originals" for his own solution.

CASE 1

The first example is drawn from Joel Sayre's "Berlin Letter," published in the *New Yorker* during the disturbed occupation period in the summer of 1946.[1]

The story of the blind man in the Knesebeckstrasse gives some idea of how Berliners' minds are working. Late one afternoon, a young woman was on her way home from her office when, on the Knesebeckstrasse, a residential street in a badly bombed neighborhood, a blind man bumped into her while she was waiting for a traffic light. He was a tall, gaunt, middle-aged man, wearing black spectacles, an old sweater, and plus-fours that reached almost to his ankles, and he was feeling his way with a cane. In his other hand, he was carrying a letter. On one arm was the yellow brassard, marked with a pyramid of three black balls, which all blind or deaf Germans are supposed to wear on the street. The blind man apologized for bumping into the woman. She told him that it was nothing and asked if she could be of any assistance. He said that, as a matter of fact, she could, and he handed her the letter and asked her to direct him to the address on the envelope. The letter was ad-

[1] Issue of July 20, 1946, pp. 41 f. Reprinted by permission of the author and of the *New Yorker*.

dressed to someone living quite a distance down the Knesebeckstrasse, and the woman told the man that he had many blocks to travel. "*Ach, Gott,* I've walked so far today!" he said. "Could you possibly deliver it for me?" She told him that she'd be glad to; she'd be passing the address on her way home anyhow, so it would be no trouble at all. The blind man thanked her warmly, the two said *auf Wiedersehen,* and he tapped off down the street, in the direction she had come from. She had gone twenty or thirty yards when she happened to glance back to see if the blind man was making out all right. He was indeed making out all right: he was walking rapidly along the sidewalk with his cane under his arm. There was no mistaking those long plus-fours. Instead of delivering the letter, the woman took it to a police station and told how it had come into her possession. The police went to the apartment the envelope was addressed to and found there two men and a woman and a quantity of meat that, upon inspection, was declared by a doctor to be human flesh. The letter in the envelope consisted of a single sentence: "This is the last one I am sending you today."

Comment. The reporter who offers this tasty morsel appends his own analysis:

This story is pure myth. Yet all the Germans I know in Berlin, as well as a number of others I have questioned, have heard it, and ninety-five percent of them have believed it. Quite frequently, some man I've discussed the story with has given me a hint, a sort of mustache-twirling implication, that he was personally acquainted with the young woman who so narrowly escaped being sold by the pound. Plump, she has been described to me as being; plump but exceedingly pretty. For quite a while, I found almost no Berliner who doubted the blind-man story. There are two reasons for this. First, it's hard to imagine anything so outré that it couldn't happen in Berlin these days, and, secondly, most Berliners over thirty can remember a historical precedent. In 1925, Fritz Haarmann, or the Hanover Ogre, as he was known all over Europe, was executed for doing in two dozen male adolescents and selling choice cuts of them to the public. He also confessed to the processing and distribution of several dozen more youths not even mentioned in the testimony—thirty or forty, he couldn't be sure. Almost the entire population of Hanover went on a vegetarian diet for several years afterward, I'm told.

THE ANALYSIS OF RUMOR

The reporter makes two excellent points, undoubtedly the two most important for explaining this particular gruesome tale.

1. The story reflects primarily the violent disruption of the economic and moral life of Berlin, brought about through a series of unprecedented catastrophes: bestial persecutions, bombings, starvation, defeat. The wilder the social disruption, the wilder the rumors—"it's hard to imagine anything so outré that it couldn't happen in Berlin these days." People are profoundly suggestible because their mental life is completely "unstuck." If some unbelievable things happen, why not others?

2. The factor of *assimilation* looms large. The population is continually preoccupied with food; likewise with physical safety. The cheapening of life, gruesome dealings with human bodies (in concentration camps and in bombings) form an additional part of the immediate apperceptive mass. This general sanguinary background of interest is reinforced through a more specifically cannibalistic memory of the Ogre of Hanover. This particular bit of macabre history is the one "kernel of truth" that appears in the entire situation, but it resides not in the incident which is the "proposition for belief" (and widely believed) but in the apperceptive context to which the story is assimilated. What has happened is that current and past events have become *condensed* and *contemporized*.

In addition to these two major principles of hearsay, the Berlin tale illustrates others:

3. It is obvious that the basic rumor formula applies. Food and safety are matters of utmost *importance* to the distressed population, and the disrupted communications of the town together with the breakdown of its established

moral codes creates a situation of maximum *ambiguity,* where "anything might happen."

4. The story serves the psychological function of explaining and relieving the current emotions of anxiety over the quality of food and the safety of human life. These two anxieties become *fused* for the time being in the listener's mind. The tale justifies one's apprehensiveness, and, when shared, brings others into the circle of sympathy and suffering.

5. For all its mythical nature the story has *good continuation* and a pseudo-logicality to assist the listener and teller in their "effort after meaning." The victim of the butchering racket is described as plump; her kindness to the "blind" villain and his fictitious affliction provide motive and pathos. Longer than most rumors in the telling, this one is dramatically sharpened, and fortified with much concrete and circumstantial detail which, although it seems elaborate, is well assimilated to the principal theme.

6. According to the reporter this hearsay is exceedingly widespread and almost universally believed. It is not restricted to a limited rumor public. The prevalence of anxiety and food interest in the city make it a rumor coin good for universal circulation, for in respect to the underlying interests the entire population is homogeneous.

7. The excessive morbidity of this story gives it a special emotional appeal. It would not, however, circulate in a safer social atmosphere, where there was less hunger or less fear. Morbidity is an interest fed by the deepest of all human anxieties—fear of pain and death, omnipresent mysteries. Whenever melancholy social conditions prevail, morbid stories are one of the dependable subjects of gossip. Through them somber emotions are relieved, justified, explained.

Case 2

Immediately after the San Francisco earthquake, April 18, 1906, the wildest rumors were afloat in the city. Four of these as recounted by Jo Chamberlain in the Baltimore *Sunday Sun* (March 31, 1946) follow:

a. That a tidal wave had engulfed New York City at the same time as the San Francisco quake
b. That Chicago had slid into Lake Michigan
c. That the quake had loosed the animals in the zoo, and that these were eating the refugees in Golden Gate Park
d. That men were found with women's fingers in their pockets, not having had time to take the rings off. In these stories the ghouls were always strung up to the nearest lamp post.

Comment. The suspicious reader may wonder whether rumors recounted forty years after their circulation may not have suffered considerable additional sharpening and other distortion in the interim. An example, perhaps, might be the word "always" in rumor d. It would certainly be difficult to prove that this ghoulish story *invariably* was accompanied by the denouement of summary justice. It is true, however, that the rumors circulating after the catastrophe were recorded at the time and we may assume, for purposes of our analysis, that they did not differ greatly from those listed above.

1. One obvious principle illustrated in this series is the *fecundity of rumor.* Prodigious *importance* and vast *ambiguity* conspired in the manufacture of one wild story after another, many of which were merely slight variations of others. The chain of associations is simple: one big city has been destroyed, why not others? The fecundity makes for *sharpening* through a *multiplication* of catastrophes.

2. The disturbed population is trying to gauge the im-

portance of the event as one phase of its *effort after meaning*. Rumors succeeded in the almost impossible task of exaggerating the effects of the catastrophe. Yet from an *appraisive* point of view they express fairly accurately the private significance of the event. Metaphorically they were saying "things just couldn't be more horrible." Having lost home and perhaps loved ones, they underlined their feelings of anxiety and desolation by adding the ravages of wild beasts, or ghouls, and the destruction of an additional metropolis or two. Through these embellishments the sense of total disaster is metaphorically conveyed.

3. In their effort after meaning people also drew many inferences, some plausible. Among the more reasonable of the inferences is the possibility that the quake might have liberated animals from the zoo (rumor *c*). Whether there was a kernel of truth in this statement we do not now know, but even if shattered cages permitted *some* animals to escape, it is likely that in the telling many qualifying phrases were *leveled* out. The extent of the stampede was sharpened, and it seems probable that *condensation* brings in the gruesome fate of the refugees. Animals were in Golden Gate Park; refugees were in Golden Gate Park. The latter are "condensed" into the maws of the former. Imagination (in rumors as in dreams) often unifies separate events, drawing simplicity out of multiplicity and a specious order out of confusion.

4. The hanging of the ghouls (rumor *d*) represents a *moralized closure* and a fantasied revenge. The vast frustrations engendered by the catastrophe had no personal cause. The despoiler of the dead was the only accessible scapegoat in a cataclysm brought on by an act of God.

5. Panic rumors such as these correspond to the fourth stage of riot rumors. Nothing is too wild to be believed pro-

THE ANALYSIS OF RUMOR 207

vided it somehow explains or relieves the current excitement. But unlike riot rumors the tales nourished by panic do not have preceding stages of build-up, unless, of course, the panic itself is a gradual development—a rather unusual situation.

6. As in the case of the Berlin rumor there is no evidence here for rumor chains. The catastrophe forged so complete a unity of interest that we can well imagine a survivor telling these stories to a complete stranger. We cannot, however, imagine citizens of New York or of Chicago believing the tales of destruction of their own cities. Dwellers in each metropolis had their own secure standards of evidence making such tales impossible. It is doubtful too that the press published any of the rumors that could be so readily checked. Yet many of the *unverifiable* stories were published on hearsay evidence alone and were believed widely throughout the country until the quake was no longer a subject of topical interest.

7. One can easily imagine *prestige* accruing to the teller of such horror stories. The whole nation was in a state of agitation and eager for news of any kind. As soon as the outlines of the catastrophe became known, details to fill in the picture were greedily grasped, and a neighbor who supplied latest bits of "news" was welcomed and eagerly listened to.

Case 3

In Great Britain after World War I a story was told concerning an Englishman bathing in the Channel. He wore a bathing suit lent him by an American. The upper part of the suit bore the embroidered legend, "America Won the War." A friend on the beach said to the Englishman, "You had better watch out for sharks." The Englishman replied, pointing to the words on his suit, "Oh, I'm not afraid; no shark would swallow that stuff."

In America during World War II the story was told of an American about to take a swim at Miami Beach. His suit had been lent to him by an Englishman. Warned against sharks he replied, "Don't worry; no shark would swallow that stuff," and pointed to the legend on his suit which read, "There'll always be an England."

Comment. Here we have (no pun intended) what Bysow calls a *diving* rumor (p. 171). In this case the story dove under the Atlantic and emerged on a different continent a generation after its first period of currency. In the course of its travels it reversed the direction of its "tendency wit," and substituted one victim of its jibe for another.

1. All diving rumors depend for their successive periods of popularity upon the recurrence of comparable psychological conditions. The conditions in both wars were closely similar. Bound together as allies, it was inevitable for British and Americans to be thrown together on many occasions. Even individuals who were unfriendly toward one another, nourishing perhaps a strong prejudice against each other's nation, were compelled to engage in mutual activities. The lending of the bathing suit reflects the closeness of the contacts—and betokens a degree of mutuality and friendliness that the point of the rumor itself denies. One of the quaint characteristics of this story is its reflection of this ambivalence of both intimate and hostile relationships between the two allied nations.

2. Basically the story is of the hostility type, though the animus is not particularly acute. The emotion expressed is not hatred of the other fellow so much as scorn for his smugness and a feeling of rivalry. Unlike most rumors this

THE ANALYSIS OF RUMOR

one contains wit (if of a slightly trite variety). Indeed, were it not for its *tendency wit* one wonders whether it would survive at all, because the degree of importance is relatively slight to most tellers. Few Americans or British feel strongly enough about the eccentricities of the other to spread wholly hostile rumors. This one merges into a joke and its viability depends at least partly upon the desire to provoke a laugh through the humorous incongruity involved in the pun on the word "swallow." It is the sort of chatter that we use to fill in awkward conversational gaps. Serious and whole-hearted rumors against Britain are more likely to deal in a sinister fashion with her imperialistic plots and with her ability to "play America for a sucker." Such completely hostile stories would circulate, of course, only among the part of the American population that has an appreciable anti-British bias.

3. So prominent is the joke aspect of this story that we find ourselves on the borderline of rumor. The alert reader may point out that the example does not fit our definition of a "proposition for belief." The listener is expected to laugh, not believe. The reader is right. Between rumor and humor there is no sharp line of demarcation, though the latter tends to deal frankly in make-believe, whereas the former tends toward seriousness. Yet in this case, as in many others, make-believe expresses true hostility under the guise of amusement. The narrator is saying in an appraisive-poetic fashion, "What fools the smug Americans (British) are!" Though, strictly speaking, the story is not truly a rumor, in so many respects it behaves like one that it merits inclusion in our gallery.

4. *Assimilation* to the current scene is clearly illustrated. What happened after World War I at a bathing resort on

the English Channel has no interest for the public. Hence the venerable story is given a modern setting and thus *contemporized*.

CASE 4

Rumor is no respecter of learning. Even cold science comes in for its share of distortion and falsification, as Dr. G. G. Simpson of the American Museum of Natural History regretfully discovered. Here is a report of his experience as he tells it in a brief article entitled "The Case History of a Scientific News Story" published in *Science* (see Simpson, 1940). We have somewhat condensed this account.[2]

On August 21, 1937, the United States National Museum published a bulletin written by me and entitled "The Fort Union of the Crazy Mountain Field, Montana, and Its Mammalian Faunas." Highly technical in character, this publication of 287 pages described the geology and paleontology of Middle and Upper Paleocene strata in central Montana. As is their custom, the officials of that museum released to the press a nontechnical résumé of this publication. It was a rigidly correct and yet easily comprehensible summary, carefully avoiding any sensational claim or misstatement. Less than one-fourth of this version refers to the oldest known primates included in the faunas described in the bulletin. The bulletin and the original release emphasized that these are not in a direct line of modern primates or man, but that they are very ancient representatives of the same broad group of mammals. They also pointed out that it was not I who discovered these ancient primates. A clipping service sent in versions of this story as it appeared in ninety-three different papers from Maine to California.

Even in the reprints of the whole release a few errors crept in. Among them a statement that the fossils in question are seventy million years old, a considerable exaggeration. The headlines were innocuous, although the Butte, Montana, *Standard* spread across three columns, "Montana's Crazy Mountains Listed as Cradle of Animal Life to which Man Belongs," which escapes falsity largely by being nonsensical.

The Associated Press used the release as a basis for a rewritten and much modified dispatch that appeared in thirty-four papers. The tone of this is set by its first

[2] Reprinted by permission of the author.

sentence: "Man instead of having descended from the monkey probably ascended from a four-inch-long tree-dwelling animal which was the ancient grand-daddy of all mammals on the earth today." It went on to suggest that I held that man might have originated in the western United States rather than in Asia. The headline writers outdid themselves on this version of the story:

MONKEY FATHER OF MAN? NOPE, A MOUSE—Sacramento, Calif., *Union*.

FOUR-INCH TREE ANIMAL SEEN AS MAN'S ANCESTOR —Shreveport, La., *Times*.

STUDY OF MAMMALS BRINGS ABOUT NEW EVOLUTION THEORY—Newport News, Va., *Press*.

Incidentally the recurrent theme of rats and mice in these various versions is the result of saying that some of these early mammals were as small as rats and mice. Of course, they were not rats or mice, nor was such a statement made in the original release.

Only four papers seem to have written their own unsyndicated accounts. Two of them, like several that used accredited press services, have me discovering the missing link.

This furor died down in October, 1937, and I sighed in relief and set about trying to live down the newspapers' ideas of what I had said. Then, on April 18, 1938, the Gloversville, N. Y., *Leader* published an account of the Mohawk Valley Kennel Club's show in the course of which they gave me (under a wrong but all too recognizable name) as authority for the existence seventy million years ago in Montana of dogs as large as Kodiak bears. Then another town had a dog show and this time it appeared that I had not only discovered such dogs but had described sixty different species of them. This is appalling fertility of imagination, for the original release contained no mention whatever of the discovery of dogs whether as large as Kodiak bears or as small as mice. Dog fanciers and newspaper exchanges being what they are, I subsequently enjoyed another period of fame—this time as the discoverer of the great seventy-million-year-old Kodiak bear-dogs which no more existed and which are no more my invention than the rats ancestral to man.

Out of nearly one hundred papers whose stories finally came back to me, about one-tenth had reports that were neither seriously wrong scientifically nor obnoxious to me personally. In view of the great need for popular presentation of the results of research, this is a serious matter despite its humorous side. It is fairly typical of what still happens to scientific news, and it has a moral, in fact several of them, that will be obvious to the reader.

Comment. (1) The first striking aspect of this "scientific" rumor is the fact that the distortion occurs wholly in print. It is a newspaper rumor and illustrates various aspects of the kinship between word-of-mouth and press distortion discussed on pages 186-189.

2. In applying the rumor formula we note that ambiguity is inherent in the subject matter. Even to a specialist the problem of man's descent is still far from settled; to the layman the facts are even more ambiguous, and he has no standards by which to separate the evidential wheat from the speculative chaff. Though the problem is not personally important, it is certainly one of perennial interest. The essential lack of genuine "importance" in the original news release furnishes one clue to the type of distortion that occurred. The original news release had nothing whatever to do with man's descent, but in order to make the story appear newsworthy the reporters and headline editors had to tie it in with this one and only topic of related interest. News value, like rumor value, requires a report to fit *some* interest system of the individual. Distortion inevitably resulted from the effort to force the objective facts into a mold of preestablished interest. The author was made to say something that could be assimilated to the *expectancy* of the reader, the descent of man being the one and only intelligible subject in the vast field of paleontology which to the reader was of potential interest.

3. It is inevitable that in popular accounts of scientific research the dry-as-dust listing of safeguards and qualifica-

THE ANALYSIS OF RUMOR 213

tions will be *leveled* out. Statements of caution, contingent propositions, limitations of the research, are pared away. What is wanted is the nub of contribution without pedantry. A good example of leveling occurs in the statement that rats and mice were the ancestors of man. The original statement read that the primates in question (not claimed to be man's ancestors) were "as small as" rats and mice. The simile was leveled out.

4. *Sharpening* is obvious. The age of primates, considerable enough when conservatively estimated, is blown up to seventy million years. The remote kinship among mammals is sharpened so that the small vertebrates are made to appear as the direct ancestors of man; and the tree of evolution is planted squarely in Montana, on good American soil.

5. *Assimilation* appears in many forms. The linguistic cliché, "the missing link," was bound to find its way into a story having some remote bearing on evolution. Assimilation to expectancy, to language habits, to interest are well illustrated. Dog fanciers assimilated the whole story to the genealogical self-interest of canines. This particular redaction is sharpened by *multiplication* so that reports speak of "sixty species" of such imaginary pre-dog families. Sharpening of *size* occurs in the *importation* "as large as Kodiak bears." Leveling again plays upon the simile, and we find that the outsized imaginary dogs have become "Kodiak beardogs."

6. The introduction of the "missing link," "Kodiak bear," "monkey ancestry," "evolution theory"—all products of assimilation to expectancy and to verbal habit—illustrates also the *conventionalizing* tendency in rumor. Current folklore and popular phrases seem, like a lightning rod, to attract "propositions for belief" and to channel them into a limited

set of grooves. Scientific rumors, like other types of rumor, thus become grounded in familiarity.

7. The author laments that the wilder version of the story was ascribed to him "under a wrong but all too recognizable name." His plaint reminds us of the principle that proper names are especially liable to distortion. The case also illustrates the instability of statements regarding time and number.

Case 5

Our next problem, drawn from World War I, also involves the public press. We do not wish to point too many accusatory fingers at newspapers, but printed rumors are accessible to scrutiny and hence especially suitable for analysis.

A fascinating instance of snowballing in a series of newspaper reports was uncovered by Ponsonby and published by him in *Falsehood in Wartime*.[8] It is rare to be able to spot successive stages in the transformation of rumors in this manner. The accounts, taken from the European press, deal with the fall of Antwerp to the German Army in November, 1914.

> When the fall of Antwerp became known, the church bells were rung [meaning in Germany]. *Kölnische Zeitung*

> According to the *Kölnische Zeitung*, the clergy of Antwerp were compelled to ring the church bells when the fortress was taken. *Le Matin*.

> According to what *Le Matin* has heard from Cologne, the Belgian priests who refused to ring the church bells

[8] Copyright 1928, by E. P. Dutton & Co., Inc. Reprinted by permission.

THE ANALYSIS OF RUMOR 215

when Antwerp was taken have been driven away from their positions. *The Times*

According to what *The Times* has heard from Cologne via Paris, the unfortunate priests who refused to ring the church bells when Antwerp was taken have been sentenced to hard labor. *Corriere della Sera*

According to information to the *Corriere della Sera* from Cologne via London, it is confirmed that the barbaric conquerors of Antwerp punished the unfortunate Belgian priests for their heroic refusal to ring the church bells by hanging them as living clappers to the bells with their heads down. *Le Matin*

Comment. 1. Typical of most wartime *bogies,* this one arises from the essential ambiguity and emotional importance of the war situation. Its sustaining motive is *hostility* toward the enemy. (Many wartime "hate rumors," as we have noted, are directed not toward the enemy but toward local groups of fellow citizens who serve as objects of displaced aggression.) In this case hatred of Germany is nicely *justified* in the course of the rumor.

2. The kernel of original truth is the simple, verifiable fact that church bells were rung in Germany to celebrate the taking of Antwerp. But the kernel is lost through its assimilation to pre-existing hate and to the *expectancy* that the Huns will under most circumstances commit atrocities.

3. Through all the serial reproductions the church bells (a familiar *symbol*) are retained as a center of interest, and become sharpened in successive versions, finally being equipped with human clappers. *Sharpening* is illustrated also by the fact that priests are first punished by removal

from their parishes, then by hard labor, and finally by a horrible and fanciful type of capital punishment.

4. Starting with a mention of church bells, the *importation* of priests was a reasonably mechanical association due to contiguity. Thus, the operation of *cognitive* as well as *motivational* assimilation is illustrated.

5. Perhaps the most important shift in this serial reproduction occurs immediately following the original *Kölnische Zeitung* statement. The Cologne paper took it for granted that it was in *Germany* that the church bells were rung. But the French editor located them in *Belgium*. This major misstep (which invited an elaborate *rationalization* to explain why church bells should ring in a defeated city) is like the distortions that sometimes start through an innocent *verbal misunderstanding*. Once a verbal misapprehension has created a condition of ambiguity it may easily invite both nonmotivational and motivational rationalizations.

6. In stories of this type the operation of *complementary projection* is obvious. Wickedness in the Germans justifies (by complementing) the hatred we feel. The possibility of *direct projection* likewise cannot be ruled out. What the Allies would *like* to do to the Germans is not far removed in murderous inclination from what the Huns do to the Allies. But since it is, supposedly, the Huns and not the Allies who commit atrocities, there is in the situation a perfect opportunity for Allies to *evade guilt* for their own repressed sadism.

Case 6

The following story circulated during the visit of Madame Chiang Kai-shek to America in 1943. The scene of the incident is usually said to be Baltimore. One day, the story goes, a gentleman entered a jewelry store and asked for a

$500 watch. The jeweler did not carry such expensive stock, but finally managed to find several high-grade timepieces for his customer to choose from. The purchaser selected in all $7000 worth of watches and jewelry. When asked by the proprietor how they were to be paid for, the customer replied that he was Madame Chiang's secretary and requested that his purchase be charged to Chinese lend-lease.

Comment. This was typical of the World War II *wedge-driving* rumors, whose effect was to divide the United States from its allies. It was such stories that gave government officials grave concern. (Of the same stamp was the tale that the Russians were using lend-lease butter to grease their guns, and that the British were using the aid to purchase in the United States nylon stockings and other scarce and luxurious articles, thus depriving our own citizens of the coveted goods.)

1. Evidence shows that we may expect such stories to circulate only among a limited rumor public. The Madame Chiang scandal would appeal to people possessing a pre-existing grudge against China or, more probably, against the Democratic administration in Washington (cf. p. 4).

2. Like hostility rumors generally, this one is a product of *frustration,* much of the resulting aggression being *displaced.* Wartime shortages were annoying and high taxes aggravating. If short goods are going abroad and tax revenue being squandered recklessly by a prodigal administration, why should we not feel annoyed? Oh, of course, we are willing to make sacrifices for the war—but, after all, it is not the war we are complaining about, it is the scandalous inefficiency of that radical set of long-haired professors and "that man" in Washington. The rumor represents a subtle fusion of antipathies and frustrations, and serves to explain and justify our political animosities.

3. The motivation may also entail *guilt evasion*. During the wartime boom many people indulged in luxuries which they could not afford in peacetime and which were hardly compatible with the wartime emphasis upon self-sacrifice and the purchase of war bonds. But our petty extravagances could easily be forgotten and forgiven in the face of the blatant self-indulgence of one of the most prominent of wartime personages, wantonly wasting *our* national funds in the purchase of fabulous luxuries.

4. There may be an element of *assimilation* to the widely current belief in the waste and corruption of high officials in China. But this factor, if present, is minor since the victims of the animus are more apparently the American "crackpot" officials.

5. We find the use of *concreteness* to lend plausibility to the story. The precise amounts—$500 and $7000—are mentioned. The case is like that of the Berlin gossip which described in detail the clothes of the blind villain and the street on which the incident occurred. Part of the rationalizing process is to surround the item with the pseudo-authority of detail.

6. Although the locale of this story was not always given as Baltimore, yet we know that when a scene is set, the *label* conferred upon the incident (especially if the label introduces the story and thus benefits from the *primacy* effect) tends to remain unchanged (p. 96).

7. Had the story been told without introducing the name of Madame Chiang its essential function would have been unchanged. But to specify a well-known individual is a common device for *personalizing* a rumor and for *assimilating* it to common and conventional subject matter of *current* interest.

THE ANALYSIS OF RUMOR

Case 7

The war produced a rumor about rumor. At one period the story spread that the government had passed legislation penalizing all rumor mongers. According to the report, persons convicted of spreading rumors were liable to fines of $10,000 or a term in prison.

Comment. 1. Perhaps the most prominent principle at work in this mild bogy is *assimilation*. There was on the statute books a sedition act forming part of the Federal Code. This law, well publicized in wartime, provides fines not exceeding $10,000 or imprisonment for spreading of reports which might interfere with the successful prosecution of the war. (The phrase "not exceeding" was *leveled* out.) Because of the campaign for security of information and because of the prominence given to the subject of harmful gossip by the rumor clinics, the public became aware of the topic of rumor and easily assimilated the relatively innocent type of chatter everywhere current to the sedition act itself. In reality, of course, it would be only a rare and peculiarly vicious rumor monger (presumably an Axis agent) who would be prosecuted under the act.

2. But such legal distinctions were beyond the power of most people to make. The situation for them was highly *ambiguous*, for to the general population *secure standards* in the realm of jurisprudence are lacking.

3. The issue was of some *importance*, not only because of the amount of publicity given to rumor and because of the general sense of insecurity in wartime, but also because of the *guilt* which many loyal citizens undoubtedly felt due to their own minor tale-bearing. Knowing that his loose talk was not helping his country, the average rumor spreader may have been fantasying a punishment for himself. Even

in cases where the rumor did not play the part of a *relief* in this particular manner, it did *metaphorically* express the solemnity people felt about the necessity of obeying wartime restrictions. The feelings of fear, guilt, solemnity may, of course, be fused in different proportions in different individuals.

GUIDE FOR THE ANALYSIS OF RUMOR

THE reader is now invited to make his own analysis of additional cases, selected from the concluding section of this chapter if he chooses, or from his own daily intake of rumor, if he prefers. In undertaking his analysis he may find the following guiding questions helpful. Without exception they are based on the principles presented in earlier chapters. Needless to say, not all the questions are applicable to all samples of rumor. To use them intelligently presupposes an accurate and flexible comprehension of the definitions and discussion that have gone before. Furthermore, the analyst may find that in order to interpret some fresh rumor adequately he will need to apply some psychological or sociological principle that is relevant to the case but not sufficiently common to find a place in our list.

1. Is the story a proposition for belief of topical reference?
2. Do teller and listener lack secure standards of evidence for its verification?
3. Are ambiguity and importance both present? Which factor is more prominent?
4. In what way does the rumor reflect an effort after meaning?
5. Does it offer an economical and simplified explanation of a confusing environmental or emotional situation?
6. Does it explain some inner tension?

GUIDE FOR THE ANALYSIS OF RUMOR

7. Is the tension primarily emotional or nonemotional?
8. Is the tension anxiety, hostility, wish, guilt, curiosity, or some other state of mind?
9. Does it justify the existence in the teller of an otherwise unacceptable emotion?
10. What makes the story important to the teller?
11. In what sense does the telling of the rumor confer relief?
12. What elements of rationalization are present?
13. Does it contain possibilities of projection, direct or complementary?
14. Does it resemble a daydream? If so, how?
15. May it serve the function of guilt evasion?
16. Does it reflect displaced aggression?
17. In telling it, is the teller likely to acquire prestige?
18. Might it be told to please a friend or confer a favor?
19. Might it serve as small talk?
20. Can one detect the kernel of truth from which it probably developed?
21. Is it a home-stretch rumor?
22. Might there have been errors in the initial perception?
23. What might have been the course of the creative embedding?
24. Is it likely that it contains elaboration; if so, of what type?
25. Does it probably suffer from a distortion of names, dates, numbers, time?
26. Does its label or locale persist?
27. Is there likely to have been a complete shift of theme?
28. Is there evidence of conventionalization? moralization?
29. What cultural assimilations does it seem to reflect?
30. Does it partake of the character of a legend?
31. Could it conceivably contain a reversal to truth?

32. Does it contain tendency wit?
33. Do the conditions underlying its circulation illustrate the fecundity of rumor?
34. What may have become leveled out?
35. Have oddities or perseverative wording persisted in the telling?
36. Has there been sharpening through multiplication?
37. Have movement, size, or familiar symbols played a part in the sharpening?
38. Has there been concretization or personalization?
39. What closure tendencies may be illustrated?
40. Does it deal with current events?
41. Does it contemporize past events?
42. Primarily does it seem to reflect relatively more intellectual, or relatively more emotional, assimilative tendencies?
43. Are all details assimilated to the principal theme?
44. May condensation of items have occurred?
45. Is there evidence of good-continuation?
46. In what way is assimilation to expectancy shown?
47. Is there assimilation to linguistic habits?
48. Has there been assimilation to occupational, class, racial, or other forms of self-interest?
49. Is there assimilation to prejudice?
50. Is it conceivable that any part rests on verbal misunderstanding?
51. What is the expressive (metaphorical) signification of the rumor?
52. Does it perhaps represent a fusion of passions or antipathies?
53. Does it probably travel in a rumor chain? What is its public? Why?

ORIGINALS FOR SOLUTION

54. Are people suggestible to this particular tale because their minds are "unstuck" or "overstuck"?
55. Could it be classified as a bogy, wedge-driver, pipe dream? Or as creeping, impetuous, diving?
56. Could it be part of a whispering campaign?
57. What relation, if any, does it bear to news? to the press?
58. Is the story labeled rumor or fact, or ascribed to an authoritative source? with what effect?
59. What might be the best way to refute it?
60. Does it perhaps represent any of the four stages in crisis (riot) rumor spreading?

ORIGINALS FOR SOLUTION

Case 8

Twenty-four hours before a sizable contingent of Navy men were to receive their honorable discharges from the service, a rumor spread among them that the commanding officer had announced that they must wait two weeks longer for their discharges until the ship on which they were serving had been decommissioned.

Case 9

The Russians, it is said, "nationalize their women."

Case 10

Every few years a story reappears to the effect that a sea serpent has been seen in Loch Ness, Scotland.

Case 11

In the early days of the war it was rumored that the Philippine Islands (also the Panama Canal) had been attacked by the Japanese a whole week before the Pearl Harbor assault, but that the news of this attack had been withheld from the public.

CASE 12

Before taking off on a combat mission many squadrons were plagued with rumors to the effect that their equipment was in some way defective, that the target was almost inaccessible because of antiaircraft protection, that the enemy had recently perfected a new and dreadful defense weapon that would almost certainly be employed against the squadron.

CASE 13

Workers in a New England manufacturing town during the darkest days of the depression in the 1930's believed that the rich were running over the children of the poor in their elegant cars and never caring; also that the whole depression was some sort of plot by the upper classes to cut the wages of the workers.—Cited by Leighton (1945).

CASE 14

During the Civil War opinion in the North was largely shaped by the belief that tens of thousands of Union soldiers were deliberately shot to death, as at Fort Pillow, or frozen to death, as at Belle Island, or starved to death, as at Andersonville, or sickened to death by swamp malaria, as in South Carolina.—Cited by Buck (1937).

CASE 15

In Mr. C. K. Munro's play, *At Mrs. Beam's*, a few boardinghouse gossips are curdling each other's blood by talking about Landru, the French "Bluebeard." Their prattle runs somewhat as follows:

> They say he has killed *dozens* and *dozens* of women.
> And *eaten* them!
> No. No; I hardly believe that; I doubt that.
> I understand that he *always* eats them.
> Well, at all events, he has killed *hundreds* of women.
> No, my dear. Let us be just. We must agree to be just. Not hundreds. *Thirty-nine*. That is a better figure. Yes; we can agree, I think, on thirty-nine.

BIBLIOGRAPHY

ADAMS, J. T., 1932. Our whispering campaigns (*Harper's Magazine*, 165, 444-457).

ALLPORT, F. H., and M. LEPKIN, 1945. Wartime rumors of waste and special privilege: why some people believe them (*Journal of Abnormal and Social Psychology*, 40, 3-36).

ALLPORT, G. W., 1930. Change and decay in the visual memory image (*British Journal of Psychology*, 21, 133-148).

ALLPORT, G. W., and J. M. FADEN, 1940. The psychology of newspapers: five tentative laws (*Public Opinion Quarterly*, 4, 678-703).

ALLPORT, G. W., and L. POSTMAN, 1945. The basic psychology of rumor (*Transactions of The New York Academy of Sciences*, Series II, 8, 61-81).

BARTLETT, F. C., 1932. *Remembering* (Cambridge: Cambridge University Press).

BARTLETT, F. C., 1940. *Political Propaganda* (Cambridge: Cambridge University Press).

BINET, A., 1900. *La suggestibilité* (Paris: Schleicher Frères).

BORST, M., 1904. Recherches experimentales sur l'éducabilité et la fidélité du témoignage (*Archives de Psychologie*, 3, 203-314).

BRITT, S. H., 1941. *Social Psychology of Modern Life* (New York: Farrar & Rinehart, Inc.).

BRUNER, J. S., 1941. The dimensions of propaganda (*Journal of Abnormal and Social Psychology*, 36, 311-337).

BRUNER, J. S., and J. SAYRE, 1941. Shortwave listening in an Italian community (*Public Opinion Quarterly*, 5, 640-656).

BUCK, P. H., 1937. *The Road to Reunion* (Boston: Little, Brown & Company).

BYSOW, D. A., 1928. Gerüchte (*Kölner Vierteljahrsschrift für Soziologie*, 7, 301-308).

CANTRIL, H., and G. W. ALLPORT, 1935. *Psychology of Radio* (New York: Harper & Brothers).

CANTRIL, H., H. GOUDET, and H. HERZOG, 1940. *The Invasion from Mars* (Princeton: Princeton University Press).

CARMICHAEL, L., H. P. HOGAN, and A. A. WALTER, 1932. An experimental study of the effect of language on the reproduction of visually perceived form (*Journal of Experimental Psychology*, 15, 73-86).

CHADWICK, T., 1932. *The Influence of Rumour on Human Thought and Action* (Manchester: Sherratt and Hughes).

CLAPARÈDE, E., 1906. Expériences sur le témoignage: témoignage simple; appréciation; confrontation (*Archives de Psychologie*, 5, 344-387).

DASHIELL, J. F., 1935. Experimental studies of the influence of social situations on the behavior of individual human adults, in C. Murchison, *Handbook of Social Psychology* (Worcester: Clark University Press).

FRENKEL-BRUNSWIK, E., and R. N. SANFORD, 1945. Some personality factors in anti-Semitism (*Journal of Psychology*, 20, 271-291).

FREYD, M., 1921. A test series for journalistic aptitude (*Journal of Applied Psychology*, 5, 46-56).

GIBSON, J. J., 1929. Reproductions of visually perceived forms (*Journal of Experimental Psychology*, 12, 1-39).

HARTGENBUSCH, H. G., 1933. Untersuchungen zur Psychologie der Wiedererzählung und des Gerüchts (*Psychologische Forschung*, 18, 251-285).

HARVARD UNIVERSITY, DEPARTMENT OF PSYCHOLOGY, 1943. *ABC's of Scapegoating* (Chicago: Central Y.M.C.A. College).

IRVING, J. A., 1943. The psychological analysis of wartime rumor patterns in Canada (*Bulletin of the Canadian Psychological Association*, 3, 40-44).

BIBLIOGRAPHY

KIRKPATRICK, C., 1932. A tentative study in experimental social psychology (*American Journal of Sociology*, **38**, 194-206).

KNAPP, R. H., 1944. A psychology of rumor (*Public Opinion Quarterly*, **8**, 23-37).

KOFFKA, K., 1935. *Principles of Gestalt Psychology* (New York: Harcourt, Brace and Company, Inc.).

LANGENHOVE, F. VAN, 1916. *The Growth of a Legend: a study based upon the German accounts of Francs-Tireurs and "atrocities" in Belgium* (New York: The Knickerbocker Press).

LAPIERE, R. T., and P. R. FARNSWORTH, 1936. *Social Psychology* (New York: McGraw-Hill Book Company, Inc.).

LAZARSFELD, P. F., B. BERELSON, and H. GOUDET, 1944. *The People's Choice* (New York: Duell, Sloan and Pearce, Inc.).

LEE, A. M., and N. D. HUMPHREY, 1943. *Race Riot* (New York: Dryden Press).

LEIGHTON, A. H., 1945. *The Governing of Men* (Princeton: Princeton University Press).

LITTELL, R., and J. J. M'CARTHY, 1936. Whispers for sale (*Harper's Magazine*, **172**, 364-372).

LYONS, E., 1935. Stifled laughter (*Harper's Magazine*, **170**, 557-567).

M'GEOCH, J. A., 1928. The influence of sex and age upon ability to report (*American Journal of Psychology*, **40**, 458-466).

M'GREGOR, D., 1938. The major determinants of the prediction of social events (*Journal of Abnormal and Social Psychology*, **33**, 179-204).

M'LEAN, H. V., 1946. Psychodynamic factors in racial relations (*Annals of the American Academy of Political and Social Science*, **244**, 159-166).

MENNINGER, K., 1930. *The Human Mind* (New York: Alfred A. Knopf, Inc.).

MORENO, J. L., 1934. *Who Shall Survive? A new approach to the problem of human interrelations* (Washington, D. C.: Nervous and Mental Disease Publishing Co.).

MORRIS, C., 1946. *Signs, Language, and Behavior* (New York: Prentice-Hall, Inc.).

MURRAY, H. A., et al., 1938. *Explorations in Personality* (Oxford: Oxford University Press).

MYRDAL, G., 1944. *An American Dilemma* (New York: Harper & Brothers).

NEVINS, B., 1938. *Gateway to History* (New York: D. Appleton-Century Company, Inc.).

ODUM, H. W., 1943. *Race and Rumors of Race: Challenge to American crisis* (Chapel Hill: University of North Carolina Press).

OFFICE OF WAR INFORMATION, 1942. Intelligence report: *Rumors in wartime.*

PONSONBY, A., 1928. *Falsehood in Wartime* (New York: E. P. Dutton & Company, Inc.).

RUCH, F. L., and K. YOUNG, 1942. Penetration of Axis propaganda (*Journal of Applied Psychology*, 26, 448-455).

SELDES, G., 1935. *Freedom of the Press* (Indianapolis: Bobbs-Merrill Company).

SIMPSON, G. G., 1940. The case history of a scientific news story (*Science*, 92, 148-150).

SMITH, G. H., 1947. The effects of fact and rumor labels (*Journal of Abnormal and Social Psychology*, 42, 80-90).

STEFANSSON, V., 1928. *The Standardization of Error* (London: Kegan, Paul, Trubner and Co.).

STERN, W., 1902. *Zur Psychologie der Aussage* (Berlin: J. Guttentag).

STERN, W., 1938. *General Psychology from the Personalistic Standpoint* (New York: The Macmillan Company).

TAYLOR, E., 1940. *Strategy of Terror* (Boston: Houghton Mifflin Company).

WECKLER, J. E., and T. E. HALL, 1944. *The Police and Minority Groups* (Chicago: The International City Managers' Association).

WHIPPLE, G. M., 1909. The observer as reporter: a survey of the 'psychology of testimony' (*Psychological Bulletin*, **6**, 153-170).

WULF, F., 1922. Über die Veränderung von Vorstellungen (*Psychologische Forschung*, **1**, 333-373).

YOUNG, K., 1936. *Social Psychology* (New York, F. S. Crofts & Company).

ZERNER, E. H., 1946. Rumors in Paris newspapers. (*Public Opinion Quarterly*, **10**, 382-391).

APPENDIX

STANDARDS FOR AGENCIES WORKING ON THE PREVENTION AND CONTROL OF WARTIME RUMOR

(Devised and circulated by the Massachusetts Committee on Public Safety in cooperation with the Boston *Herald-Traveler* Rumor Clinic.)

I. *Personnel*
   1. The responsible head of this work must be an individual with maturity, good judgment, and common sense.
   2. The responsible head as well as his staff must have some knowledge of the psychology of rumor.

II. *The Advisory Board*

   It is essential that the advisory staff be competent and active. This staff should include three types of persons. Since the treatment of rumors often involves considerable delicacy of judgment, it is important that advisors be available to protect the executive against his individual blind spots and habits of thought.
   1. Technical advisors. In this group should be included psychologists or psychiatrists. A background in social psychology and abnormal psychology is essential for a full interpretation of the rumor phenomena encountered.
   2. Representative advisors. Since rumor agencies are often confronted with problems of diplomatic complexity, it

is necessary to have a wide representation of religious, labor, business, racial and cultural organizations. All appearance of partisanship must be avoided.
3. *Prestige advisors.* These persons are selected because of their prominence and influential position in the community. They lend the dignity and respectability so imperative for its successful operation. In addition they may often serve as the authorities who are quoted in the refutation of rumors. It is desirable to include in this group representatives of the local Army or Navy command, OPA, OCD, etc.

III. *Public Cooperation in Reporting Rumors*

The agency must be widely publicized as the place to which anyone may report harmful rumors. Care must be taken to reach all levels of the population.
1. Special persons may be appointed throughout the community and assigned the task of noting and reporting all rumors which come to their attention. To facilitate their operation a questionnaire may be sent them every two weeks. In addition to serving as a listening network, this group, if properly selected, can be used as a public opinion panel.
2. Citizens should be encouraged to report by mail all rumors coming to their attention. All letters should be courteously acknowledged.
3. Every precaution should be taken to assure the confidence of the public in the high intentions and sincerity of the agency.
4. The agency should never undertake the police function of reporting or reprimanding particular persons for disseminating rumors.

IV. *Checking and Refuting Rumors*

Rumors should be refuted only by competent authorities. It is most important, therefore, that the agency establish

APPENDIX

sound relations with the highest authorities of responsible public agencies (the Army, Navy, OPA, FBI, etc.). In other instances responsible community leaders may be employed to disinfect some troublesome rumor.

1. Rumors should always be referred to other agencies for refutation. No rumor clinic should answer a rumor on its own authority.
2. Refutation must be logical and factual. A single poor or inconclusive answer does great damage to the public's confidence in the entire enterprise.

    The standards of writing in a newspaper rumor clinic should be far higher than in ordinary journalism, because the readers are hypercritical of illogicality in those who are pretending to be logical, and are suspicious of those who are attempting to contradict some current common beliefs or ingrained prejudices.
3. Don't overstate the case. Many rumors have a kernel of fact. The public's confidence will be enhanced if a policy of complete candor is followed.

    Where the rumor is substantially true as well as harmful, it is best not to give it still wider circulation.
4. Don't imply that all rumors are of Nazi origin.

    It discredits confidence in the agency if the Axis origin of rumors is overemphasized. Better tell the public that a few current stories correspond to themes coming over the Axis short-wave radio, and there let the matter rest.
5. Embed the rumor in a context of negation.

    Before stating the rumor, damn it; after stating it, damn it again.
6. Do not print or otherwise publicize vicious rumors carrying striking slogans. Break up the striking phrase so that it will not be remembered. The danger is that, even though refuted, slogans and aphorisms will be retained because of their striking character.

For example, instead of saying that a rumor reports that domestics in the South are organizing Eleanor Clubs, whose motto is "Every white woman in her own kitchen by Christmas"—better say "Rumor has it that domestic servants in the South are organizing Eleanor Clubs, whose purpose is to force white women to do their own kitchen work."

7. Plenty of time should be allowed for the advisory board to read copy of the rumor clinic before it is sent to press. It takes two or three days for advisors to receive, read, and report back any criticisms they may have regarding the copy.

8. Experience shows that only about 10 percent of the rumors received merit publication. The responsible head must be prepared to deal with the remainder on an individual basis: about half will need to be referred to other organizations (OPA, Red Cross, Port Authorities) and answered on an individual basis. Others must be forwarded to the FBI or the correspondent told where an answer may be found. A few merit only wastebasket disposal. The handling of rumors is a time-consuming proposition, and should not be lightly undertaken.

9. In denying racial rumors, as a rule, do not feature the race that is being attacked. Discuss all scapegoats together (e.g., Negroes, Jews, labor organizers, capitalists, Irish, Congress, British, etc.) and show how the same malicious talk is heard about each and all of those groups.

10. A rumor clinic must never be used to advance the editorial point of view of the paper. The highest standards of objectivity must be maintained. To use this new invention to advance editorial causes would debase newspaper ethics.

11. Rumors should not be presented in a context that would

APPENDIX

make them seem to be a mere joke. The public should not regard the matter as a merely humorous entertainment.
12. Radio programs dealing with rumor should exercise the greatest caution against unwittingly furthering rather than discrediting rumors.

V. *Methods of Operation*

The agency must be prepared to fulfill various functions in the field of morale service.
1. Many problems will be brought in that require good judgment, a knowledge of community resources, and a willingness to help in the morale building of the locality.
2. The agency should be prepared to employ all or most of the following methods:
    a. *Investigating Committees.* Some rumors may be combated by appointing a committee of investigation to determine the facts. Committee's report is then released along with the rumor.
    b. *Posters and Graphic Methods.* Most posters depict rumor merely as a source of information for the enemy. The demoralizing effect of wedge-driving rumors is probably much more serious and is readily adaptable to graphic illustration.
    c. *Propaganda Literature.* Leaflets, diagrams, booklets, etc., if well written and accurate, are an effective instrument for conveying information and admonition about rumor.
    d. *Radio Programs.* Two types of radio programs are effective in combating rumors. The first of these is the "facts" programs. The basic logic of this approach is that if facts are available and complete, rumors will have no room to thrive. The second

type of program deals with rumor and gossip generally. These illustrate the ridiculousness, dangers, and menace of rumor in time of war. Considerable caution, however, must be exercised lest rumors be spread by broadcasting them over the radio. Remember: people tune in late and tune out early.

   e. Speaking Staff. Speakers appearing before all manner of organizations, discussing current rumors, and illustrating the dangers of rumor are a valuable asset to any antirumor campaign.

   f. Morale Wardens. These are people within the community whose prime duty is to report rumors. They constitute a listening network and serve as a public opinion panel.

   g. Feature Stories. This type of publicity is illustrated by the article appearing in *The Reader's Digest* of September, 1942, entitled *Boston Makes War on Rumor*. Other articles and stories could well take up the subject of wartime rumor, the relation of rumor to propaganda, etc.

   h. Films. Although the cinema is a very effective method of bringing the subject to the public, to date it has been put to very little use. *Mr. Blabbermouth*, however, is a notable example of an excellent film dealing with this subject.

VI. *Points of Attack on Rumor*

A publicity campaign attacking rumor may pursue the following lines:

1. Rumor is untrustworthy, almost always false. No sensible person relies on it.
2. Rumor may be an instrument of enemy propaganda.
3. Rumors are destructive of morale: it is unpatriotic and shameful to spread them.

APPENDIX

4. The person who spreads rumors is a foolish, malicious, or dangerous person.
5. Rumor mongering is usually a type of scapegoating, and takes the form of blaming an innocent party for one's own troubles.

INDEX

Adams, J. T., 185
Administration, hostility rumors against, 4, 12, 36, 40, 217
Allport, F. H., 4, 27, 42, 181
Allport, G. W., 75, 141 f., 187
Ambiguity
  as condition of myth, 165
  as condition of rumor, 2, 4, 8, 9, 28, 31, 33-36, 40, 43-45, 137, 162, 204, 205, 219
  as determinant of prediction, 43-45
  in news, 2, 4, 9, 33, 187
Appraisive significance, 167-169, 198 f., 206
Army rumors, 10, 11, 14, 15 f., 18-21, 31 f., 34, 40, 224
Assimilation
  cognitive processes in, 99 f., 139-144, 216
  condensation in, 103
  definition of, 100
  emotional processes in, 44, 99 f., 152-154
  expectation in, 47 f., 62 f., 103 f., 136-138, 145, 212, 215
  familiarity in, 56
  good continuation in, 102 f., 141, 204
  importations in, 101
  interest in, 58, 105-115, 117, 203
    occupational, 84-86, 108 f.

Assimilation (Cont.)
  interest in (Cont.)
    self-, 108 f., 112-115, 202
    sex-determined, 105-107
  inventions in, 119-121
  linguistic habit in, 101, 104 f., 112, 140 f., 142 f., 156 f., 213
  motivated, 105-115, 136-138, 216
  perceptual, 138-144
  prejudice in, 111 f., 174-179, 218
  principal theme in, 101 f., 137 f., 204
  protocols showing, 105, 106 f., 109, 110 f., 112 f., 114 f.
  unmotivated, 100-105
Association of ideas, 101, 137, 141
Atomic bomb rumors, 2 f., 36
Atrocity stories, 174 f., 189
Audience effect, 73 f., 120
Aussage, 49-60
Axis broadcasts, 14, 29, 30, 46, 235

Bartlett, F. C., 55-60, 83 f., 120, 135, 139 f., 143 f., 153, 154 f., 157 f., 186
Basket-case rumor, 6 f.
Binet, A., 50
Bogy rumors, 6 f., 10-14, 31, 98, 215
Borst, M., 53
Britain
  blitz rumors in, 1
  hostility rumors against, 40, 208

241

Britt, S. H., 166
Broadcasting (See Radio broadcasting)
Bruner, J. S., 30, 47
Buck, P. H., 224
Bysow, D. A., 135, 170-172, 208

Cantril, H., 181
Carmichael, L., 142 f.
Catholics, hostility rumors against, 21-23, 40, 174 f.
Chadwick, T., 159 f.
Chamberlain, J., 205
Children, testimony of, 53
Children's reports
  effect of age differences upon, 127-129
  enumerative tendency in, 123, 128-130
  leveling in, 127-129
  protocols involving, 123, 128 f., 131 f.
  racial factor in, 130-133
Claparède, E., 53
Cliché, in reporting, 52, 104 f., 112, 213 (See also Stereotype)
Closure, 37, 56, 97 f., 102
  moralized, 206
Cognitive processes, 49-59, 99 f., 139-144, 216
Committee on Propaganda Analysis (Massachusetts), 24
Concreteness of detail, 164 f., 204, 218
Condensation, 103, 155, 203, 206
  stereotypes in, 155 f.
Contemporization, 91 f., 97, 143, 203, 210
Conventionalization, 60, 97, 105, 144, 156-158, 213
  cultural, 154, 157 f.
  linguistic, 156 f.

Conversation, as medium of rumors, 46, 182 f.
Creative embedding, 145-149
Creeping rumors, 170
Curiosity rumors, 11, 37 f., 46 f.

Dashiell, J. F., 74
Daydreams, 39
Democracy, rumor in, 16
Distortion
  basic pattern of, 44, 134-158
  of perception, 44, 102, 135, 138-146
  in personality tests, 144-146
  universality of, 138-147
Diving rumors, 171 f., 208

Effort after meaning, 5, 37 f., 40, 45, 56, 97, 121, 137, 147, 206
Ego involvement, 45, 176
Elaboration
  effect of cultural differences on, 153 f.
  emotional, 153
  extent of, 56 f., 119-121, 144, 153-155
  function of, 153 f.
Eleanor Club rumors, 11, 175-177
Embedding process, 145-149
Enumeration, in reports, 121, 123, 128-130
Exaggeration, 149-153
Expectancy, 9, 47 f., 62 f., 103 f., 212, 215
Eyewitness testimony, 49-60, 135

Faden, J., 187
Falsification (See Distortion)
Familiarity, in memory, 56, 140, 143, 213
Farnsworth, P. R., 163

INDEX

Fear
  explained by rumor, 4 f., 37, 176 f., 203
  of inversion of status, 176 f.
Fear rumors, 6 f., 9, 10-16, 36 f.
Federal Bureau of Investigation, 16, 29, 235 f.
Frenkel-Brunswik, E., 42
Freyd, M., 43
Frustration, as cause of rumor, 4, 40, 217
Fusion of antipathies, 173-179, 217

Gavin, W. G., 18
Geographical orientation, 96, 124 f.
Gibson, J. J., 140 f.
Goal gradient effect, 9, 47 f., 62 f.
Good continuation, 102 f., 141, 204
Guilt evasion, 41 f., 177-179, 216, 218

Hall, T. E., 194 f.
Hallucinatory rumors, 196 f.
Hartgenbusch, H. G., 116
Hate, as motive for rumor, 10, 15, 36 f., 137, 173-179, 215
Headlines, distortion in, 186 f.
Henry, Patrick, 176
Historical rumors, 159-161, 224
Hitler, rumors concerning, 1, 8, 192
Hogan, H. P., 142 f.
Home-stretch rumors, 9, 47 f., 62 f.
Hostility rumors, 10-16, 36, 40, 98, 134-138, 173-179, 207, 208, 214, 215, 217
Humor, 191-193, 207-209
Humphrey, N. D., 194-196

Impetuous rumors, 170 f.
Importance
  as condition of legend, 163
  as condition of myth, 165

Importance (Cont.)
  as condition of rumor, 2, 4, 8, 28, 31, 33-36, 40, 43-45, 137, 203, 205, 219
  as determinant of prediction, 43-45
Importations, 101, 153 f., 216
Inflammatory rumors, 195 f.
Informative significance, 167-169, 198 f.
Insight, 35
Inventions, 101, 119-121, 153 f., 216
Irving, J. A., 172

Japan, rumors concerning, 2, 36, 223 f.
Jews
  belief in rumors, 14
  hostility rumors against, 10 f., 15 f., 21-23, 37, 40, 42, 174

Kirkpatrick, C., 66, 189 f.,
Knapp, R. H., 10-12, 24
Koffka, K., 101

Labels
  effect on rumor, 189-191
  fact, 191 f.
  perceptual, 140 f., 142 f.
  sharpening, 96, 218
Langenhove, F. van, 163, 175
LaPiere, R. T., 163
Lazarsfeld, P. F., 182 f.
Lee, A. M., 194-196
Legends
  aphoristic, 83
  biographical, 165
  elaboration of, 154
  explanatory function of, 45
  metaphorical significance of, 166-169

Legends (Cont.)
  symbolic function of, 164-169
  themes of, 163-166
Leighton, A. H., 197, 224
Lepkin, M., 4, 27, 42, 181
Leveling
  of dates, 57
  effect of audience on, 76-80
  enumerative, 121, 123
  extent of, 75 f.
  of geographical setting, 124-126
  graph of, 76
  limits of, 80 f.
  of names, 57, 83-86, 124-126, 214
  of numbers, 57
  perceptual, 138-144
  progressive, 56, 57, 75, 120, 134 f., 143 f., 153, 212 f.
  protocols showing, 77-80, 81-83, 84-86
  rate of, 75
  rote effect on, 81-83
  selective, 83-86, 134 f., 144, 212
  in slogans, 83
  of time data, 84-86, 126 f.
Linguistic habits, 101, 104 f., 112, 140 f., 142 f., 156 f., 213
Littell, R., 185
Lyons, E., 192

McCarthy, J. J., 185
McGeoch, J. A., 127
McGregor, D., 43-45
McLean, H., 179
Memory
  autonomous changes in, 101, 138 f., 141
  constructive nature of, 55-60
  emphasizing process in, 138 f., 153
  individual and social, 49, 58-60, 143 f.

Memory (Cont.)
  normalizing process in, 138 f.
  perception and, 51-60
  temporal changes in, 51-53, 100 f., 138-144
Memory traces, 100 f., 138-144
Menninger, K., 39
Metcalfe, J. C., 62 f.
Misunderstanding, verbal, 122 f., 216
Morale, 6-13
Morbidity, 204
Moreno, J. L., 182
Morris, C., 167
Motivation (See specific motivation, e.g., Fear, Hate)
Munro, C. K., 224 f.
Murray, H. A., 41
Myrdal, G., 176
Myth, 45, 164

Navy rumors, 10 f., 40, 224 f.
Nazi rumors, 28, 235
Negroes, hostility rumors against, 10 f., 21-23, 40, 175-179
Nevins, B., 166
News (See also Press rumors)
  ambiguity in, 2, 4, 9, 33, 187
  availability of, 1-3, 15, 31 f., 161 f.
  public distrust of, 4, 28, 33, 189

Occupational differences, 31 f., 84 f., 108 f., 180
Occupational interest, as rumor motive, 108 f.
Odum, H. W., 175, 177
Office of Facts and Figures, 15
Office of Price Administration rumors, 27 f., 40, 42
Office of War Information, 183 f.
  rumor policy of, 1 f., 15 f., 25 f.

INDEX

Patterson, B., 32
Peace rumors, 1 f., 8 f.
Pearl Harbor rumors, 1, 3-6, 37
Perception
  assimilative processes in, 138-144
  basic pattern of distortion in, 138-144
  closure in, 37, 56, 91 f., 102
  emotional distortion in, 44 f., 135
  good continuation in, 102 f., 141
  memory in, 51-60, 135, 138-144
  Prägnanz in, 138, 141 f.
  role of expectancy in, 103 f., 144-146
Perseveration, 154
Pipe-dream rumors, 7 f., 10-13, 31, 36
Place errors, 84-86, 124-126
Ponsonby, A., 214
Postman, L., 75
Prägnanz, 138, 141 f.
Prejudice, as rumor motive, 21-23, 111 f., 174-179, 218
Prejudice rumors, 10, 21-23, 111 f., 174-179
Press rumors, 1-3, 186-189, 206, 210-216
Prestige, as rumor motive, 46 f., 207
Primacy effect, 96, 124
Principal theme
  assimilation of, 101 f., 137 f.
  persistence of, 116-119, 148 f.
  shift in, 116-119, 152 f.
Projection
  complementary, 40, 160, 216
  in daydreams, 39
  definition of, 38
  direct, 41 f., 216
  in dreams, 38
  limitations of, 44 f.

Projection (Cont.)
  in rumor, 39-43
  examples of, 39 f.
Projective techniques, 45, 145 f.
Propaganda, 14, 28, 29-31
Propaganda analysis, organizations for, 23, 24, 233-239

Racial rumors, 110-115, 130-133, 136, 193-196
Radio broadcasting
  Axis, 29, 235
  propaganda rumors in, 14, 30
  rumor defense by, 3, 5 f., 15, 25-27
Rationalization, 36-38, 43-45, 98, 144, 177-179, 216
Reader's Digest, 10
Recall, 49-60
Recurrent rumors, 159, 171 f., 208
Red Cross rumors, 40
Reporting, 54-60
Reversal to truth, 120, 122 f.
Riots, 193-198, 206 f.
Roosevelt, Franklin D.
  anti-rumor speech, 3, 5 f., 15
  hostility rumors against, 11, 29, 174
  rumors after death of, 2
Rorschach Test, 145
Rosten, L., 15
Ruch, F. L., 14
Rumor
  basic law of, 2, 3 f., 8, 28, 31, 33-36, 43-45
  belief of, 14, 24-28, 147-149, 183 f.
  classification of, 10-13, 169-173
  effect of label on, 189-191
  experimental method of studying, 61-74

Rumor (Cont.)
  explanatory function of, 4 f., 5, 38, 40 f., 43, 98, 174-179, 204
  fecundity of, 205
  formula for, 33, 43
  as justification of emotions, 36-38, 43, 98, 174-179, 204, 215
  personification in, 179, 218
  relief of emotions through, 36-38, 43, 174-179, 204 f., 219 f.
Rumor analysis
  examples of, 134-138, 200-220
  guide for, 220-226
Rumor chain, 49, 182
Rumor clinics, 15, 18-28, 232-239
Rumor defense, 5 f., 14-29, 36, 199 f., 232-239 [199
Rumor immunity, 28, 35 f., 189,
Rumor offensives, 29-32
Rumor propaganda, 14, 28, 29, 30, 181 f.
Rumor prophylaxis, 31 f.
Rumor publics, 14, 35, 180-184, 203 f., 217
Rumor wardens, 23 f., 234
Russia, rumors concerning, 12, 36 f., 40, 190 f., 223

Sanford, R. N., 42
Sayre, Jeanette, 47
Sayre, Joel, 201
Security of information, 12, 16-18
Seldes, G., 186 f., 188
Self-interest, as rumor motive, 108 f., 112-115, 203
Serial reproduction
  accuracy of, 58-60
  conventionalization of, 60, 97
  idiosyncratic responses in, 60, 156 f.
  individual differences in, 120 f.
  method of, 58-60, 143 f.

Sex interest, 36, 177-179
Sex-determined interest, 105-107
Sharpening
  closure in, 97 f., 102
  in current events, 96
  definition of, 86
  exaggeration by, 149-153
  explanatory, 98, 121
  of familiar items, 97, 125, 144, 215 f.
  of labels, 96
  of movement, 92-95, 97
  numerical, 91, 151 f., 205, 213
  of oddity, 52, 89-91
  perceptual, 138-144
  by professional interest, 84-86, 108
  protocols showing, 87-91
  of selected features, 57, 117 f., 135 f., 143 f., 152 f., 213
  of size, 95 f., 213
  of stereotypes, 111-115, 136, 151 f.
  temporal, 91 f.
Simpson, G. G., 210
Slogans, 83, 120
Smith, G. H., 190 f.
Social participation, 183 f.
Sociometry, 182
Standardization of error, 168
Stefansson, V., 168
Stereotype, 97, 103, 104, 111-115, 136, 155 f. (*See also* Cliché)
Stern, W., 50-53
Subjectifying process, 146 f.
Suggestibility, 180-182
Symbolization, 101

Taylor, E., 29 f.
Tendency wit, 192 f., 209
Terminal reports, 68-73
Testimony, 49-60

INDEX

Thematic Apperception Test, 45, 145 f.
Time errors, 84-86, 124-126
Truth, kernel of, 9, 33, 117, 134, 148 f., 165, 203, 215

U.S.S.R., rumors concerning, 12, 36 f., 40, 190 f., 223

V-E Day rumors, 47 f.
V-J Day rumors, 2, 47 f., 61-63
Verbal misunderstanding, 122 f., 216

Walter, A. A., 142 f.
Weckler, J. E., 194 f.
Wedge-driving rumors, 10-13, 31, 36, 40, 98
Whipple, G. M., 49 f., 53
Whispering campaigns, 184-186
Wish, as rumor motive, 7 f., 9, 10-13, 36, 47 f., 62 f.
Wulf, F., 138-141

Young, K., 14, 164

Zerner, E. H., 187

www.ingramcontent.com/pod-product-compliance
Lightning Source LLC
Chambersburg PA
CBHW070729160426
43192CB00009B/1372